ative Suite® 6

Premium

OOM IN A BOOK®

g workbook from Adobe Systems

Printed and bound in the United States of America

ISBN-13: 978-0-321-83268-9

ISBN-10:   0-321-83268-X

9 8 7 6 5 4 3 2 1

WHAT'S ON THE DISC

Here is an overview of the contents of the Classroom in a Book disc

The *Adobe Creative Suite 6 Production Premium Classroom in a Book* disc includes the lesson files that you'll need to complete the exercises in this book, as well as other content to help you learn more about Adobe Creative Suite 6 Production Premium and use it with greater efficiency and ease. The diagram below represents the contents of the disc, which should help you locate the files you need.

These same disc files are available to eBook users via electronic download. Please click here to go to the last page in your eBook for instructions.

Lesson files

Each lesson has its own folder inside the Lessons folder. You will need to copy these lesson folders to your hard drive before you can begin each lesson.

Name
▶ Lesson01
▶ Lesson02
▶ Lesson03
▶ Lesson04
▶ Lesson05
▶ Lesson06
▶ Lesson07
▶ Lesson08
▶ Lesson09
▶ Lesson10
▶ Lesson11
▶ Lesson12

Online resources

Links to Adobe Community Help, product Help and Support pages, Adobe certification programs, Adobe TV, and other useful online resources can be found inside a handy HTML file. Just open it in your Web browser and click on the links, including a special link to this book's product page where you can access updates and bonus material.

Adobe Press

ADOBE PRESS

Find information about other Adobe Press titles, covering the full spectrum of Adobe products, in the Online Resources file.

Adobe

CONTENTS

GETTING STARTED

The tools for creating and broadcasting a professional-quality video have never been as accessible as they are today, thanks to more affordable and powerful recording equipment and computers, broadband Internet, and user-friendly software.

The Adobe® Creative Suite® 6 Production Premium® offers industry-standard applications for project organization, video and audio editing, animation, and final encoding for delivery.

About Classroom in a Book

Adobe Creative Suite 6 Production Premium Classroom in a Book® is part of the official training series for Adobe graphics and publishing software. The lessons are designed so you can learn at your own pace. If you're new to Adobe Creative Suite 6 Production Premium, you'll learn the fundamental concepts and features you'll need to use the program. This book also teaches many advanced features, including tips and techniques for using the latest version of this software.

You'll learn how to:

- Format a script in Adobe Story and learn the basics of its online features to collaborate with other members of your creative team.

- Ingest footage and add searchable metadata to your video clips with Adobe Prelude CS6.

- Use Adobe Premiere Pro CS6 as your main creative hub in which you'll do a refined edit of your movie and add visual effects and titles.

- Use Adobe Photoshop CS6 Extended to edit a still image utilizing the Mercury Graphics Engine to view your changes in real time.

- Use the Image Trace feature in Adobe Illustrator CS6 to create a vector logo graphic.

- Create motion graphics in Adobe After Effects CS6 and optimize your system to leverage the new Global Performance Cache.

- Create the final audio mix of your edit using Adobe Audition CS6.
- Use the enhanced Three-Way Color Corrector effect in Adobe Premiere Pro to color correct your edit.
- Apply color grading presets with Adobe SpeedGrade CS6.
- Create files for the Internet and mobile devices with Adobe Media Encoder or send a sequence to Adobe Encore CS6 without rendering or intermediate exporting to output to DVD, Blu-ray Disc, or Adobe Flash.
- Apply a media playback skin to your exported movie file with Adobe Flash Professional CS6.

Adobe CS6 Production Premium is available for both Windows and Mac OS.

Prerequisites

Before beginning to use *Adobe Creative Suite 6 Production Premium Classroom in a Book*, make sure your system is set up correctly and that you've installed the required software and hardware. You can view updated system requirements by visiting www.adobe.com/products/creativesuite/production/tech-specs.html.

You should have a working knowledge of your computer and operating system. You should know how to use the mouse and standard menus and commands, and also how to open, save, and close files. If you need to review these techniques, see the printed or online documentation included with your Windows or Mac OS system.

Installing Adobe CS6 Production Premium

You must purchase the Adobe CS6 Production Premium software separately from this book. It can be purchased as a stand-alone product or included in the Creative Suite or Creative Cloud families. Install Adobe CS6 Production Premium from the software DVD onto your hard drive; you cannot run the program from the DVD. If you purchased a downloadable version, follow the instructions included with the download for launching the installation process.

Adobe CS6 Production Premium trial

Adobe offers a 30-day trial of Adobe CS6 Production Premium. You can download this trial from the Adobe product website. After 30 days, the software will stop functioning. If you decide to purchase Adobe CS6 Production Premium, you can enter your purchased serial number into the trial version you have installed to convert it to a full version of Adobe CS6 Production Premium.

Hardware requirements

The most basic hardware requirements needed to run Adobe CS6 Production Premium include:

For Windows

- Intel® Core™2 Duo or AMD Phenom® II processor with 64-bit support; Intel Core i7 processor required for Adobe® SpeedGrade™
- Microsoft® Windows® 7 with Service Pack 1 (64 bit)
- 4 GB of RAM (8 GB recommended)
- 10.5 GB of available hard-disk space for installation; additional free space required during installation (cannot install on removable flash storage devices)
- Additional disk space required for disk cache, preview files, and other working files (10 GB recommended)
- 1280×900 display with 16-bit color and 512 MB of VRAM; 1680×1050 display required and second professionally calibrated viewing display recommended for Adobe SpeedGrade
- OpenGL 2.0–capable system
- 7200 RPM hard drive (multiple fast disk drives, preferably RAID 0 configured, recommended)
- Sound card compatible with ASIO protocol or Microsoft WDM//MME
- DVD-ROM drive compatible with dual-layer DVDs (DVD±R burner for burning DVDs; Blu-ray burner for creating Blu-ray Disc media)

● **Note:** For more hardware information, refer to the Adobe CS6 Production Premium system requirements at www.adobe.com/products/creativesuite/production/tech-specs.html.

For Mac OS

- Multicore Intel processor with 64-bit support

- Mac OS X v10.6.8 or v10.7

- 4 GB of RAM (8 GB recommended)

- 10.5 GB of available hard-disk space for installation; additional free space required during installation (cannot install on a volume that uses a case-sensitive file system or on removable flash storage devices)

- Additional disk space required for disk cache, preview files, and other working files (10 GB recommended)

- 1280×900 display with 16-bit color and 512 MB of VRAM; 1680×1050 display required and second professionally calibrated viewing display recommended for Adobe SpeedGrade

- OpenGL 2.0–capable system

- 7200 RPM hard drive (multiple fast disk drives, preferably RAID 0 configured, recommended)

- DVD-ROM drive compatible with dual-layer DVDs (SuperDrive for burning DVDs; Blu-ray burner for creating Blu-ray Disc media)

Optimizing performance

Editing video is memory- and processor-intensive work for a computer. A fast processor and a lot of RAM will make your editing experience faster and more efficient; 4 GB of RAM is the minimum, and 8 GB or more is best for high-definition (HD) media. Adobe CS6 Production Premium takes advantage of multicore processors on Windows and Macintosh systems.

A dedicated 7200 RPM or faster hard drive is recommended for HD media. A RAID 0 striped disk array or SCSI disk subsystem is strongly recommended for HD. Performance will be significantly affected if you attempt to store media files and program files on the same hard drive. Be sure to keep your media files on a second drive if at all possible.

The Mercury Playback Engine in Adobe Premiere Pro and the Global Performance Cache in Adobe After Effects can operate in software-only mode or GPU acceleration mode. The GPU acceleration mode provides significant performance improvement. GPU acceleration is possible with select video cards. You can find a list of these video cards on the Adobe website at www.adobe.com/products/premiere/tech-specs.html.

Copying the lesson files

The lessons in *Adobe Creative Suite 6 Production Premium Classroom in a Book* use specific source files, such as video clips, audio files, and image files created in Adobe Photoshop CS6 and Adobe Illustrator CS6. To complete the lessons in this book, you must copy all the files from the *Adobe Creative Suite 6 Production Premium Classroom in a Book* DVD (inside the back cover of this book) to your hard drive. You'll need about 11.3 GB of total storage space. This includes 780 MB for the file from the DVD in addition to the 10.5 GB you need to install Adobe CS6 Production Premium. It is also recommended that you have at least 10 GB of additional storage space for disk cache, preview files, and other working files.

Although each lesson stands alone, some lessons use files from other lessons, so you'll need to keep the entire collection of lesson assets on your hard drive as you work through the book. Here's how to copy those assets from the DVD to your hard drive:

1 Open the *Adobe Creative Suite 6 Production Premium Classroom in a Book* DVD in My Computer or Windows Explorer (Windows) or in Finder (Mac OS).

2 Right-click (Windows) or Control-click (Mac OS; if you're using a super mouse or pen, you can right-click) the folder called Adobe CS6 Project Assets, and choose Copy.

3 Navigate to a location on your hard drive (such as your desktop) where you will copy your Adobe CS6 Project Assets folder.

   We will refer to this folder throughout the lessons in this book, so make sure this location on your hard drive is easy to find again.

4 Right-click (Windows) or Control-click (Mac OS) inside the designated folder, and choose Paste.

Following these steps will copy all the lesson assets to your local folder. This process may take a few minutes to complete, depending on the speed of your hardware.

Relinking the lesson files

It is possible that the file path to the lesson files may need to be updated.

If you open an Adobe Premiere Pro project and it cannot find a media file, a dialog may open and ask *Where is the File MEDIA.mov?* If this happens, you'll need to navigate to one of the offline files to reconnect. Once you've reconnected one file in the project, the rest should reconnect.

If you open an Adobe After Effects project and it cannot find a media file, a window will open telling you that a number of files are missing. Look through your Project panel to find italicized filenames of imported media. Double-click on each of these filenames and navigate to the offline files to reconnect them. To find the files:

- You can navigate to the same location where you put the files you copied from the DVD. You may need to look in some of the included folders to find the media file.
- You can use the search field in the OS dialog to search for the file by name.

When you locate a file, just select it and click the Open button.

How to use these lessons

Each lesson in this book provides step-by-step instructions for creating one or more specific elements of a real-world project. The lessons stand alone, but most of them build on previous lessons in terms of concepts and skills. So, the best way to learn from this book is to proceed through the lessons in sequential order.

The organization of the lessons is workflow-oriented rather than feature-oriented, and the book uses a real-world approach. The lessons follow the typical sequential steps that creative media makers use to complete a project, starting with script writing, acquiring video, laying down a cuts-only sequence, adding effects, creating a motion graphic sequence, sweetening the audio track, color-correcting video clips, and ultimately exporting the project to the web, a portable device, a DVD, a Blu-ray Disc, or Flash.

Additional resources

Adobe Creative Suite 6 Production Premium Classroom in a Book is not meant to replace documentation that comes with the program or to be a comprehensive reference for every feature. Only the commands and options used in the lessons are explained in this book. For comprehensive information about program features and tutorials, please refer to these resources:

Adobe Community Help. Community Help brings together active Adobe product users, Adobe product team members, authors, and experts to give you the most useful, relevant, and up-to-date information about Adobe products.

To Access Community Help. To invoke Help, press F1 or choose Help > [name of CS6 application] Help.

Adobe content is updated based on community feedback and contributions. You can add comments to content and forums (including links to web content), publish your own content using Community Publishing, or contribute Cookbook recipes. Find out how to contribute at www.adobe.com/community/publishing/download.html.

See community.adobe.com/help/profile/faq.html for answers to frequently asked questions about Community Help.

Adobe Creative Suite 6 Production Premium Help and Support. www.adobe.com/support/creativesuite is where you can find and browse Help and Support content on *adobe.com*.

Adobe Forums. forums.adobe.com lets you tap into peer-to-peer discussions, questions, and answers on Adobe products.

Adobe TV. tv.adobe.com is an online video resource for expert instruction and inspiration about Adobe products, including a How To channel to get you started with your product.

Adobe Design Center. www.adobe.com/designcenter offers thoughtful articles on design and design issues, a gallery showcasing the work of top-notch designers, tutorials, and more.

Adobe Developer Connection. www.adobe.com/devnet is your source for technical articles, code samples, and how-to videos that cover Adobe developer products and technologies.

Resources for educators. www.adobe.com/education offers a treasure trove of information for instructors who teach classes on Adobe software. Find solutions for education at all levels, including free curricula that use an integrated approach to teaching Adobe software and can be used to prepare for the Adobe Certified Associate exams.

Also check out these useful links:

Adobe Marketplace & Exchange. www.adobe.com/cfusion/exchange is a central resource for finding tools, services, extensions, code samples, and more to supplement and extend your Adobe products.

Adobe Creative Suite 6 Production Premium product home page. www.adobe.com/products/creativesuite/production.html.

Adobe Labs. labs.adobe.com gives you access to early builds of cutting-edge technology as well as forums where you can interact with the Adobe development teams building that technology and with other like-minded members of the community.

Adobe certification

The Adobe training and certification programs are designed to help Adobe customers improve and promote their product-proficiency skills. There are four levels of certification:

- Adobe Certified Associate (ACA)
- Adobe Certified Expert (ACE)
- Adobe Certified Instructor (ACI)
- Adobe Authorized Training Center (AATC)

The Adobe Certified Associate (ACA) credential certifies that individuals have the entry-level skills to plan, design, build, and maintain effective communications using different forms of digital media.

The Adobe Certified Expert program is a way for expert users to upgrade their credentials. You can use Adobe certification as a catalyst for getting a raise, finding a job, or promoting your expertise.

If you are an ACE-level instructor, the Adobe Certified Instructor program takes your skills to the next level and gives you access to a wide range of Adobe resources.

Adobe Authorized Training Centers offer instructor-led courses and training on Adobe products, employing only Adobe Certified Instructors. A directory of AATCs is available at partners.adobe.com.

For information on the Adobe Certified programs, visit www.adobe.com/support/certification/index.html.

Checking for updates

Adobe periodically provides updates to its software. You can easily obtain these updates through Adobe Updater as long as you have an active Internet connection.

1 In Adobe Premiere Pro, for example, choose Help > Updates. Adobe Updater automatically checks for updates available for your Adobe software.

2 In the Adobe Application Manager, select the updates you want to install, and then click Update and Install Updates to install them.

For updates and bonus material, visit the book's page on the web at www.peachpit.com/cs6pcib.

1 WORKING IN ADOBE CREATIVE SUITE 6 PRODUCTION PREMIUM

Lesson overview

Becoming familiar with the applications in Adobe CS6 Production Premium and learning about the basic digital video workflow are essential to successfully complete a project. In this lesson, you will learn about:

- The general workflow of creating a video
- The role of each application in Adobe CS6 Production Premium
- The components of the Adobe CS6 Production Premium user interface
- The various types of media files and what they are typically used for in your workflow
- Linking a project with media files

 This lesson will take approximately 20 minutes to complete.

A final motion graphic created in Adobe After Effects CS6. Using the applications in the Adobe CS6 Production Premium, you'll assemble raw sample video footage and a music track into a rough cut, add some visual effects, animate a motion graphic, create a final audio mix, and then generate exports of the final video.

The "planning to playback" video-production workflow

The tools for creating and broadcasting a professional-quality video have never been as accessible as they are today, thanks to more affordable and accessible recording equipment and computers, broadband Internet, and user-friendly software.

Adobe Creative Suite 6 Production Premium offers industry-standard applications for project organization, video and audio editing, animation, and final encoding for delivery.

The lessons in this book take you through the process of creating a promotional video for the San Francisco-based music collective Afrolicious, featuring an interview with the band leader and DJ, Joey. Assets provided include interviews, music clips, and footage from a recording session and from a live performance. Using all of the applications in the Adobe CS6 Production Premium, you'll assemble the raw video footage and a music track into a rough cut, add some visual effects, animate a motion graphic, create a final audio mix, and then generate exports of the final video.

This book is intended for those who have some experience in part or all of the creative process or who have never used the Adobe Creative Suite. After completing these lessons, you'll have a basic understanding of the creative process and how the applications in Adobe CS6 Production Premium can play an integral role in that process.

The creative process of making a broadcast-quality video consists of three phases—preproduction, production, and postproduction. Each phase has its own procedures.

Preproduction

In preproduction you generate all of the big-picture ideas and concepts, and establish general creative guidelines and styles. Once you formulate a concept, you then write your scripts and draw your storyboards. These will serve as your points of reference as you proceed to the production phase. As a result, preproduction can be the most creative phase of the entire process, and it will establish a general direction for all work to follow.

In Chapter 2 you'll learn how to use Adobe Story to create and format a film script.

Production

In the production phase you shoot any video footage and record any audio that is unique to a given project. This is also when you gather additional media—stock images, logo graphics, music and sound effects—that you want to include in your project. Just as much care and planning should go into the production phase as the preproduction phase because without good video, audio, and other media to work with, the next phase of the creative process cannot happen.

Also in Chapter 2 you'll learn how to use Adobe Prelude CS6 to ingest raw footage to your computer's hard drive, which is a task that, thanks to video cameras with tapeless media, is now possible during the production phase.

Postproduction

When you have all of your raw media, you are ready to put all of the pieces together. Postproduction is when you edit your video, mix your audio, animate your motion graphics, generate final composites, apply color-correcting techniques, output your final video master file, compress your video for web and mobile devices, and deliver your final output to the client or end user.

The lessons in this book use raw video footage and audio that has already been created and provided for you, and primarily focus on the postproduction phase:

- In Chapter 3 you'll create a rough edit of your movie with Adobe Premiere Pro.

- In Chapter 4 you'll refine your Adobe Premiere Pro edit by applying video effects and transitions.

- In Chapter 5 you'll edit a layered image with Adobe Photoshop Extended and convert that layered image into a motion graphic with Adobe After Effects. You'll add this motion graphic to your edit in Adobe Premiere Pro.

- In Chapter 6 you'll refine your motion graphics sequences in Adobe After Effects by adding a vector graphic from Adobe Illustrator.

- In Chapter 7 you'll create a final audio mix with Adobe Audition.

- In Chapter 8 you'll use Adobe Premiere Pro and Adobe SpeedGrade to apply color-correcting techniques. You'll also use Adobe Media Encoder to export your final edit for optimized playback on multiple devices.

- In Chapter 9 you'll use Adobe Encore to create a DVD menu for your movie that can be mastered to a standard DVD. You'll also use Adobe Flash Professional to apply a media playback skin so that your final movie can be embedded in a web page.

Learning the role of each component in the suite

The applications in Adobe CS6 Production Premium perform different functions in the creative process. The following applications are included when you purchase the entire suite:

- **Adobe Bridge.** Manage all of your digital assets, including photos, video clips, audio clips, and other media.

- **Adobe Story.** Write your script using formatting presets and collaborate online with members of your creative team. Adobe Story Free can be downloaded for free and Adobe Story Plus is available for purchase at www.adobe.com.

- **Adobe Prelude.** Ingest your raw footage and create an assembly edit right away, adding searchable markers and temporal metadata.

- **Adobe Premiere Pro.** The hub of your video editing processes. Edit your video and audio in a Timeline, apply color correction, and create an audio mix.

- **Adobe After Effects.** Create motion graphics in 3D space, composite multiple layers of video and images, and generate visual effects.

- **Adobe Photoshop Extended.** Create multilayered bitmap image documents, edit still images, and create 3D graphics.

- **Adobe Illustrator.** Create multilayered vector image documents and design logo graphics and digital illustrations.

- **Adobe Audition.** Edit, mix, and restore multitrack audio.

- **Adobe SpeedGrade.** Color grade your final video edit using presets or customized settings.

- **Adobe Media Encoder.** Create multiple encoded versions of source files, Adobe Premiere Pro sequences, and Adobe After Effects compositions.

- **Adobe Encore.** Create DVDs, Blu-ray Discs, and web DVDs, all from one application.

- **Adobe Flash Professional.** Create animation and interactive multimedia content for the web and mobile devices.

The lessons in this book touch on all of these applications to help you become familiar with them; however, they do not go deeply into using each one. Rather, this book focuses on the recommended workflows and the right tools for the job when using the applications together for your video projects. You'll learn video-making concepts along the way, and this book will point out other *Classroom in a Book* titles for your reference if you want more in-depth information on particular Adobe software applications.

Understanding the Creative Suite user interface

Although each application performs a different function and features different tools, the overall look and feel of the applications in Adobe CS6 Production Premium share many common elements. We'll touch on these elements here, but you'll learn more about each one in context with the particular application covered while going through the lessons in the book:

- **Toolbars.** Each application has its own set of tools located in a toolbar at the top of the interface. The Selection, Hand, Zoom, Pen, and Type tools all work the same way across the suite. By hovering your cursor over a tool in the toolbar, you can see a tool tip that shows the keyboard shortcut to access the tool.

- **Workspaces.** All CS6 applications have customizable workspaces that allow you to move interface panels to fit your needs, as well as convenient presets for commonly used workspaces.

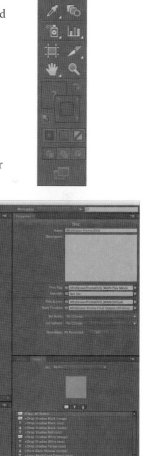

- **Timelines.** Time-based applications like Adobe Premiere Pro, After Effects, Audition, Encore, Prelude, and Flash all have a Timeline panel that enables you to play back and quickly scan through layers or footage by adjusting a current time indicator (CTI).

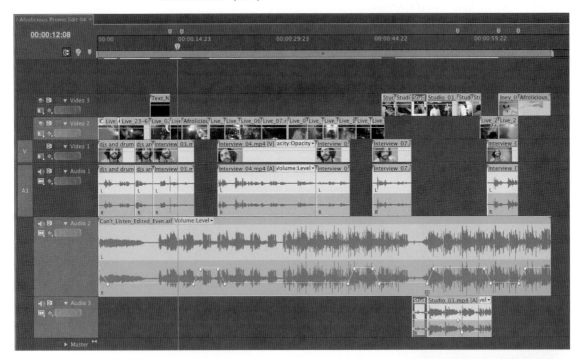

- **Layers.** Image applications like Photoshop Extended and Illustrator allow a single image document to contain a stack of multiple layers of image data; each can have its own unique settings. After Effects compositions also use layers as objects stacked in a Timeline.

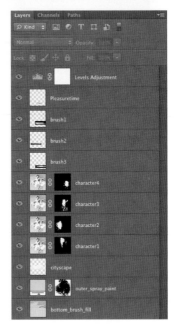

- **Folders and bins.** These are commonly used across Adobe CS6 Production Premium to organize project media within an application.

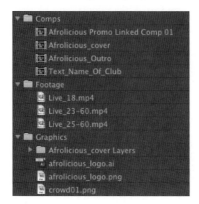

Using Dynamic Link

Adobe Premiere Pro, After Effects, and Encore all feature Dynamic Link, which enables you to send project elements between applications without any intermediate rendering. This greatly speeds your workflow and saves you time.

For example, if you create a motion graphic in After Effects and want to add it to a sequence in Adobe Premiere Pro, you can import the raw unrendered After Effects composition into your Adobe Premiere Pro project. Any changes you make to the After Effects composition reflect automatically in your Adobe Premiere Pro sequence. This is explained in further detail in Chapter 5.

You can also send your projects from Adobe Premiere Pro to Encore using Dynamic Link without rendering or saving an intermediate file. You'll learn more about this in Chapter 9.

Working with media files in video production

It's important to know the difference between the types of media files and the ideal applications you use to edit them:

- **Video clips** are movie files that originate from a video camera or exist as prerendered animations or other edited videos. Typical formats for these include .mov, .mp4, and .avi. These are typically used in Adobe Premiere Pro, After Effects, Encore, Flash, and Prelude.

- **Audio clips** are audio files that usually contain music, sound effects, and voice-over recordings. Typical formats for audio clips include .aiff, .wav, and .mp3. Although these can be used in Adobe Premiere Pro, After Effects, and Flash as raw media, editing and mixing of audio clips should be done in Audition. Be advised that .aiff and .wav allow for uncompressed audio data, whereas .mp3 is a compressed format and should not be used for raw audio in your edits.

- **Bitmap images** are still images that are pixel-based and are typically photographs or still frames from video. Some bitmap image file formats include .jpg, .tif, .png, and .tga. There are a few factors to consider when using one bitmap image format over another. For instance, consider whether you need a bitmap image format that supports layers (.psd and .tiff support layers, whereas .jpg, .png and .tga do not); whether you need a bitmap image format that supports embedded transparency, also referred to as an alpha channel (.psd, .tif, .png, and .tga do, whereas .jpg does not); and whether the format supports uncompressed image data (.psd, .tif, .png, and .tga do, whereas .jpg does not). You should use Photoshop to edit bitmap image files. Photoshop's native .psd format can contain layers, alpha channels, and uncompressed image data.

- **Vector images** are still images or graphics that are vector based, meaning they are resolution independent. Because of this versatility, vector images are typically used for logo graphics. Typical vector image formats are .eps and the Adobe Illustrator native format, .ai. You should use Illustrator to create or edit vector images. By default, Adobe Illustrator CS6 will save graphics as a .ai file, which may not be compatible on systems that don't have Adobe Illustrator installed. However, because the .eps format is not application-specific, these images are good to use as deliverable vector images.

Video format compatibility

Some video files will not play back on your system if the appropriate software is not installed. Formats like .avi and .wmv were developed for playback on the Windows operating system and may not play back on Mac OS X. Apple's .mov format is native to the Apple QuickTime media player, and the .mp4 format is cross-platform. They each have different ways of storing video data, which may result in compatibility issues when transferring from one device to another. Fortunately, Apple QuickTime can be downloaded to Windows and Linux machines to provide them with the ability to play .mov files. Media players like VLC by VideoLAN are available for download on Mac computers to provide support for Windows-based .avi files. Adobe Premiere Pro CS6 is able to edit nearly any type of video file that is playable on your computer, and Adobe Media Encoder can convert these playable media files into a grand array of different formats.

Codecs and Extensions

The video codec, as its etymology "*compressor-de*compressor" indicates, compresses information into a convenient file and then later reverses the process by decompressing the data for interpretation by a playback system. Codecs are like languages; if your computer does not have a specific codec installed, it will not be able to read or write in that particular language. As newer codecs introduce better ways of encoding and decoding media, older codecs become antiquated and are less commonly used. The most commonly used codec for video sharing today is H.264, which is rooted in the cross-platform MPEG-4 format. Unlike other codecs that were developed for one specific usage, H.264 is renowned for its versatility among web, mobile, Blu-ray, and high-definition recording.

A video's codec relates to its file extension, but they are not synonymous. A video file's extension (like .mp4, .mov, .avi) reflects how data is stored and organized within its file. The container format also determines how the metadata and audio/video components interrelate. A container format like .mov can be encoded in one of many different codecs. Therefore, the extension does not describe how the file is encoded and decoded but rather how the data is internally structured. Both the codec and the file extension are elements that have a direct impact on the quality and the accessibility of a file.

You'll learn more about the importance of compression and file formats when exporting files in Chapter 8.

Adobe Photoshop Extended and Adobe Illustrator documents (.psd and .ai, respectively) exist as self-contained files. As new layers and additional graphics are introduced into these multilayered documents, their file sizes will, in turn, get larger.

However, link-based project files, like those generated by Adobe Premiere Pro, After Effects, Encore, and Flash, are not self-contained and act as "hubs" for all related project media. Project files exist separately from media files on your computer. This means that for a project file to function properly, it must be linked with all related media on your system.

Self-contained files, like .psd or .ai, can be moved from system to system and edited without requiring linkage to any other media files. Link-based project files, like those used by Adobe Premiere Pro, After Effects, Encore, and Flash, do require active links to all associated media files. When you're working with link-based project files, it's best to store all associated media in a local project folder accompanied by the project files. This will make it easier to move projects between systems without breaking links to the media files.

Linking a project with media files

Let's do an exercise that will give you a glimpse of working with Adobe Premiere Pro CS6 and also show you how to link a project to media files. Make sure you've copied the Adobe CS6 Assets folder from the DVD to your hard drive.

1 Launch Adobe Premiere Pro CS6. You'll see the Welcome screen with a list of recently opened projects (if any) as well as three buttons at the bottom.

2 Click the Open Project button. Navigate to the Lesson 01 folder (Adobe CS6 Project Assets > Lessons > Lesson 01) on your hard drive. Select the Lesson_01 Start.prproj file and click Open.

The Adobe Premiere Pro user interface appears.

At the bottom left you'll see a Project panel with a list of folders (called bins) that have media organized in them. You'll also see a Timeline panel at the bottom right that has clips in an edited sequence. The Timeline has a CTI that looks like a red vertical line with a yellow handle at the top. At the top right of the interface, you'll see a Program Monitor that shows the frame of your edited sequence that the CTI is currently parked on.

3 Click on the CTI's yellow handle and drag to the right, thereby moving through time in your sequence. This action is referred to as *scrubbing*. As you do this, notice that the Program Monitor shows many offline clips in the Timeline.

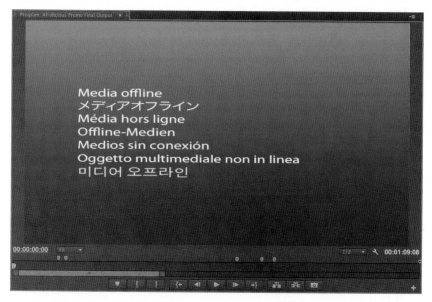

This is a fairly common occurrence, especially if a project file and project media have been copied to a different computer than the one on which the project originated. Although the project file opens and references to the media exist in the project, it still needs to be linked to all of the related media files for you to work with the media in the project.

Fortunately, link-based project files, like those from Adobe Premiere Pro and After Effects, allow you to easily fix the links in the project to the media files on your hard drive.

4 Using Finder on Mac OS X or Explorer on Windows, navigate to your Adobe CS6 Project Assets folder. Notice the subfolders for Audio, Exports, Footage, Graphics, and Lessons. It's good working practice to keep all of your project-related files organized so that they are easy to find when you need them.

5 Switch back to Adobe Premiere Pro.

If you have a project file open and you are about to make one or more changes to it, it's also good working practice to save a version of your project file so that the older version is preserved in case you need to reference it later.

6 Choose File > Save As. Navigate to your Lesson 01 folder and type **Lesson_01_Relinked** in the Save As dialog. Then click the Save button.

Let's fix the offline media links in this project. You'll first open the bin for the offline media.

7 In the Project panel, double-click on the Live bin.

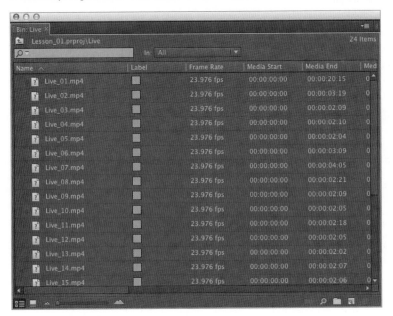

It will open as a floating panel in your interface and show a list of all of the Live clips, which are the ones currently offline. Notice that the icon next to each of these media files, or clips, currently looks like a document with a question mark, indicating that the media is offline.

8 Because you need to relink all of these clips to files on your hard drive, select them all by pressing Command+A (Ctrl+A).

All of the clips in the bin will become highlighted, indicating that they are selected. Often, operations can only be performed on project items, such as clips in a bin or in the Timeline, if they are selected. On the other hand, it's important to keep track of what is selected in your interface so that you don't accidentally apply changes to them.

9 With all of the clips in the Live bin selected, choose Project > Link Media.

10 A file navigation window appears. Navigate to Adobe CS6 Project Assets > Footage, select Live_01.mp4, and click Open.

Conveniently, because all of these offline clips were in the same folder, relinking one of them relinks all of them.

11 Select the Live bin and press Command+W (Ctrl+W) to close it.

12 Now scrub the CTI through your Timeline. You should see that all of the Live clips have been relinked and now appear in your Program Monitor.

13 Press the Home key or scrub your CTI all the way to the left to go to the beginning of the edited sequence. Press the spacebar to play the sequence.

Note that there are a couple of clips in sequence that may not play back in real time, particularly the very last clip in the sequence. These are Dynamically Linked clips from Adobe After Effects, and they will be explained in forthcoming lessons in this book.

> ▶ **Tip:** Press the spacebar to start and stop playback of a sequence in your Timeline.

> ▶ **Tip:** It's a good idea to save your work often.

14 Press Command+S (Ctrl+S) to save your Adobe Premiere Pro project file.

You should now be familiar with the concept of linking a project file with project media on your system.

15 Choose Premiere Pro > Quit Premiere Pro (File > Exit) to quit Adobe Premiere Pro because you won't need it for the remainder of this lesson.

Real-time playback and editing

Improvements in Adobe CS6 Production Premium yield speed enhancements to Adobe Premiere Pro, Adobe After Effects, Adobe Photoshop Extended, and Adobe Illustrator.

The Mercury Playback Engine

The Mercury Playback Engine brought extraordinary performance and stability to Adobe Premiere Pro CS5 and CS5.5. In Adobe Premiere Pro CS6, performance and stability have been boosted yet again, thanks to optimizations and enhancements that let you smoothly play and scrub through multilayer, multiformat sequences that include HD, 5K, and even higher-resolution footage containing effects. The enhanced Mercury Playback Engine is dynamically scalable, natively 64-bit, GPU-accelerated, and optimized for today's multicore CPUs—and has improved support for third-party hardware. It delivers this kind of performance with or without a GPU. This allows you to work on dense, complex projects using a fast, GPU-enabled workstation, and then bring them onto a lesser-powered computer and continue working without missing a beat.

To check whether you are using GPU acceleration in Adobe Premiere Pro CS6, under Video Rendering and Playback, choose Project > Project Settings > General.

Only systems with GPUs that support CUDA technology or OpenCL technology allow Adobe Premiere Pro CS6 to utilize the Mercury Playback Engine.

For more information on the Mercury Playback Engine and supported GPUs, go to www.adobe.com/products/premiere/mercury-playback-engine.html.

For more information on CUDA and OpenCL technologies in general, go to http://blogs.adobe.com/premiereprotraining/2011/02/cuda-mercury-playback-engine-and-adobe-premiere-pro.html.

Global Performance Cache

The Global Performance Cache feature is a revolution "under the hood" that makes Adobe After Effects faster and more responsive by taking full advantage of your computer's hardware. Global Performance Cache comprises a set of technologies: a global RAM cache, a persistent disk cache, and a new graphics pipeline.

The Global Performance Cache is covered in more depth in Chapter 5.

Mercury Graphics Engine

The new Mercury Graphics Engine in Photoshop CS6 Extended uses the power of your computer's GPU to speed up the performance of Photoshop. Many features in Photoshop Extended take advantage of the Mercury Graphics Engine, including the all-new Crop tool, Puppet Warp, Liquify, Adaptive Wide Angle, and the Lighting Effects Gallery. Doing 3D work in Adobe RayTrace mode in Photoshop CS6 Extended is also quickened thanks to the Mercury Graphics Engine.

Mercury Performance System

The new Mercury Performance System in Adobe Illustrator CS6 speeds up your workflow when creating and editing your vector graphics. Native 64-bit support on Mac OS and Windows provides access to all the available RAM on your system. Overall performance optimization is apparent when you open, save, and export large files. Previews are faster, and interaction in general is more responsive.

Creating a disk image to back up your system regularly

Your system hard drive holds your operating system files and your applications. After continual use of the applications, cached data and preference files tend to accumulate and slow your computer's performance. It is recommended that you create an archive of your system hard drive that has a fresh install of the operating system and all regularly used applications. Such an archive can be saved as a disk image file on a separate hard drive.

To do this, you first create a fresh install of your operating system and applications on your system hard drive. Don't copy any project files or media to your system drive after you do this. Your system drive should only have the operating system and applications, nothing else. Then you create an archive of your system drive. On Mac OS X, you can use Disk Utility to create a disk image of your system drive. On Windows, you can use the "Back up your files" feature to create a system image.

In the event that you'd need to restore your operating system and applications due to unbearably slow performance or a complete hard drive failure, all you'd need to do is simply restore your system drive from your system archive rather than be forced to spend time reinstalling your operating system and applications one at a time.

To go one step further, if your computer allows you to easily remove the physical system hard drive and replace it with another, it's recommended that you have at least one spare hard drive that has your operating system and applications already installed on it. Restoring your system hard drive should be done monthly or on an otherwise regular basis.

Review questions

1 What is the difference between a Timeline and a bin?

2 What is Dynamic Link?

3 What are some common file formats for video clips?

4 What is a codec?

5 In Adobe Premiere Pro, how do you relink offline media in your project?

Review answers

1 A bin is used to store raw project media that can be included in multiple Timelines, whereas a Timeline contains instances of project media that were added from bins.

2 Dynamic Link is a feature that enables users to send project elements between Adobe Premiere Pro, After Effects, and Encore without any intermediate rendering.

3 Common file formats for video clips include .mov, .avi, and .mp4.

4 A codec is a compression/decompression algorithm that allows a video file size to be shrunk so that the video clips are more manageable on a wider range of computer systems.

5 To relink media, select the clips in a bin that need to be relinked (a document with a question mark indicates the media is offline) and choose Project > Link Media. Navigate to the media you want relinked when the file navigation window opens. Select the media and click Open. The clips will relink and appear in your Program Monitor.

2 ORGANIZING THE MEDIA FILES FOR YOUR PROJECT

Lesson overview

The way you plan and organize your media files at the beginning of a project affects how easily and efficiently you can work in the later phases. In this lesson, you'll learn how to do the following:

- Use Adobe Bridge to manage, preview, and add metadata to your media files

- Understand basic film script page elements

- Use Adobe Story to write and collaborate on a script

- Use Adobe Prelude to ingest and add comments to video clips

- Create bins to organize your media files

- Assemble a rough cut

- Add time-based comments

- Export your Adobe Prelude project for use in Adobe Premiere Pro

 This lesson will take approximately 30 minutes to complete.

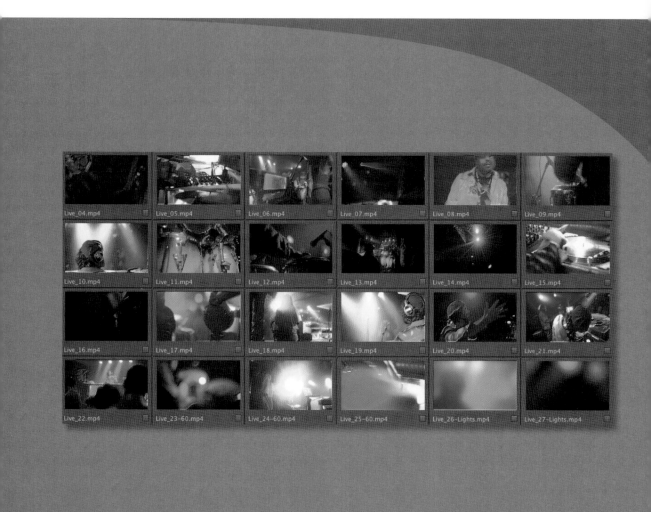

Previewing clips in Adobe Prelude CS6.

About Adobe Bridge

Adobe Bridge CS6 digital asset management software provides integrated, central-ized access to your project files and enables you to quickly browse through your creative assets visually—regardless of what format they're in—making it easy for you to locate, organize, and view your files.

In addition, Adobe Bridge CS6 allows you to add searchable keywords to your files to make these files easier to find. You can add frequently accessed folders on your system to a Favorites list as well. Adobe Bridge CS6 also can do batch processing of media files, such as applying a Photoshop Action to a folder of images or renaming several files for more efficient organization.

Naming and managing your project and media files

Having a strategy for how you name and organize your files is fundamental. When possible, use clear, simple naming that describes what is in the file or folder. Organize your media files into folders based on category.

You'll use Adobe Bridge to browse through the media files that we've included for you to work with in this *Classroom in a Book*. We've named the files and organized them into folders based on a simple, effective strategy that you can use in your own productions.

Navigating and previewing media

When you're beginning the postproduction of a video project, it's good working practice to look at all of the footage and media before you start editing. You become familiar with the material you'll be working with and also discover anything that might be wrong with the footage.

Adobe Bridge CS6 allows you to browse through your footage and other media, and it can provide technical details about your footage and media.

1 Launch Adobe Bridge.

2 Using the Favorites panel in the upper-left corner of the interface, navigate to the Adobe CS6 Project Assets folder.

3 Double-click on the Adobe CS6 Project Assets folder to reveal its contents.

The assets are organized by category: Audio, Exports, Footage, and Graphics. This is a simple way to organize assets at a high level in any video project.

4 Double-click on the Footage folder, and then double-click on the Interview folder to reveal its contents.

The interview clips are all named "interview" with the take number. They are grouped together in this folder for easy access later in the editing process.

5   Click the clip Interview_01.mp4 to select it.

The clip is now visible in the Preview panel.

▶ **Tip:** You can also drag the playback bar to scrub forward and back through the video, which is useful when you're choosing which clips to use.

6   In the Preview panel, click the Play button to preview the clip. When you're finished, click the Pause button to stop playback.

Media asset management storage and integration

If you work in a facility with other video professionals, it is usually advantageous to have a shared asset management and storage system to streamline workflow and minimize costs.

Many Adobe partners offer products and services to help you do just that, such as online storage, asset management, hardware solutions for video acquisition and conversion, and software solutions for creating broadcast graphics.

You'll find a current list on the Adobe website at www.adobe.com/solutions/broadcasting/partners.html.

Working with metadata

Simply put, *metadata* is data about your data.

Looking at a video file, you'd have no idea what is contained within the file without metadata. For example, what video format is it? What is the frame size and frame rate? What is the duration? Is this a good take or a bad take? Metadata describes these and other attributes of the media files you use in video production.

One of the advantages of using Adobe Bridge as a file management tool is that you can create custom metadata fields, and then add them to your media files. Because the metadata stays with the media, it will be usable in all facets of your workflow down the line. For example, if you enter comments about the video in Adobe Bridge, you'll be able to see those comments when you're working with that video later in the other components of Creative Suite 6 Production Premium.

In the Metadata panel in Adobe Bridge, you'll see some of the metadata attached to the Interview_01.mp4 clip that you currently have selected.

You can add your own metadata to any file using Adobe Bridge.

Adding metadata to your media

Adobe Bridge CS6 provides an easy way to add metadata to your footage for future reference when editing.

Metadata can include information like scene description, shot number, and shooter's name. You can also add a comment about qualitative information, such as whether a take is usable or not, which can help streamline the editing process. This process of adding comments to your media is known as logging clips.

Let's look at the basics on adding metadata by adding a "Best Take" comment.

1 Using the scroll bar in the Metadata panel, scroll down until the Video category is visible.

2 Click the gray space directly to the right of Log Comment.

3 Type **Best Take**.

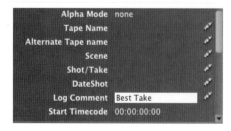

4   In the Content panel, click on the clip's thumbnail.

5   In the dialog that appears, click the Apply button to apply your metadata changes.

6   The comment is now attached to the file and will stay with it throughout the rest of the workflow.

When you're logging clips, it's very useful to add notes about camera angles or different takes, making it much easier to find and work with your clips.

About Adobe Story

Now that we've discussed some basics about naming files and adding metadata, let's change gears and talk about Adobe Story, which is an application that simplifies formatting scripts for film, television, and other outlets so that you can focus on writing your story.

Adobe Story is more than just a script writing application. During the preproduction phase of a project, scriptwriters can use Adobe Story to store their scripts in the cloud. After all of the footage has been shot, video editors can import an Adobe Story Script Format file to Adobe Premiere Pro to compare the dialogue in the script with a speech analysis of selected clips. This makes it easier for editors to locate segments of footage with certain dialogue.

With a paid subscription to Adobe Story Plus, you can automatically synch scripts and other Adobe Story documents with other collaborators. Because scenes are numbered in the script, this information can be used during the production phase. Producers can use Adobe Story Plus to automatically generate production reports and schedules that relate to certain scenes.

The first exercise in this section is intended to give you a brief overview of how to properly format film script page elements with Adobe Story, and the subsequent exercise covers some of the collaboration features found in Adobe Story Plus.

Basic film script page elements

● **Note:** The definitive guide to formatting film scripts is The Complete Guide to Standard Script Formats by Judith H. Haag and Hillis R. Cole (CMC Publishing,1989).

A screenplay is more than just a script with scene descriptions and character dialogue: It's also a blueprint for producers and directors that makes it easy for them to break down what is needed to shoot a movie and helps them to budget costs for equipment, actors, locations, and so on. A screenplay follows a certain format that is based on standards that were established in the 1980s. These standards have been adopted in screenwriting software and are still in use today.

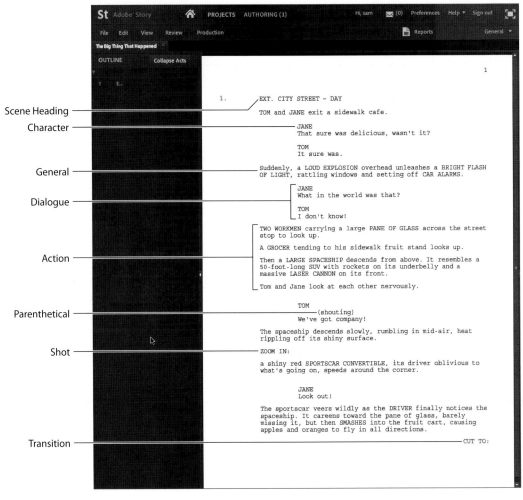

The following is a brief list of screenplay formatting elements that you can use in your script when you're writing with Adobe Story:

- **Scene Heading.** This is a brief indicator of the location of a scene and what time of day it takes place. Interior and exterior locations are denoted by the abbreviations INT and EXT.

- **Character.** When a character is introduced in a screenplay, it is important to clearly indicate this to the reader, which is why the character's name is written in capital letters. This element also allows a producer to see at a glance how many actors will be needed to shoot a scene or a movie when a script is being budgeted.

- **General.** At the beginning of a scene, it's a good idea to describe what you intend the viewer to see. If your script needs to indicate the presence of props, visual effects, sound effects, or anything that the producer might need to include in the production's budget, indicate those items with capital letters.

- **Dialogue.** When a character has a spoken line of dialogue, the character's name (using capital letters) and the dialogue are indented to the center of the page.

- **Action.** When something happens in a scene that is not dialogue, write a brief visual description of it. Be as concise as possible; a screenplay is not a novel.

- **Parenthetical.** This element is brief stage direction that is indented on the page with dialogue so that the flow of the scene is not interrupted with a separate general description. Keep parenthetical directions very brief.

- **Shot.** Whenever a specific camera direction (pan, zoom, dolly, etc.) is needed for a shot, indicate this using capital letters. The producer can then see at a glance if any extra camera equipment (special lenses, camera crane, etc.) will be required and needs to be included in the production budget.

- **Transition.** This element indicates a specific type of transition (cut, dissolve, wipe, etc.) at the end of a scene as a general guideline for the editor(s).

Starting a new script in Adobe Story

To become familiar with what Adobe Story can do, let's write a sample page of film script.

1 Open your web browser.

2 In the Address field, type the URL **story.adobe.com** and press Return (Enter).

3 On the Adobe Story homepage, click Sign In.

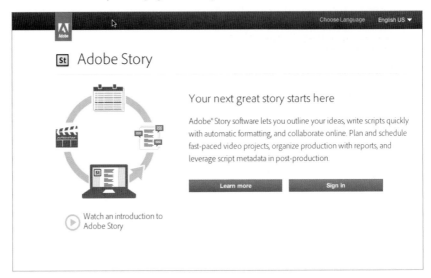

4 In the Sign In window that appears, enter your Adobe ID and Password, and then click Sign In. If you don't already have an Adobe ID, follow the onscreen instructions to create one. Accept the terms of use as well.

Your web browser will load the Story interface.

5 Click the Projects menu at the top left of the interface and choose New Project.

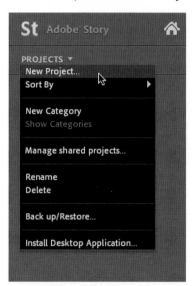

6 In the Create New Project dialog enter a name for your project (you can type in **The Big Thing That Happened**, which is the name of our hypothetical script, or any other name of your choosing), and then click Create.

7 At the top of the Story interface, click the + New button to create a new script in your project.

8 In the Create New Document - Adobe Story window, click the Type menu and choose Film Script.

9 Double-click in the Title field and type **The Big Thing That Happened**.

10 Click Create. The script's title page appears.

11 Notice that Adobe Story has formatted your title page by placing your script title and your name automatically.

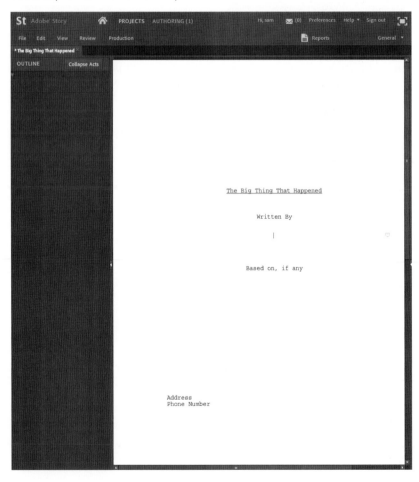

12 Scroll down to the first page of the script to where you see the placeholder text ENTER SCENE HEADING. Click on that text and type in the new scene heading **EXT. CITY STREET – DAY**.

As you are typing the word EXT, Story anticipates that you want to type a commonly used scene heading by showing the word EXT in a floating menu below your cursor. You can either continue typing, or you can choose the desired word from the floating menu.

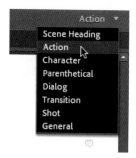

13 Press Return (Enter) to start a new line of text.

Next, you'll write a brief bit of action.

14 Type **TOM and JANE exit a sidewalk cafe.**

Note that in the Formatting menu at the top right of the interface, Story has automatically formatted this line of text as Action.

15 Choose from the Formatting menu to manually format any text in your script.

Let's write some dialogue.

16 Press Return (Enter), click the Formatting menu, and choose Character.

17 Type **jane** and then press Return (Enter). The formatting automatically changes to Dialogue.

18 Type **that sure was delicious, wasn't it?**

Notice that Story automatically and conveniently formats character names with all capital letters and adds a capital letter to the start of the dialogue.

Collaborating with others on your script

The free version of Adobe Story, which is available with your Adobe ID account, gives you the ability to craft your story using industry-standard formatting. However, many collaboration features are only available with a paid subscription to Adobe Story Plus.

The following exercise takes advantage of these collaboration features. If you do not have a paid subscription to Adobe Story Plus, proceed to the next exercise in the section "About Adobe Prelude."

Adobe Story Plus

If scriptwriting is a regular part of your workflow, it might make sense to upgrade to Adobe Story Plus. Not only does it feature enhanced scriptwriting tools, like trackable history of changes, customizable script templates, and industry-standard formatting, but it also allows you to collaborate with project team members online. Many of the online features include tools for scheduling and reporting, such as permission assignment, email notifications, and the ability to organize and synch scene elements like props and costumes.

One of the primary advantages of using Adobe Story Plus to write your scripts is that it enables you to collaborate with others and track changes in a single interface. This removes the "what version is this" factor of sharing and working on the same document with multiple contributors.

Adobe Story Plus helps to ensure that any changes to dialogue, shot lists, or other copy in a script is associated with a specific user and when those changes were made.

1 Choose File > Share.

2 In the dialog that appears, enter the email addresses of people you want to collaborate with, and assign them roles (co-author, reviewer, or reader).

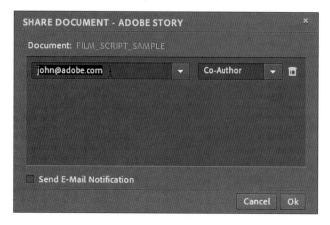

3 Select the Send E-Mail Notification check box.

4 Click OK to add your collaborators and send them an email inviting them to collaborate on your script.

5 Choose Review > Start Tracking Changes.

6 Choose View > Track Changes Toolbar.

Now you'll be able to see, in red text on your script, what changes have been made and by whom.

About Adobe Prelude

With modern digital video cameras that use memory cards, it has become possible during the production phase of a project to not only view footage immediately after it is shot, but to transfer the footage to a computer's hard drive while on set.

Adobe Prelude CS6 allows you to begin organizing your footage right after the footage has been transferred to a computer from a camera. Prelude was also designed for producers (and non-editors) to be able to mark up clips for their editors, as part of a collaborative workflow. You can ingest entire raw clips or selected portions of clips to a Prelude project. Once clips are ingested to Prelude, you can add descriptive metadata to them, mark subclips, and insert searchable comments. This added metadata will be saved with the clips when you send your rough cut from Adobe Prelude to Adobe Premiere Pro, which can help streamline the editing process.

In this exercise you'll ingest the Afrolicious raw clips to a project in Adobe Prelude CS6, apply metadata to some clips, create a rough cut of the clips, and then send the rough cut to Adobe Premiere Pro CS6.

Ingesting footage

Let's go through the process of ingesting the raw footage for the project into Adobe Prelude CS6 so that you can begin logging and commenting on the footage.

1 Launch Adobe Prelude and click New Project.

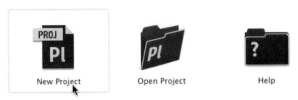

2 By default, Adobe Prelude saves a new project to its own Projects folder. But instead, navigate to the Lesson 02 folder (Adobe CS6 Project Assets > Lessons > Lesson 02) and open it.

3 Name your project **Afrolicious Ingest**, and then click Save.

4 Click the Ingest button. The Ingest panel opens.

Similar to Adobe Bridge, you'll see a list of the contents of your computer's hard drive(s) on the left of the interface.

5 Navigate to the Adobe CS6 Project Assets folder and then to the Footage folder to reveal its contents.

By default, the contents of the Footage folder are displayed as a list, but it can be more useful to display the contents as thumbnails.

6 Toggle the Thumbnail view by clicking the Thumbnail button.

You can hover your cursor over a thumbnail and scrub through it to preview its contents.

7 Drag your cursor to one of the thumbnails and park it there, but do not click on the thumbnail.

8   Move your mouse left and right to scrub through the video.

If you want to ingest just a portion of a video clip, you set In and Out points, defining the portion of the video to be ingested.

9   Click on any of the thumbnails in the Ingest panel.

10 Drag the scrubber to a frame toward the beginning of the clip.

11 Press the I key to set an In point.

12 The thumbnail now shows a shortened Timeline, indicating that the portion of the video prior to the In point will not be ingested.

13 Drag the scrubber to a frame toward the end of the clip.

14 Press the O key to set an Out point.

Note that to ingest only part of a clip, Prelude would need to make a trimmed copy of the file, and it would only do that if the Transfer Clips to Destination check box is selected along with Transcode.

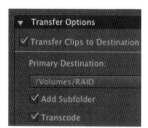

Because you actually want to ingest this entire clip, reset the In and Out points to their original locations.

15 Drag the scrubber to the beginning of the clip and press the I key.

16 Drag the scrubber to the end of the clip and press the O key.

▶ **Tip:** The shortcut for marking clips is to press the V key. You can then select multiple clips and press the V key to mark all selected clips for ingest.

17 You can select which clips and folders you want to ingest simply by selecting the check box under their corresponding thumbnails. Deselected clips and folders will not be ingested into your project. However, in this exercise you'll be ingesting all the clips and folders contained within the Footage folder.

18 Click the Check All button at the bottom of the ingest window to select all the clips.

19 Click the Ingest button to ingest your selected clips.

Copying and transcoding footage to a new location

In most scenarios you'll be ingesting media from data cards or a hard drive and copying it to a different location. Prelude can automatically copy your media to your destination of choice as part of the ingest process.

To set Prelude to do this, locate the Transfer Options on the right side of the Ingest dialog, and select the Transfer Clips to Destination check box. Then choose a Primary Destination folder on your computer. You can add more destinations by clicking the Add Destination button.

In some cases you may receive media that needs to be transcoded—or saved as a different file format and/or with different video and audio settings—to work with Adobe Premiere Pro. If this is the case, select the Transcode check box in the Ingest dialog and use the Transcode presets to save the media with your desired settings upon ingest.

Adding notes to footage

The log comment you added in Adobe Bridge, in the earlier section "Adding metadata to your media," remains attached to the file as metadata. You can view this comment in Prelude and add new comments.

A typical workflow involves ingesting files and then adding the notes or log comments. Prelude is perfectly suited for this.

1 In the Project panel, double-click the first clip Interview_01.mp4.

2 Choose Window > Metadata. Click the disclosure triangle next to Dynamic Media, and then scroll down the list until the Log Comment field is visible.

   Note that the comment you entered in Adobe Bridge is still attached to the file.

3 In the Project panel, double-click the clip Interview_02.mp4.

4 In the Metadata panel, type **Alternate take** in the Log Comment field, and then press Return (Enter). Close out of the Metadata panel in preparation for the next lesson.

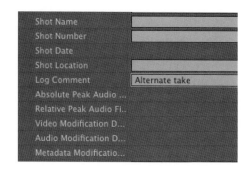

The comment is added to the file and will be attached to the clip throughout the rest of the workflow.

Creating bins

In film and video production, the folders you create to organize your media files are called *bins*. The term bins dates back to traditional film editing when you literally sorted your physical clips of film into bins.

It's essential when starting a video editing project to organize your media into bins. This will help you to quickly locate specific clips when the editing process is underway.

1   In the Project panel, click the New Bin icon. A new bin appears in the Project panel.

2   Name the bin **Joey**, and then press Return (Enter) to confirm.

3   Click on the Joey_01.mp4 clip to select it, and then hold down the Shift key and click on the Joey_02.mp4 clip to select it.

▶ **Tip:** Bins can be placed inside other bins for better organization.

4   Drag the selected clips into the Joey bin.

5   Now create a new bin by clicking the New Bin icon. Name this new bin **Interview**. Select Interview_01.mp4, hold down the Shift key, and then click Interview_08.mp4 to select all clips in between. Drag these selected interview clips into the Interview bin.

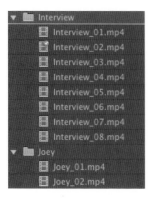

Assembling a rough cut

You can begin creating simple, assembly edits in Prelude, either to get a head start on editing or to assemble clips for another editor if you're working on a project as part of a team.

1 Click the Create a New Rough Cut icon.

2 In the Create Rough Cut dialog, enter the name **Studio Assembly** and save the rough cut to your Lesson 02 folder. The rough cut now appears in your Project panel.

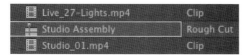

3 Double-click the Studio Assembly rough cut to open it in the Timeline.

   Let's add some clips to the rough cut.

4 Drag the clip Studio_01.mp4 to the Timeline panel.

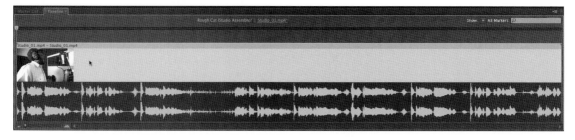

5 Drag the clip Studio_02.mp4 to the right of the first clip in the Timeline panel and drop it there. The second clip is now inserted after the first clip.

6 Drag the clip Studio_03.mp4 to the left of the first clip in the Timeline panel and drop it there. The third clip is now inserted before the first clip.

7 Drag the clip Studio_04.mp4 in between the first two clips on the Timeline. The fourth clip is now inserted in between the existing clips.

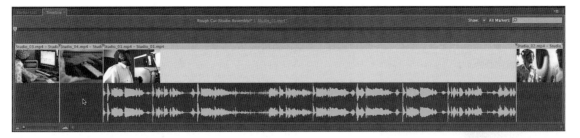

8 Drag and drop the clips on the Timeline to rearrange them in any order.

9 Press the spacebar to play back your rough cut.

10 Choose File > Save to save your project.

Adding time-based comments

You may want to specify which segment of a clip you want to use in the edit. You can enter comments on clips in your Prelude Timeline that pertain to specific parts of your clips. These comments will be available in Adobe Premiere Pro when you move to the editing part of the workflow.

1 In your Timeline, double-click the clip Studio_01.mp4.

2 In the Marker Type panel, click the Comment button.

3 Type **use this section** to enter the comment, and then press Return (Enter).

You'll see the comment in the Timeline starting at whatever frame your current time indicator (CTI) was parked on. You can adjust the In and Out points of the comment to indicate which portion of the clip it pertains to.

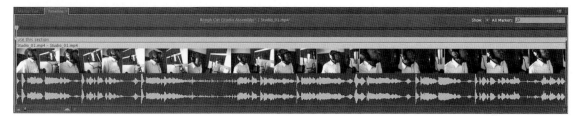

4 Drag the left edge of the comment to a new location on the Timeline to set its In point.

5 Drag the right edge of the comment to a new location on the Timeline to set its Out point.

▶ **Tip:** It's helpful to add comments about camera movements and live audio.

It's also possible to set comment In and Out points by scrubbing your CTI in the Timeline and then clicking the In and Out buttons in the Marker Inspector panel.

6 To return to the rough cut, click the underlined text Rough Cut (Studio Assembly) at the top of the Timeline.

Sending your project to Adobe Premiere Pro

All of the work you've done so far is prep work for the next step of the workflow, which is to edit your project in Adobe Premiere Pro. A single menu selection is all it takes to move your project from Prelude to Adobe Premiere Pro.

1 Click the Project panel.

2 Choose Edit > Select All to select all of the items in the project.

If you want to send just certain items to Adobe Premiere Pro, not your entire project, simply select those items in the Project panel. Any items not selected will not be sent to Adobe Premiere Pro.

3 Press Command+S (Ctrl+S) to save your project. Then choose File > Send to Premiere Pro.

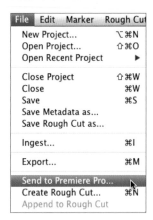

Adobe Premiere Pro will launch, if it is not already open, and will create a new project for you.

Note: If Adobe Premiere Pro is already open when you send a rough cut from Prelude, the currently open Adobe Premiere Pro project will receive the rough cut.

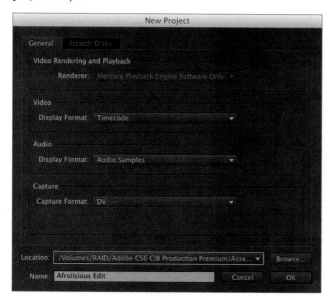

4   In the New Project dialog, click the Browse button.

5   Navigate to your Lesson 02 folder and click Choose.

6   In the Name field type **Afrolicious Edit** and click OK.

All of your footage (with metadata still attached), the bin you created, and the rough cut you created are now in your Adobe Premiere Pro project.

Review questions

1 What is a simple and effective way of organizing your media into folders?

2 What is metadata, and why is it useful?

3 How do you format text in a script?

4 How do you collaborate with others on your script?

5 When ingesting media, how do you ingest only a portion of a clip?

6 How do you send footage and rough cuts from Prelude to Adobe Premiere Pro?

Review answers

1 Organizing your media by asset type (Footage, Audio, Graphics) is simple and effective.

2 Metadata is information about your data. It contains information such as frame resolution, frame rate, clip duration, and so on. Metadata provides useful information to streamline your video production workflow.

3 The Formatting menu in Adobe Story lets you easily format your script the preferred, industry-standard way.

4 Choosing File > Share in Adobe Story lets you invite and assign roles to collaborators.

5 Setting In and Out points on a clip in the Adobe Prelude Ingest panel lets you specify which portion of the clip is ingested, but only if it's marked for transcoding.

6 Select all desired clips and rough cuts in the Prelude Project panel, and then choose File > Send to Premiere Pro.

3 CREATING A BASIC EDIT

Lesson overview

The editing tool is the hub of the video postproduction workflow, so understanding how to do basic editing with Adobe Premiere Pro CS6 is a fundamental skill. In this lesson, you'll learn how to do the following:

- Create a new project and import media files with the Media Browser

- Interpret and view footage

- Organize your project by creating bins

- Create subclips

- Use the Timeline to create and edit a sequence

- Work with tracks on the Timeline

- Reorder and remove clips from your sequence

- Adjust audio levels

- Trim your edit points and use the new Dynamic Timeline Trimming feature in Adobe Premiere Pro CS6

- Add markers to clips and sequences

- Use the Snap feature in the Timeline

 This lesson will take approximately 90 minutes to complete.

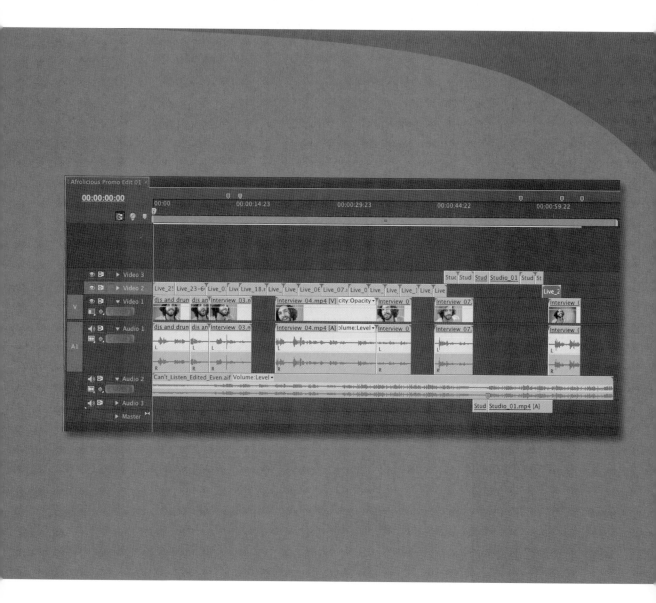

An edited sequence in the Adobe Premiere Pro Timeline.

About Adobe Premiere Pro

Adobe Premiere Pro CS6 is your nonlinear video editing system. It offers lots of intuitive and powerful features that simplify the postproduction phase of your project.

As the hub of your postproduction workflow, Adobe Premiere Pro is not only where you compose your edited piece, but it's also where you bring together the rest of the work that you will create in the other components of Creative Suite 6 Production Premium.

In addition, Adobe Premiere Pro allows you to link dynamically to project assets from other applications in Adobe CS6 Production Premium so that intermediate rendering is not required.

Linear editing vs. nonlinear editing

Linear editing is a method of editing video using a system in which you record each edit sequentially onto videotape. If any changes are required to an edit that has already been recorded to tape, all edits after that change need to be re-recorded in sequence onto the tape. Linear editing systems are largely obsolete now due to the introduction of nonlinear editing systems in the 1990s.

Nonlinear editing is a method of editing video using software on a computer that enables you to manipulate the sequence of digitized video clips before exporting the entire sequence to videotape or as a digitized movie file. Changes can easily be made in the software before output, allowing for maximum flexibility. Adobe Premiere Pro CS6 is an example of nonlinear editing software.

One way to summarize the difference between linear video editing and nonlinear video editing is to compare them, respectively, to typing onto a piece of paper with a typewriter versus using a word processor on a computer.

Optimizing performance

Your hardware requirements for running Adobe Premiere Pro will largely depend on which video file formats you will be editing, as well as the types of tasks you are performing. Adobe Premiere Pro CS6 is able to perform well on high-end systems as well as lower-spec machines, such as laptops, thanks to the Mercury Playback Engine (see Chapter 1 for more details).

The video files we've provided for you to work with in this *Classroom in a Book* are H.264 files, which were encoded to a bitrate that will play back in real time on most computers. However, in film production, you'll likely encounter other video formats, such as 2K and 4k, which require much more horsepower to play back in real time.

What is H.264?

H.264 is a standard for video compression and has become widely used as a standard for web video on sites such as YouTube and Vimeo, allowing high-definition (HD) video to play online. H.264 is also a standard compression used on Blu-ray Discs. Modern video cameras commonly use H.264 as a means of internally compressing raw footage.

2K, 4K, and high frame rates

The terms 2K and 4K refer to video standards that describe the pixel width of a digitized frame of film. For example, a 4K frame can have 4096×3072 pixels, whereas a 2K frame can have 2048×1080 pixels.

Many cameras on the market today can acquire imagery at high frame rates and at a resolution that is higher than standard HD.

Acquiring video footage at resolutions higher than the standard 1920×1080 pixel frame size gives you the flexibility to crop regions of the frame in postproduction and create simple postproduction pans and zooms. High frame sizes may also be required when producing movies for theatrical release. However, as a result of having a greater amount of pixels per frame, 2K and 4K footage can be a bit unwieldy and require more storage space, transfer speed, and processing power.

Shooting at a high frame rate yields more frames per second of playback, which can be interpreted in Adobe Premiere or Adobe After Effects to achieve a dramatic slow-motion look. When shooting at a high frame rate, there is less time to capture each frame; therefore, more light is required.

Many of the cameras made by RED can shoot at frame rates of up to 300 frames per second, whereas cameras manufactured by Phantom HD can shoot close to 10,000 frames per second. These cameras tend to be more expensive than digital SLR cameras (which can shoot at up to 60 frames per second) and require more camera support, such as rigging and additional crew assistance.

The most current tech specs for Adobe Premiere Pro CS6 can always be found on the Adobe website at www.adobe.com/products/premiere/tech-specs.html.

The general rules of thumb for improving performance in Adobe Premiere Pro CS6 are:

- Add as much RAM as your computer is capable of taking.

- Keep your media on a separate drive from the hard drive that your OS and applications are on. A RAID is recommended if you are editing a media format that has a high data rate, or at the very least a 7,200 RPM hard drive.

- Add an Adobe-certified graphics card for GPU acceleration.

Note: For more information on recommended graphics cards for use with Adobe Premiere Pro CS6, go to www.adobe.com/products/premiere/tech-specs.html.

What is a RAID?

A Redundant Array of Independent Disks (RAID) is a combination of multiple hard drives recognized by a RAID hardware controller or by the operating system as a single hard drive. RAID configurations were originally developed for the purpose of security and redundancy where multiple disks would store redundant data. Because hard drives tend to fail over time due to physical friction and heat, redundancy of data decreases the probability of data loss.

Today, RAID configurations are signified by a number from 0 to 6. Common RAID configurations include the following:

- **RAID 0.** Two or more hard drives configured to alternate in reading and writing of data in small blocks. A RAID 0 offers no redundancy but can achieve exponentially higher speeds with the inclusion of more physical hard drives. RAID 0 configurations are ideal for media storage in video postproduction. It's important to accompany RAID 0 configurations with some external means of redundancy, because a RAID 0 has no inherent redundancy.

- **RAID 1.** Two or more hard drives configured to mirror each other for maximum redundancy and security. A RAID 1 is ideal for archiving media, because it provides inherent redundancy that a RAID 0 does not.

- **RAID 5.** Three or more hard drives configured for speed and redundancy. A RAID 5 is capable of operating even if one hard drive in the array has failed.

Creating a new project in Adobe Premiere Pro

Note: P Note: For in-depth coverage on Adobe Premiere Pro CS6, it's recommended that you read Adobe Premiere Pro CS6 Classroom in a Book.

If you're continuing from the previous lesson in Lesson 2, you'll already have the media, bins, and rough cut you created in Prelude in your Adobe Premiere Pro project. In a real-world workflow you would continue building your edit from here.

If you're continuing from Lesson 2, skip these steps that follow and begin with the section "Understanding the Adobe Premiere Pro user interface."

Let's start by exploring how to create a new project in Adobe Premiere Pro!

1   Launch Adobe Premiere Pro CS6.

The Welcome screen appears.

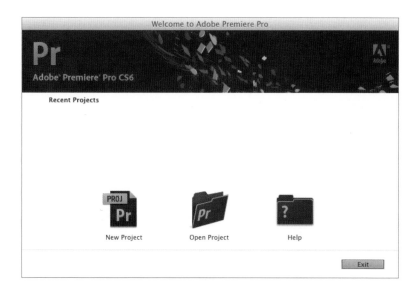

2 Click the New Project icon to open the New Project window.

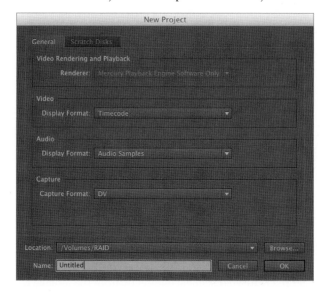

3 Click the Browse button. Navigate to the Lesson 03 folder on your hard drive and click Choose.

4 Double-click in the Name field to select the default name, type **Afrolicious Promo**, and click OK.

● **Note:** Refer to the section "Copying the lesson files" in the "Getting Started" section at the beginning of the book.

5   The New Sequence dialog appears. On the left, you'll see a list of Available Presets to match the specifications of various video footage standards.

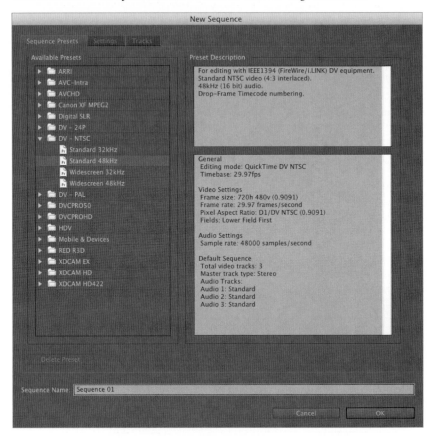

You can create your first sequence here by selecting the format you created your footage in from the Available Presets. A *sequence* is a series of edits arranged in the Timeline panel that when played from beginning to end shows the order of your chosen clips and transitions. You'll learn more about them later in the chapter.

In most cases it's easier to create your sequences directly from the footage you'll be importing, so you'll skip this step.

6   Click Cancel.

Your new project is now open in Adobe Premiere Pro.

Understanding the Adobe Premiere Pro user interface

Now that you have a project open in Adobe Premiere Pro, let's take a look at the interface.

When you launch Adobe Premiere Pro for the first time, you'll be presented with the default Editing workspace. This workspace puts the most commonly used panels at your fingertips. Adobe Premiere Pro allows you to configure the layout panels in multiple ways, to suit your particular way of working, and those configurations are saved on a file-by-file basis.

To reset the Editing workspace to its default settings, do the following:

1 Choose Window > Workspace > Editing.

2 Choose Window > Workspace > Reset Current Workspace.

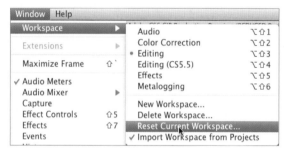

3 In the dialog that appears, click Yes.

Six panels are visible on the surface of the Editing workspace:

- The Source Monitor is where you preview your footage, audio, and graphics clips, and set In and Out points for editing them into your sequence.

- The Program Monitor is where you view the edit that you assemble on your Timeline.

- The Project panel is where you organize your media files, sequences, and other components of your project, as well as create bins.

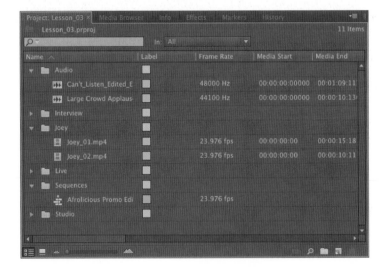

- The Tools panel is where you select different tools used in the editing process.

- The Timeline panel is where you compose and adjust your edit. You work on sequences within the Timeline.

- The Audio Meters display the master audio level of your edit.

The Tools panel   Audio Meters

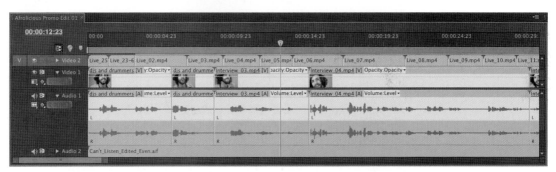

The Timeline panel

Importing footage and other media using the Media Browser

The Media Browser is where you browse the contents of any of the drives or cards connected to your computer, and it provides one way to add those files to your project.

1 Click the Media Browser tab.

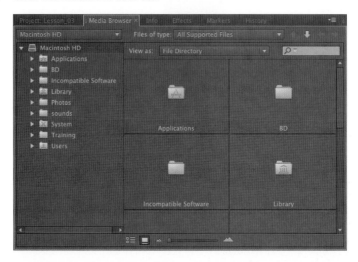

2 Navigate to your Adobe CS6 Project Assets folder, click the disclosure triangle next to Adobe CS6 Project Assets to expand the list of folders (also referred to as twirling down), and then click on your Footage folder.

The contents of the Footage folder appear in the Media Browser.

You can display the contents of a folder in List view or Thumbnail view.

3 Click the Thumbnail View icon at the bottom of the Media Browser.

You can preview the content of the footage by hovering your cursor over any clip's thumbnail and scrubbing left to right.

4 Drag your cursor so it's over the Joey_01.mp4 clip and park it there.

5 Move your cursor left and right to preview the contents of the clip. This is called a *hover-scrub*. This is a new feature in Adobe Premiere Pro that was added in the CS6 release. By doing this, you can scrub through the frames of this clip for faster previewing.

6 You can import individual clips or entire folders full of clips. In this case, import the entire contents of the Footage folder, including clips and subfolders.

7 Click on the Joey_01.mp4 clip to select it.

8 Press Command+A (Ctrl+A) to select all the clips.

9 Right-click and choose Import.

10 Click on the Project panel.

All of the media is imported into your project.

11 Press Command+S (Ctrl+S) to save your project.

Capturing from tape

The workflow you are learning in this *Classroom in a Book* uses media that was captured in a file-based format. Most modern video cameras record video to a memory card or other type of solid state media. Older cameras record to a tape-based format.

If you are editing media from a videotape, you'll need to capture that media with Adobe Premiere Pro to create files that you can edit on your computer.

The standard workflow is to connect your camcorder or tape deck to your computer via FireWire, and then open the Capture tool in Adobe Premiere Pro by choosing File > Capture.

In this workflow, you use the Capture tool to control your camcorder/tape deck and tell Adobe Premiere Pro which section of the tape to capture and what you want to name the resulting files.

If your workflow involves capturing media from tape, you can find more detailed instruction in *Adobe Premiere Pro CS6 Classroom in a Book* (Adobe Press, 2012).

Understanding the Project panel

The Project panel is where you organize all of the assets in your project. By default, it displays all of the items in Icon view, which can be useful because this view displays thumbnails, giving you a visual representation of what is contained within each file.

Viewing your Project panel in List view is also useful, because it gives you an overview of information about each clip and also makes it easy to organize your clips.

Let's explore the Project panel.

1   In the Project panel, click the List View button at the bottom left.

The items in the Project panel now display as an alphabetized list. You can click on the column headings to sort your Project panel in a variety of ways.

2 Click on the right edge of the Project panel and drag it to the right to make it wider.

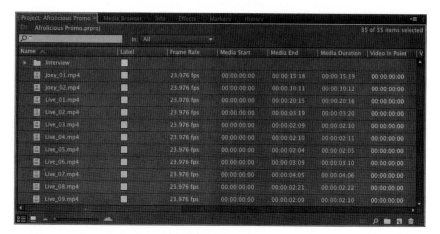

3 Click on the Media Duration heading.

The clips are now sorted based on their duration, from shortest to longest.

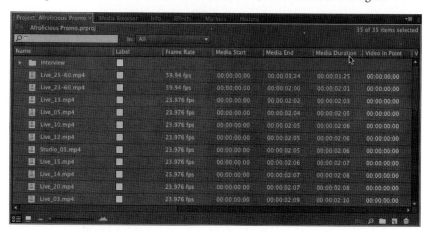

4 Click on the Name heading.

The clips are once again sorted alphabetically.

If you completed the previous chapter, you know that any metadata you add to a video clip in Adobe Bridge or Prelude stays attached to that clip and can be used in Adobe Premiere Pro as well as the other components of Production Premium. The Log Notes entered on these clips can be viewed in the Log Note column of the Project panel.

5 Using the scroll bar at the bottom of the Project panel, scroll to the right until the Log Note column heading is visible.

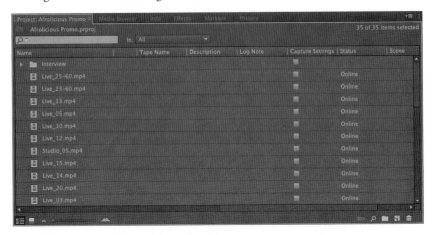

▶ **Tip:** By hovering your cursor over a panel and pressing the tilde (~) key, you can toggle maximizing the panel to fill your screen.

6 Twirl down the Interview bin to reveal its contents.

Note that the Log Notes entered on the Interview_01.mp4 and Interview_02.mp4 clips are visible.

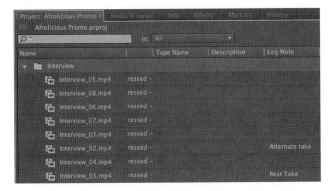

You can reorder the columns of information in the Project panel so you can easily access the information most important to you.

7 Click on the Log Note column heading, and drag it to the left.

8 Drop the Log Note column heading to the left of the Label column.

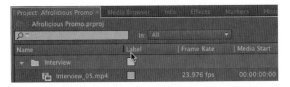

The Log Note column now displays next to the file name, making it easy to view your Log Notes.

Interpreting Footage

Most of the video clips that you imported were shot at a frame rate of 23.976 frames per second (fps). Your final movie will be set to play back at that same frame rate; therefore, the clips that were originally shot at 23.976 fps will play back at that same speed, and the motion in the clips will appear to be at a normal speed.

About seconds and frames

When a camera records video, it captures a series of still images of the action. If there are enough images captured each second, it looks like moving video when played back. Each picture is called a *frame*, and the number of frames each second is usually called *frames per second* (fps). The fps will vary depending on your camera format and settings. It could be 23.976, 24, 25, 29.97, 50, or 59.94 fps. Some cameras allow you to choose between more than one frame rate with different options for accompanying frame sizes. Adobe Premiere Pro will play back video at all common frame rates.

However, you have a few video clips that were shot at 59.94 fps. If these clips were played back at 59.94 fps, the motion in the clips would appear normal as well. But if these clips were played back at 23.976 fps, the motion in the clips would appear slower than normal.

Adobe Premiere Pro can interpret the native frame rate of a video clip as a different frame rate. By interpreting these 59.94 fps clips as 23.976 fps, they can be slow-motion clips in your sequence and give your final movie added production value.

In this exercise, you'll interpret the footage and set the frame rate to 23.976.

1 Deselect all clips by pressing Command+Shift+A (Ctrl+Shift+A).

2 In the Project panel, select the clip Live_23-60.mp4. Hold down the Command (Ctrl) key and select Live_24-60.mp4 and Live_25-60.mp4.

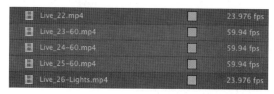

3 Choose Clip > Modify > Interpret Footage. The Modify Clip window appears. This is where you'll set the clips' interpreted frame rate.

4 Select "Assume this frame rate," and type **23.976** in the fps field. Click OK.

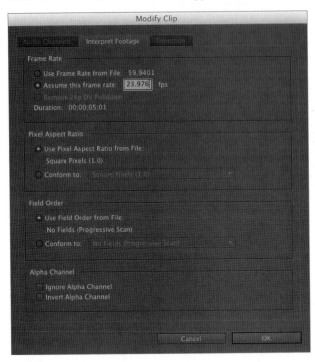

5 Double-click on Live_23-60.mp4 to open it in the Source Monitor. Press the spacebar to play the clip to verify that it is now in slow motion.

Creating bins

As mentioned in Chapter 2, bins are folders you create to sort and contain your media files. For an efficient workflow, it's essential to sort your media into bins in a way that will make it easy to find the clip you need when you need it.

Importing assets as a bin

In some cases you may already have your media sorted into folders on your hard drive. We've provided a folder called Audio with your assets that you'll now import into your project as a bin.

1 Click the Media Browser tab.

2 Navigate to your Adobe CS6 Project Assets folder, and then click on the Audio folder to select it.

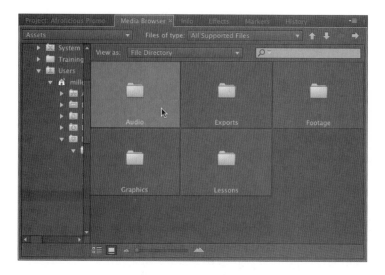

3   Choose File > Import from Media Browser.

4   Click the Project tab.

▶ **Tip:** Use the keyboard shortcut Command+Option+I (Ctrl+Alt+I) to import the selected item from the Media Browser.

You'll see that the Audio folder has been imported into your project as a bin.

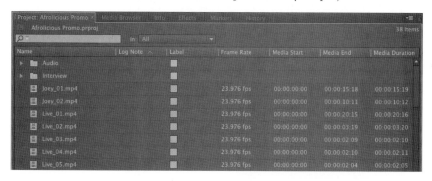

5   Double-click the Audio bin.

The Audio bin opens in a new floating panel. You'll see two audio files contained within, which you'll use later on.

6   Press Command+W (Ctrl+W) to close the Audio bin panel. Press Command+Shift+A (Ctrl+Shift+A) to deselect all.

Creating a new bin

Now you'll create a new bin from scratch.

1   In the Project panel, click the New Bin icon.

A new bin appears in the Project panel.

● **Note:** After naming a bin, if you press Return, Adobe Premiere Pro will highlight the next bin. Pressing Enter will register the name of the current bin. If you're using a laptop and have no Enter key, click on a blank area in the Project panel to register the bin name.

2   Type **Studio** to name the bin, and then press Enter.

You now have a new bin called Studio. You'll put the clips from the Studio shoot into this bin.

3   Scroll down until all the Studio clips are visible (you may need to make your Project panel bigger to see them all).

4   Place your cursor to the left of the first Studio clip, click and drag down and to the right until all seven Studio clips are selected, and release the mouse button. This is called *marquee-selecting*.

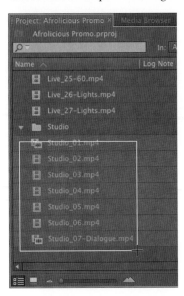

5 Click and drag your selected clips into the Studio bin. Press Command+Shift+A (Ctrl+Shift+A) to deselect all.

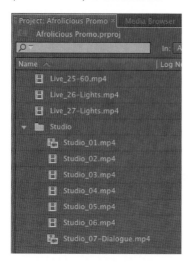

Continue by creating bins called **Joey** and **Live**, and dragging the corresponding clips into these bins. Be sure not to have a bin or any items in that bin selected when you click the New Bin icon, or the new bin will appear in the selected bin.

● **Note:** If you are continuing from Chapter 2, you should already have a Joey bin.

You can also select items in your Project panel, and then drag to the New Bin button, and a new bin will be created with the selected items contained within.

Viewing your footage

A good work practice as an editor is to take some time looking at all of your clips. Familiarize yourself with all of the well-composed moments that would help tell your story. Also become familiar with the mistakes and flubbed takes that you'll want to avoid using.

For this exercise, you'll review the raw footage for the Afrolicious promo and look at various features that might help you tell your story.

You can view your clips in the Source Monitor.

1 In the Project panel, double-click on your Interview bin to open it.

2 In your Interview bin, double-click on Interview_01.mp4. It will open in the Source Monitor.

3 Press the spacebar or click the Play icon to play the clip.

Listening to your footage

As you view your clips, look and listen for moments that stand out in terms of usable sound bites. View all of the Interview clips, one at a time, to become familiar with them.

▶ **Tip:** Depending on how much screen space you have, you may need to move the Bin panel on your screen so that the Source Monitor is not obstructed. To move it, click the top of the panel interface and drag it elsewhere.

1 Double-click on Interview_03.mp4 in the Interview bin to open it in the Source Monitor.

2 Press the spacebar to play the clip. Notice that there is an anomalous "click" sound that is not Joey's voice. Make a mental note that this will need to be fixed later.

Because these clips were shot with Joey in front of a green screen background, they may not be ideal for use as a visual element in your edit, but the audio has lots of good sound bites. You'll use these clips primarily for the audio, not the video.

3 Select your Interview bin and press Command+W (Ctrl+W) to close it.

Now let's review the Studio clips. Again, you are looking and listening for moments that would help tell your story, as well as for anomalies in your footage that you need to either fix or avoid using.

4 Go back to the Project panel, and double-click on your Studio bin to open it.

5 In your Studio bin, double-click on Studio_07-Dialogue.mp4. It will open in the Source Monitor.

6 Press the spacebar or click the Play icon to play the clip.

This clip shows a nice moment of interaction between Joey and a singer in the studio. We hear them talking about recording a vocal. Also notice that there is a low hum of background noise in this clip. That will have to be fixed later.

7 Go back to your Studio bin. Double-click on Studio_01.mp4. It will open in the Source Monitor.

8 Press the spacebar to play the clip, which shows the singer from the previous clip at the microphone, recording a vocal. So here you have two pieces of a story that would match well together in your edit.

9 View the rest of the Studio clips. Notice that all but these two don't have any audio.

10 Select your Studio bin and close it by pressing Command+W (Ctrl+W).

Viewing your Live footage

Now let's look at the Live clips. This footage was recorded during a live performance by Afrolicious, and some of it can be enhanced with visual effects.

1   In the Project panel, double-click on your Live bin to open it.

There are a lot of Live clips, so rather than viewing them as a list of clip names in the bin, switch to Icon view.

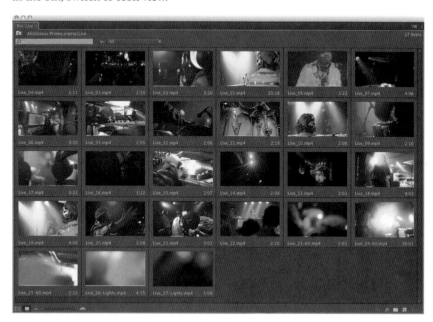

2   At the bottom left of the Live bin, click the Icon View icon. All of the clips will display as icons. You can adjust the size of the icons by using the Zoom In / Zoom Out slider next to the Icon View icon.

3   Hover-scrub Live_01.mp4.

When viewing your clips, you should also be looking for moments that could be fixed or even enhanced with a visual effect.

4   Double-click on Live_18.mp4 to open it in the Source Monitor. Press the spacebar to play it.

This clip shows the back of a musician on stage. It also shows a bright stage light shining at the camera. Symbolically, a bright light could serve to illustrate a moment of revelation or a transition of mood. This shot could be enhanced with a visual effect made in Adobe After Effects CS6, which you'll learn to do in Chapter 5.

Tip: When viewing your footage, keep your eye open for quick camera pans or movements, blurry lights, and other unintended abstract moments in your clips. You can intersperse these moments throughout your edit to give a stylistic dimension to your story.

5 Double-click on Live_26-Lights.mp4 to open it in the Source Monitor.

6 Press the spacebar to play it. You'll see that this shot is rather blurry, showing only blobs of colored light. This could have been shot by accident when the videographer pressed the Record button on his camera without realizing it. That doesn't mean you can't use it.

7 View all of these clips by double-clicking each one to open them in the Source Monitor. Press the spacebar to play a clip.

8 Set your Live bin back to List view by clicking the List View icon.

9 Close your Live bin by pressing Command+W (Ctrl+W).

Green screen footage

Now look at the Joey clips. These clips were shot with a green screen background.

1 In the Project panel, double-click on your Joey bin to open it. This bin has only two clips.

2 Double-click on Joey_01.mp4 to open it in the Source Monitor.

3 Press the spacebar to play it. The clip shows Joey doing a little dance in front of a green screen background. This has obvious potential for use in a visual effect shot, because a green screen background can be removed from a clip and the foreground subject can then be placed in front of a different background.

You'll learn about using green screen footage in Chapter 4.

4 Select your Joey bin. Close it by pressing Command+W (Ctrl+W).

5 Return to the Project panel.

Music and sound effects

You've imported a couple of clips that are just audio with no video. Let's become familiar with these clips.

1 Double-click on the Audio bin to open it. There are two audio clips in this bin.

2 Double-click on Can't_Listen_Edited_Even.aif to open it in the Source Monitor.

3 Press the spacebar to play it. This can obviously be used as the main music track in your edit.

4 In your Audio bin, double-click on Large Crowd Applause 02.wav to open it in the Source Monitor.

5 Press the spacebar to play it. This is a short sound effect clip of crowd applause. This could be used to enhance one of the Live clips.

You'll learn about editing audio using these clips in Chapter 7.

6 Select your Audio bin and close it by pressing Command+W (Ctrl+W).

After you've looked at all of your clips, think about how you'd create a compelling story with them.

About subclips

Sometimes you may have a very long clip in your bin that has two or more segments in it that can serve as stand-alone clips. You can extract these segments as *subclips.* Although a subclip is a reference to a segment of the master clip, Adobe Premiere Pro shows a subclip in a bin as a self-contained clip.

You can use a subclip in your project much like a master clip but with a few exceptions. For instance, you can trim a subclip only within its initial start and end frames. You can set new In and Out points for a subclip but only if they fall between the In and Out points you set when you first created the subclip.

A subclip is a reference to the master clip's media file. If the master clip is taken offline or deleted from the project, any subclips derived from it will remain online. However, if you remove the master clip's media file from your system, its subclips will go offline.

▶ **Tip:** Be warned that if you relink a subclip that has been taken offline, it becomes a master clip, and all connections to the original master clip are broken.

Creating a subclip

Especially with longer takes, creating a subclip is an efficient method of breaking down a piece of footage to just the components you want to use in your edit.

The first interview clip we've provided in your Adobe CS6 Project Assets folder is a long interview with Joey that you need to grab some sound bites from. So, let's do that now.

1   In your Project panel, twirl down the Interview bin triangle to reveal its contents.

2   Double-click the clip Interview_01.mp4 to open it in the Source Monitor.

3   Press the spacebar and view the contents of the clip.

This clip contains a variety of random statements about Afrolicious. You'll create some subclips containing only the best sound bites for use in your edit.

4 In the Source Monitor, drag the current-time indicator (CTI) to 00:00:22:00.

5 Press the spacebar to begin playback, and then press it again to stop playback when the CTI reaches 00:00:31:00.

The first sound bite you'll create a subclip for is "DJs and drummers, MCs, horn players, and all tied in to the dancers."

6 Drag the CTI back to 00:00:22:00 and click the Mark In icon, or press the I key.

7 Drag the CTI to 00:00:31:00 and click the Mark Out icon, or press the O key.

The sound bite is now selected in the clip.

8 Choose Clip > Make Subclip.

9 In the dialog, type **djs and drummers**, and then click OK.

The subclip is now in the Interview bin in your Project panel.

10 Double-click the **djs and drummers** subclip to load it into the Source Monitor.

11 Press the spacebar to play back the subclip.

Speech to Text workflow

If you are editing interview footage, you may want to try the Speech to Text feature in Adobe Premiere Pro CS6. This feature analyzes the audio and attempts to create a text transcript.

Simply right-click any clip containing audio in the Project panel, and choose Analyze Content.

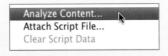

Make sure the Speech check box is selected, as well as the language your audio is in. When you click OK, Adobe Media Encoder will launch, analyze the clip, and then put the Analysis Text into the Metadata panel in Adobe Premiere Pro. Selecting the clip in the Project panel and then opening the Metadata panel will reveal the analyzed text.

Of course, in the event that the Speech to Text feature makes a few errors, they can be edited manually.

Creating the first sequence

In terms of editing in Adobe Premiere Pro, a *sequence* is a series of edits arranged in the Timeline panel that when played from beginning to end shows the order of your chosen clips and transitions. Clips can easily be added, removed, trimmed, and rearranged in a sequence. Because clips are merely instances of project media, any edits performed on clips in a sequence are nondestructive to the raw media on your system.

The easiest way to create a new sequence in Adobe Premiere Pro is to drag a clip to the New Item button. This will create a new sequence in the same video format, frame size, and frame rate as the clip.

1   Click and drag the djs and drummers subclip from the Interview bin to the New Item button.

A new sequence called djs and drummers appears in the Timeline. Adobe Premiere Pro names the sequence the same as the clip used to create it. Now you'll rename the sequence.

2   In the Interview bin, click the name of the djs and drummers sequence to rename it.

3   Type **Afrolicious Promo Edit 01** and then press Return (Enter).

Next, you'll create a bin called Sequences to contain the sequences you'll create for this project.

4   In the Project panel, click the New Bin button.

5   Type **Sequences** and then press Return (Enter).

6 Drag the Afrolicious Promo Edit 01 sequence into the Sequences bin.

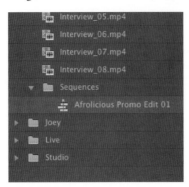

Note that the new bin is contained in the Interview bin, because that bin was already selected when you created the Sequences bin. Now you'll move the Sequences bin out of the Interview bin.

7 Click and drag the Sequences bin to the left, out of the Interview bin, so that it's listed above the Studio bin.

Working in the Timeline

The Timeline is where you'll do most of the work when you are editing. It's where you assemble and arrange your footage, add transitions and effects, and do most of the creative work involved in editing film and video.

Preparing to edit in the Timeline

The sequence you just created contains only a single video clip at this point. To fully understand the Timeline, you need to add more clips to your sequence.

1 In the Interview bin, marquee-select the clips Interview_03.mp4 through Interview_08.mp4.

2 Click and drag the selected clips into the sequence, directly to the right of the existing clip.

3 Make sure the edge of the new clips snap to the edge of the existing clip, and then drop the new clips.

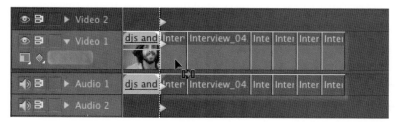

Now you have a sequence with multiple clips.

The components of the Timeline

The main components of the Timeline that you'll be working with in Adobe Premiere Pro are:

• **Video tracks.** Contain your visual elements, such as video, titles, and graphics.

• **Audio tracks.** Contain your audio, such as dialogue, soundtrack, and sound effects.

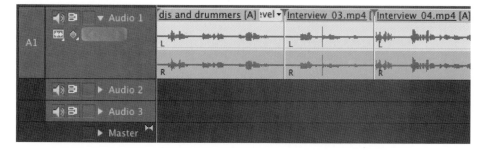

- **Current-time indicator.** Indicates which frame in your sequence you are viewing in the Program Monitor. You can drag the CTI around to change your position in time.

- **Work Area bar.** Defines the active part of the sequence in your Timeline. It is typically used to select a portion of the Timeline to render previews or export.

Editing on the Timeline

Now that you have the first set of clips on your Timeline, you'll remove one of the extraneous words from the subclip you created by marking that section of the sequence and then extracting it.

▶ Tip: If you are using a reduced size keyboard on an Apple iMac or MacBook, press Fn+left arrow to adjust your CTI to the beginning of your sequence and Fn+right arrow to adjust your CTI to the end of your sequence.

▶ Tip: To adjust your CTI to a specific frame in your sequence, click once on the Playhead Position at the top left of the Timeline panel, type in the desired timecode, and press Return (Enter).

1 Drag the CTI to the beginning of the sequence, or press the Home key.

2 Press the spacebar to begin playback, and then stop playback after the first clip.

You'll edit out the word *and* in Joey's interview to make this sound bite flow better.

3 Park the CTI at 00:00:05:00.

4 Zoom in on your Timeline by pressing the equal (=) key on your main keyboard (not the numeric keypad) three times.

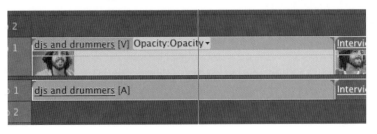

5 Drag the CTI to the right and then back to the left again, so you can hear where he says the word *and*.

When you're editing a sound bite, it can be helpful to view the audio waveform to identify when a word or phrase begins or ends.

6 Click on the Collapse-Expand Track triangle to twirl down Audio 1.

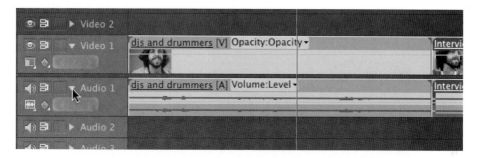

7 Hover your cursor over the divider line between Audio 1 and Audio 2 so that your cursor changes, and then drag downward to stretch Audio 1 vertically in the Timeline.

The audio waveform is now clearly visible. Next, you'll set an In and Out point to select the word *and*.

8 Drag the CTI back and forth over the word *and* so you can identify it in the audio waveform.

9 Park the CTI at 05:17.

10 In the Program Monitor, click the Mark In button.

11 Park the CTI at 06:04.

12 In the Program Monitor, click the Mark Out button.

13 Now let's remove the video and audio from this region of time. Click the Extract button. This will cut the selected region from the Timeline and move all clips in all unlocked tracks to the left to fill in the gap.

The video and audio of Joey saying the word "and" is removed, and all of the video and audio following it is moved backward in time to fill the gap.

14 Drag the CTI to the beginning of the sequence, or press the Home key.

15 Make sure that the Program Monitor is set to show the entire frame. Choose Fit from the Set Zoom Level menu at the bottom left of the Program Monitor.

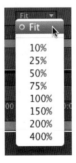

16 Press the spacebar to play back the first 15 seconds of the edit, and then stop playback.

You'll notice that the sound bite sounds great, but the video jumps where you cut it. That's OK; you'll be replacing the video of Joey with b-roll from the live show and the recording session. Joey's audio will mainly serve as a narration; viewers won't be seeing him onscreen at this point.

Working with tracks

In Adobe Premiere Pro you can add multiple layers, or tracks, of video, audio, graphics, titles, and other elements. In this exercise you'll be adding b-roll to the Video 2 track to cover the video of Joey's interview.

1 Press the backslash (\) key to zoom the sequence to fit the Timeline panel.

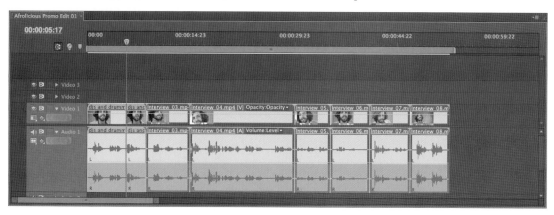

2 In the Project panel, double-click the Live bin to open it.

3 Select Live_01.mp4. Hold down the Shift key and select Live_25-60.mp4. This will select all clips in between. The clips Live_26-Lights.mp4 and Live_27-Lights.mp4 should not be selected. You'll be using those later. Drag the Live_01.mp4 clip to the Timeline, and then drop the series of clips on Video 2. These video clips have no accompanying audio.

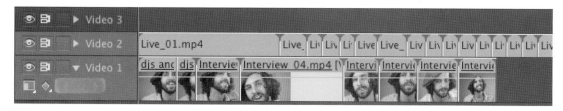

You can turn the visibility of a track on and off by clicking the Toggle Track Output button.

4 Click the Toggle Track Output button for Video 2 to make it invisible.

5 Click the Toggle Track Output button for Video 2 again to make it visible.

6 Close the Live bin by selecting it and pressing Command+W (Ctrl+W).

Reordering clips on the Timeline

You added the clips to the Timeline from the Live bin in the order in which they were listed in the bin. Now you'll rearrange some of the clips on the Timeline so they play in the desired order.

Creating the Overwrite edit

To begin with, you'll move a clip to replace another clip on the Timeline.

1 Press the backslash (\) key to zoom your sequence to fit the Timeline panel.

2 Click the last clip on the Timeline in Video 2, Live_25-60.mp4, to select it.

3 Click and drag the clip to the beginning of Video 2.

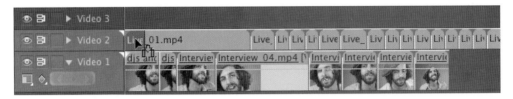

The video that was previously in that part of Video 2 has been overwritten by the clip you just dragged and dropped. This is called an *Overwrite edit*. But in this instance you want to insert the new clip, so you need to push the rest of the clips down the Timeline without overwriting what's already there.

Creating the Insert edit

Now you'll learn a technique that allows you to insert a clip between other clips without overwriting.

1 Choose Edit > Undo to undo your Overwrite edit.

2 Click the last clip on the Timeline in Video 2, Live_25-60.mp4, to select it.

3 While holding down the Command (Ctrl) key, click and drag the clip to the beginning of Video 2. Notice how the cursor changes while you do this.

The clip is now inserted at the beginning of the video and has pushed the rest of the items to the right, or later in the sequence. This is called an *Insert edit*. The only problem is that it moved all of the items on all of the video and audio tracks. In this example, you want just the items on Video 2 to adjust when you insert this clip. To do this, you need to lock Video 1 and Audio 1.

4 Choose Edit > Undo to undo your Insert edit.

5 Toggle on the Lock button on both Video 1 and Audio 1.

6 Click the last clip on the Timeline in Video 2, Live_25-60.mp4, to select it.

7 While holding down the Command (Ctrl) key, click and drag the clip to the beginning of Video 2.

Reorder an additional clip

You've successfully rearranged the clips on Video 2 without overwriting existing content on the Timeline or rearranging the other video and audio tracks. Now you'll reorder an additional clip.

1 Click the next-to-last clip on Video 2, Live_23-60.mp4.

2 While holding down the Command (Ctrl) key, click and drag the clip so it lines up with the beginning of the Live_01.mp4 clip on Video 2.

3 Release the mouse button.

> **Tip:** You can zoom in on your Timeline using the equal (=) key. Zoom out by using the minus (–) key.

The clip has now been inserted between the first and second clips on the Timeline.

4 Select the Live_02.mp4 clip on your Timeline, and while holding down the Command (Ctrl) key, drag it to the beginning of the Live_01.mp4 clip and drop it there.

5 Move your CTI to the beginning of the sequence, and start playback to review your changes.

6 Stop playback.

Removing clips

Nonlinear editing is nondestructive; therefore, anything that you delete from your sequence can be put back later if you change your mind. There is a rather long clip at the end of your sequence that can be removed.

1 Press the backslash key (\\) to show your entire sequence.

2 Select the clip at the end, Live_24-60.mp4.

3 Press the Delete key. The clip is deleted from your sequence.

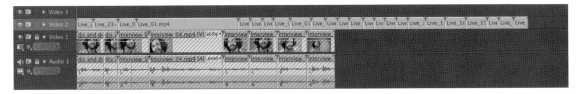

Let's remove another clip from the sequence.

4 Find what is now the second-to-last clip in Video 2, Live_21.mp4, and select it. This clip shows the back of Joey's head and is not very interesting.

5 Press the Delete key.

The clip is now removed, but notice that there is a gap where it was.

You can easily remove this gap by making any clips that appear later in the Timeline move to the left to fill in the gap. This is called a *Ripple Delete*.

6 Zoom in to your Timeline by pressing the equal (=) key.

7 Click on the gap between Live_20.mp4 and Live_22.mp4.

8 Right-click on this selection and choose Ripple Delete. Live_22.mp4 automatically moves to the left and fills in the gap.

You can use Ripple Delete to remove clips from your sequence, as well as remove gaps. Instead of deleting a clip and then Ripple Deleting the gap left behind as two separate operations, you can do both in one step.

9 Select the Live_01.mp4 clip on your Timeline.

10 Right-click on the clip and choose Ripple Delete.

The clip is now deleted from the sequence, and the clips that came later have filled in the empty space.

▶ **Tip:** You can perform a Ripple Delete by selecting a clip or a gap and pressing Shift+Delete.

Working with audio

A well-known saying in filmmaking is *audio is half the picture*. It's essential to give the same attention to audio in your productions as you do to the visual components.

In the Afrolicious Promo project, you'll be working with audio from Joey's interview, a track from the Afrolicious CD, as well as a sound effect.

Earlier in this lesson, you imported the Audio bin into your project. Now you'll add one of the files in that bin to your sequence.

1 In the Project panel, twirl open the Audio bin.

2 Double-click the file Can't_Listen_Edited_Even.aif to load it into the Source Monitor.

3 Press the spacebar to preview the audio file.

4 In the Timeline, click the disclosure triangle on the Audio 1 track to collapse the track and hide its waveform.

5 In the Source Monitor, click and drag the Drag Audio Only button to the Audio 2 track on your Timeline.

6 Make sure the beginning of the audio file lines up with the beginning of the sequence, and then release your mouse button.

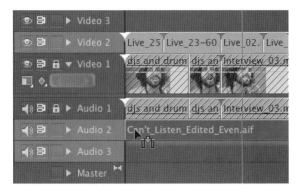

7 Adjust your CTI to the beginning of your sequence. Press the spacebar to preview the sequence with the new audio added. Stop playback when you're finished previewing.

Note that the volume of the music makes it difficult to hear what Joey is saying. You'll use the Audio Mixer to bring down the level of the music track so it's at an appropriate volume relative to Joey's voice.

8 Choose Window > Audio Mixer > Afrolicious Promo Edit 01. The Audio Mixer panel appears.

9 Press the spacebar to play back the sequence, and note how the meters in the Audio Mixer indicate the level of each audio track.

10 With the sequence playing back, click and drag down the volume fader for Audio 2 in the Audio Mixer until the volume is low enough so you can hear Joey's voice clearly. This will be in the area of –12dB.

11 Press the spacebar to stop playback.

When adjusting audio levels, your first impulse might be to raise the level on the track you want to make louder. It's usually a better idea to lower the level on the track you want to make quieter, because it will help avoid over modulated audio, which will distort and degrade in quality.

● **Note:** Audio editing will be covered in more detail in Chapter 7.

12 Press Command+S (Ctrl+S) to save your project.

Refining your story

Now that you have all of your sound bites placed on your Timeline, let's explore ways to make a more dynamic story. In this exercise, you'll learn techniques that will help you refine timing in your sequence.

Using gaps in audio

Joey is telling a story about his experience and inspiration as a musician. One way to make his story more compelling is to create gaps in the talk track so that the music can occasionally attract the viewer's attention.

1 In your Timeline, unlock Video 1 and Audio 1 by clicking their Toggle Track Lock switches.

2   Press the Home key to move your CTI to the beginning of the sequence. Press the spacebar to play your sequence. Listen carefully to the interview audio. The last clip, Interview_08.mp4, in which Joey says, "My confidence comes from the music. We can't lose with that music behind us" is a good conclusive and uplifting statement; it should go at the end.

3   Select Interview_08.mp4 and drag it to the right with the Selection tool—toward the tail (end) of the music clip in Audio 2—to put it aside for later.

The sound bite in Interview_06.mp4 is not very good. Joey makes a somewhat redundant statement, and he is mumbling.

4   Select Interview_06.mp4 and press Delete. Doing so leaves a gap in the interview audio.

5   Now click on the Toggle Track Output switch for Audio 1 to mute it.

6   Twirl open Audio 2 to show its waveform.

7   Press Home to set your CTI at the beginning of the sequence. Press the spacebar to play. This time listen closely to the music track. Pay close attention for moments in the music that stand out and would sound good during gaps in the interview audio.

For instance, at 0:00:16:00, you should hear a bass riff in the music. That would serve as a moment for the music to be heard while there is a brief pause in the interview audio.

8   Adjust your CTI to 0:00:18:11.

9   Select Interview_04.mp4, hold down the Shift key, and select Interview_05.mp4. With the Selection tool, drag these clips to the right so that the head of Interview_04.mp4 lines up with the main bass riff in the music at 0:00:18:11.

10 Click the Toggle Output switch for Audio 1 to unmute it. Click the Toggle Track Lock switches for Video 1 and Audio 1 to lock them.

11 Press Command+S (Ctrl+S) to save your project.

Trimming edits

When you have a number of clips in your sequence, you'll normally start trimming the heads (beginnings) and tails (endings) of each clip to adjust the pace and timing of your edit. In the third clip on your sequence, you'll trim the head to remove the first 12 frames from the clip.

1 Choose the Ripple Edit tool from the Tools panel.

▶ **Tip:** You can also press the B key to access the Ripple Edit tool.

2 Zoom in on your Timeline using the equal (=) key. Place the cursor at the beginning of the Live_23-60.mp4 clip on the Timeline. Note that it changes to indicate a Ripple Trim.

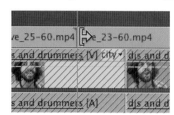

3 Click and drag the head of the clip to the right (do not release the mouse button yet).

As you drag, note that the Program Monitor has changed to show you the last frame of the previous clip on the left and the first frame of the clip you are trimming on the right. This makes it easy to preview your edit.

4 Move the mouse until you have trimmed 12 frames from the head. The timecode in the Program Monitor will show you how many frames you have trimmed.

Also notice that a tool tip next to your cursor indicates how many frames are being trimmed.

5 Release the mouse button.

Note that the sequence updates to represent your edit.

6 Move your CTI to the beginning of the sequence, and play back the first few cuts to review your changes.

Using Dynamic Timeline Trimming

Adobe Premiere Pro CS6 introduced a new feature called Dynamic Timeline Trimming, which allows you to trim your cuts in real time as the edit is playing back. You'll use this feature to perform additional trimming.

The goal with this trim is to get the beginning of the clip Live_23-60.mp4 to line up with the audio of Joey saying "MCs."

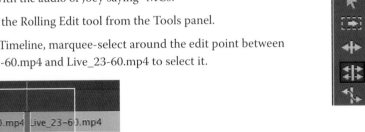

► **Tip:** You can also press the N key to access the Rolling Edit tool.

1 Choose the Rolling Edit tool from the Tools panel.

2 On the Timeline, marquee-select around the edit point between Live_25-60.mp4 and Live_23-60.mp4 to select it.

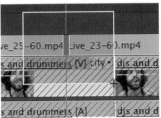

Marquee-selecting one or more edit points automatically puts Adobe Premiere Pro into Trim mode.

3 Press the spacebar to begin playback.

Note that the playback loops around your edit point. As the edit plays, you can trim the edit point by clicking the buttons in the Program Monitor.

4 Click the –1 button to trim the edit point back in time by one frame.

Note that the edit point on the sequence moves back as you trim. As the sequence loops, pay attention to where Joey says the word "MCs"; this is where you want to trim the edit point to.

5 Click the –1 button four more times, so that you trim the edit point back in time by a total of five frames.

You've now successfully trimmed the edit point so it lines up properly with the audio.

6   Click in any gray space in the Timeline panel to leave Trim mode.

7   Choose the Selection tool from the Tools panel.

8   Press the backslash key (\) to show your whole sequence in the Timeline.

9   Press Command+S (Ctrl+S) to save your project.

Tip: You can also press the V key to access the Selection tool.

Multicam editing

The project you are creating in this *Classroom in a Book* was shot with a single DSLR camera. If you are editing a project shot with multiple cameras, the Multicam editing features of Adobe Premiere Pro CS6 will help you cut between your cameras in real time, similar to editing a live TV show. Previously, you could work with multicam footage from four cameras, but now you're limited only by the formats you're working with and the power of your editing machine.

In Adobe Premiere Pro CS6, the process of creating a multicamera sequence has been greatly simplified. For more information, we recommend *Adobe Premiere Pro CS6 Classroom in a Book* (Adobe Press, 2012).

Using Markers

There are times when you'll want to mark specific frames for future reference, either to indicate when something happens in a clip or when you want something to happen in your sequence.

Adobe Premiere Pro CS6 lets you add markers to clips as well as to your sequence.

Adding a marker to a clip

In Chapter 7 you'll create an audio transition in your edit that will start with live audio of a singer recording a vocal and blend into the recorded version of the same song. So you're going to add a marker in this next exercise which you'll use later in Chapter 7.

1   In your Project panel in your Audio bin, double-click on Can't_Listen_Edited_Even.aif to open it in the Source Monitor.

2   Play the clip, and you'll hear the vocal start at 0:00:50:09. Let's add a marker to this frame in the clip.

3 At the bottom of the Source Monitor is a row of icons. Click the Add Marker icon.

You should see a marker in the Source Monitor at the current frame.

You should also see a marker on the music clip in the Timeline at the same corresponding frame.

This marker will indicate for us later when to start the video clip of the singer recording the same vocal.

Adding a marker to a sequence

In Chapter 5 you'll create a motion graphic in Adobe After Effects CS6 that will be exactly five seconds long. You'll want the end of that motion graphic to coincide with the end of the music clip in your sequence. And you'll want to save the last five seconds of your edit for the motion graphic and not put any other video clips in those last five seconds. Therefore, you need to add a marker to your sequence to indicate when the motion graphic will begin.

Tip: Pressing Shift+left arrow moves your CTI backward five frames; Shift+right arrow moves your CTI forward five frames.

1 Select your Timeline and press the End key. Your CTI will jump to the last frame of your edit, which is at 0:01:09:04. Move your CTI backward exactly five seconds to 0:01:04:04.

At the bottom of the Program Monitor is a row of icons similar to the row of icons on the Source Monitor.

2   Click the Add Marker icon to add a sequence marker at the current frame.

▶ **Tip:** Press the M key to add a marker at the current frame of a sequence.

You'll add one more marker to your sequence to mark where another shot will go.

3   In your Project panel in the Joey bin, double-click Joey_01.mp4 to open it in the Source Monitor. In Chapter 4 you'll add this clip to your sequence toward the end, right before where the end motion graphic will go.

4   Select your Timeline and go to 0:01:01:04. Add a new marker at this frame by clicking the Add Marker icon in the Program Monitor or by pressing the M key. This marker indicates where Joey_01.mp4 will go later and will remind you not to place any other video clips on the Timeline after this marker.

5   Press Command+S (Ctrl+S) to save your project.

Clip markers vs. sequence markers

A sequence marker is attached to a specific frame in the sequence, whereas a clip marker is attached to a specific frame on a clip. Sequence markers do not move as clips move in the sequence. However, if a clip with a marker on it is moved in the sequence, its marker will move in time with it.

Using Snap

Adobe Premiere Pro CS6 has a handy Snap feature, which makes it easy to move your CTI between edit points in your sequence as well as add clips to your sequence and move clips in your sequence.

Snapping between edit points

The Snap feature is turned on by default and can be toggled on and off by pressing the Snap icon at the top left of the Timeline.

1   Scrub your CTI through your Timeline with the Shift key held down. You'll notice that the CTI "snaps" between edit points and markers automatically. Edit points and marker locations appear as white triangles when the CTI is snapped to them.

2   Click the Snap icon to deactivate it. Now scrub through your Timeline. Notice how the CTI no longer snaps to edit points and markers.

3   Click the Snap icon to reactivate it.

Snapping clips into a sequence

The Snap feature also simplifies adding clips to your sequence. You'll use the Snap feature as you place clips in Video 3.

1 In your Project panel, twirl open the Studio bin, if it isn't already open.

2 Double-click on Studio_01.mp4 to open it in the Source Monitor. Play the entire clip.

You'll see the singer at the microphone as he records his vocal. The first ten seconds of the clip show some erratic camera movement as well as the singer stopping to recompose himself. You won't use that part.

However, you will use the segment starting at 00:00:11:11, as he begins singing "I can't listen..." all the way to 00:00:21:06, as he finishes singing "... I could never go for that."

3 In the Source Monitor, adjust the CTI to 00:00:11:11 and set the clip's In point by pressing the I key.

4 Adjust the CTI to 00:00:21:06 and set the clip's Out point by pressing the O key.

5 Select your Timeline, hold down the Shift key, and adjust your CTI to snap at the clip marker on the music clip in Audio 2. You may want to zoom in on your Timeline by pressing the equal (=) key a few times to make sure that your CTI is on the clip marker.

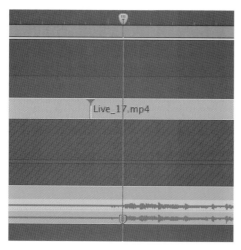

6 Go back to the Source Monitor, click on the video frame, and drag the clip directly into the Timeline on Video 3 so that the clip's head snaps to the clip marker and the CTI. The accompanying audio should land in Audio 3.

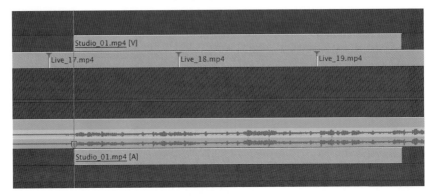

7 Adjust your CTI to a few seconds before Studio_01.mp4 and press the spacebar to play the clip.

Listen closely; you'll notice that the timing of the singer and the vocal on the music track are practically in synch. Also notice, again, how tracks operate in Adobe Premiere Pro. Because Studio_01.mp4 is on a track above Live_18.mp4, you do not see Live_18.mp4.

Snapping clips within a sequence

If Snap is enabled, when you move clips within a sequence, the clip's head or tail will snap to markers or edit points.

Let's move Interview_08.mp4 so that its tail snaps to the sequence marker at 0:01:04:04.

1 Deactivate the locks on Video 1 and Audio 1 by clicking their Toggle Track Lock switches.

2 Double click on Interview_08.mp4 in the Timeline. It will appear in the Source Monitor.

3 Play the clip. At 00:00:04:19, after Joey says, "We can't lose with that music behind us," press the O key to set the clip's Out point. You'll see that the clip's Out point has been trimmed in the Timeline as well.

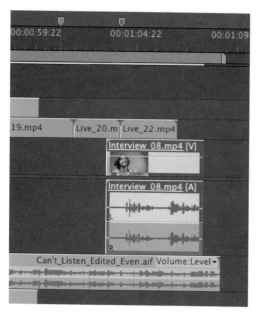

4 Select your Timeline. Hold down the Shift key and scrub your CTI so that it snaps at the marker at 0:01:04:04.

5 Click and drag the Interview_08.mp4 clip in the Timeline so that its tail snaps to the CTI.

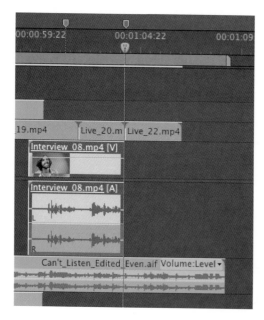

You've now set markers indicating where clips will go eventually in your Timeline, and you've set clips at specific frames in relation to markers either on other clips or in the sequence. These clips and markers will not move or have their timing adjusted. As you can see, the snap feature allows you to make precise edits to your sequence, and you are encouraged to use it.

Finishing Your Rough Edit

The rest of the edit will be motivated by moments in the interview audio or the music. If you're editing a movie that has a voice-over that drives the story, it's logical to edit video clips in your sequence that supplement what the voice-over mentions. Also, if your edit has an underlying music track, certain moments in the music, such as tempo transitions, can be enhanced by applying video edits at the same time in your sequence.

Adding more Studio clips

Let's go ahead and add some clips to accompany the voice-over.

1   Adjust your CTI to the head of Interview_07.mp4 in the Timeline and press the spacebar to play the clip.

Joey says, "We try to take some of that inspiration from a gig and turn it into a song in the studio." This sound bite could serve as a transition point to the shots of Joey and the singer in the recording studio.

2   In the Project panel, double-click on the Studio bin to open it.

3   Click the Icon View icon to display all of the clips in the bin in Icon view.

Only two of these clips have audio. You can determine this by the waveform icon at the bottom right of a clip's icon.

Trim a clip with a sound bite

As an editor, always be looking and listening for moments in your clips that could match together and give your story a consistent narrative flow.

Let's trim a clip to a usable sound bite. You'll use trimming techniques that were covered earlier in this lesson.

1 Double-click on Studio_07-Dialogue.mp4 to open it in the Source Monitor.

2 Press the spacebar to play it. In this clip, Joey and the singer are talking enthusiastically about recording a vocal. This shot would fit perfectly in your edit after the sound bite of Joey's mention of bringing inspiration from his live shows into the studio.

4 Set the CTI in the Source Monitor to 00:00:01:09 as Joey is about to say "Yo, man, we should do that vocal." Press the I key to set this clip's In point.

5 Set the CTI in the Source Monitor to 00:00:03:15 after the singer says, "Let's do it, man." Press the O key to set this clip's Out point.

6 Click on the video frame in the Source Monitor and drag the clip into your Timeline in Video 3, so that its tail snaps to the head of Studio_01.mp4. The accompanying audio will be put in Audio 3.

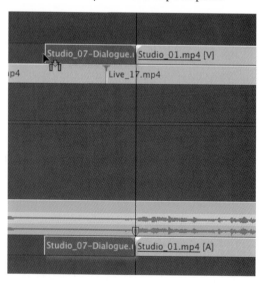

Add a Studio sound bite to your sequence

Now you'll take that sound bite you just created and add it to your sequence.

1   Adjust your CTI to just before the Interview_07.mp4 clip, and then press the spacebar to play the clip.

    Notice that there is roughly a one-second pause between Joey saying "turn it into a song in the studio" and the Studio_07-Dialogue.mp4 clip of Joey saying "Yo, man, we should do that vocal." This pause should be removed to maintain the pace of the narrative.

2   Select Interview_07.mp4 in the Timeline with the Selection tool. Drag it to the right so that its tail snaps to the head of Studio_07-Dialogue.mp4.

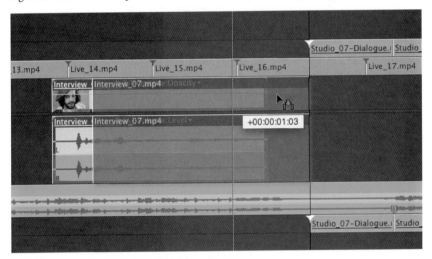

3   Adjust your CTI to just before the Interview_07.mp4 clip, and then press the spacebar to play the clip.

    The pause is now gone. Also, because you moved Interview_07.mp4 in the Timeline, there is now more of a gap between it and Interview_05.mp4, allowing the music to be heard in that gap of time.

Bridging the Live clips to the Studio clips

There are a few other Studio clips that you could use to smooth the visual transition from the Live clips to the Studio clips. Let's go ahead and edit these clips together.

1   In the Studio bin, hover-scrub Studio_03.mp4 to preview the frames in this clip, which shows Joey in his studio working with audio software on his computer.

2   Hover-scrub Studio_04.mp4 to preview the frames in this clip, which shows a close-up of Joey's hands on a synthesizer keyboard.

These two clips would not only match well together in your edit, but also reinforce the sound bite of Joey talking about working in the studio, and thus serve as a logical visual transition between the Live clips and the Studio clips.

3 Select Studio_03.mp4, hold down the Command (Ctrl) key, and select Studio_04.mp4. Drag these clips into Video 3 in your Timeline so that the tail of Studio_04.mp4 snaps to the head of Studio_07-Dialogue.mp4.

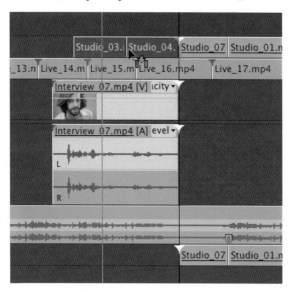

4 Adjust the CTI in your Timeline to just before Interview_07.mp4, and then press the spacebar to play back your changes.

When Joey says the word "inspiration," that could serve as an edit point between the Live clips and the Studio clips.

5 Adjust your CTI to 0:00:43:12.

6 Select the head of Studio_03.mp4 in Video 3.

7 Using the Selection tool, trim the head of this clip to the right until the cursor snaps to the CTI.

Applying an L-cut

A common editing technique called an L-cut entails letting the audio of one clip play over the video of the following clip. This type of edit not only helps quicken the visual pace of a story, but provides a narrative connection between two shots that might be unrelated.

Your viewers probably don't need to see the entire Studio_01.mp4 clip in your sequence, because the action is clearly established. You can insert other Studio clips on Video 3 that will show as the audio of the singer continues.

1   Scrub your CTI through the Timeline over Studio_01.mp4. Find the moment before you hear the singer take a breath, at 0:00:54:23.

2   Make a new marker at this frame by pressing the M key.

3   In the Studio bin, hover-scrub Studio_02.mp4. It shows the singer at the microphone recording a vocal. You probably don't want to use this clip because his visible lip movements wouldn't match the vocal heard in the edit, and that would be distracting to the viewer.

4   Hover-scrub Studio_05.mp4, which shows the singer at the microphone and Joey dancing to the music. This was taken at a reverse angle from Studio_01.mp4, so it would be a good edit match.

5   Hover-scrub Studio_06.mp4, which shows them sitting at the computer listening to their recorded track. This would logically follow Studio_05.mp4, because it shows a progression of action.

    You saw them recording the song and now they are listening to it. The magic of editing allows you and the viewer to skip ahead in time.

6   Select Studio_05.mp4, hold down the Command (Ctrl) key, and select Studio_06.mp4 so that they are both selected.

7   With the Selection tool, drag these clips to Video 3 in the Timeline, so that the head of Studio_05.mp4 snaps to the marker you had made at 0:00:54:23.

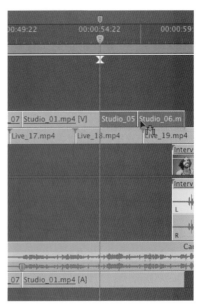

Notice that by doing this, the last half of the video frames of Studio_01.mp4 have been over-written, yet the audio remains in Audio 3.

Removing flash frames

A *flash frame* is either a very short clip (only a few frames long) or a short gap in-between clips that causes a brief "flash" during playback, which can be quite distracting to the viewer. Since we have a flash frame here, let's remove it.

1 Scrub the CTI in your Timeline back several seconds, and then press the spacebar to review your changes.

If you were paying close attention, you may have noticed that a couple of frames from Studio_01.mp4 were not overwritten by performing this edit in the previous exercise and are visible after Studio_06.mp4.

2 Scrub your CTI to the end of Studio_06.mp4. Press the equal key (=) several times to zoom in to show one-frame increments in your Timeline.

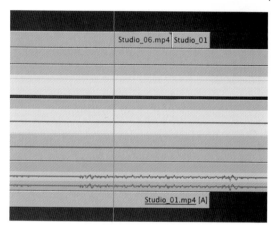

3 Select this bit of frames of Studio_01.mp4 on Video 3 and press Delete.

Final trimming

Studio_06.mp4 could probably be shortened a little, so let's do that now.

1 Zoom out by pressing the minus key (–) four times.

2 Scrub your CTI to the head of Studio_06.mp4 in your Timeline. Scrub your CTI forward and find the moment in the audio when you hear "I could never go for that." Park your CTI on the frame right before where you hear the word "go," at 0:00:58:13.

3 Select the tail of Studio_06.mp4 with the Selection tool. Drag to the left to trim the tail of this clip until it snaps to the CTI.

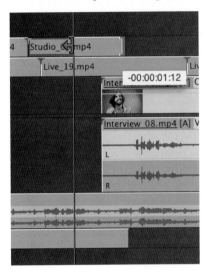

4 Select your Studio bin and press Command+W (Ctrl+W) to close it.

5 Press Command+S (Ctrl+S) to save your project.

For now, you're finished editing the Studio clips on Video 3.

Editing the Live clips

Now let's concentrate on editing the clips in Video 2.

1 Click the Toggle Track Output switch for Video 3 to turn it off.

2 Press the backslash key (\) to show your entire sequence in the Timeline.

3 Press Home to adjust your CTI to the beginning of your sequence. Press the spacebar to play the sequence. Pay attention to moments in the Interview sound bites that would serve as logical edit points for the clips in Video 2.

For instance, in Interview_03.mp4 when Joey says, "blurring lines between audience and performer," you could use that as a moment to cut between a shot of the crowd and a shot of the musicians on stage.

4 Adjust your CTI to the frame after Joey says "audience," at 0:00:11:05, and create a marker by pressing the M key.

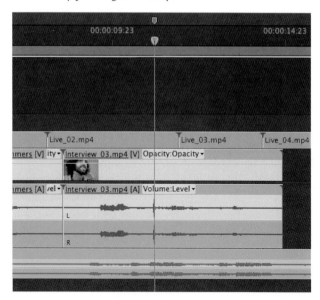

Conveniently, the next clip on Video 2, Live_03.mp4, is a shot of the crowd.

5 Zoom in on your Timeline by pressing the equal (=) key as many times as needed to see the clip names.

6 Select Live_03.mp4, and then drag it to the left until its head snaps to the marker you just made. This will create a small gap in Video 2.

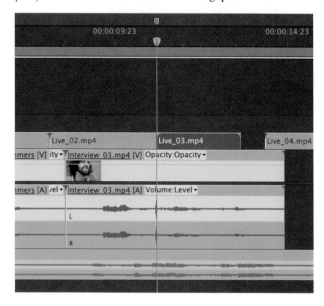

7 Now scrub the CTI forward to when Joey begins to say, "and performer," at 0:00:13:00. This is where you will place a shot of performers on stage, of which there are many.

8 Create a marker on this frame by pressing the M key.

9 Scrub forward to Live_18.mp4 on Video 2. This is the clip that shows a bright light shining on one of the musicians.

Using empty space in video tracks to rearrange clips

▶ **Tip:** Press the equal key (=) to zoom in to your Timeline. Press the minus key (–) to zoom out of your Timeline.

In Premiere Pro CS6, you can temporarily place clips in an empty region of a video track while you move other clips around in an occupied track to make room for the clips you want to place in the occupied track. While this technique may not be the most elegant way to work, sometimes rearranging clips in your sequence requires making good use of empty space in your Timeline interface. That said, be careful not to leave clips in your Timeline where they should not be. Stay organized as you work.

1 Select Live_18.mp4 in Video 2 and drag it into Video 3 so that its head snaps to the marker at 0:00:13:00.

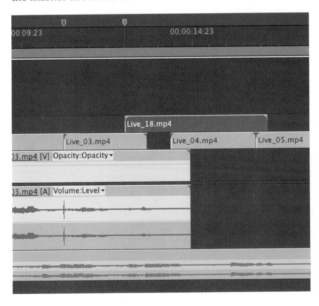

2 Show your entire sequence by pressing the backslash key (\).

3 Marquee-select all of the clips in Video 2 from Live_04.mp4 to Live_17.mp4. Be careful not to accidentally select anything in Video 3 and Video 1.

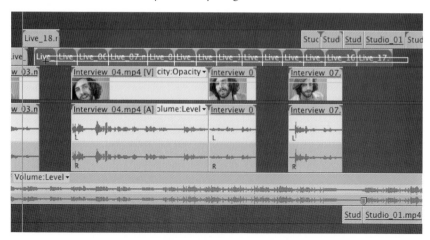

4 Click and drag these clips so that the head of Live_04.mp4 snaps to the tail of Live_18.mp4.

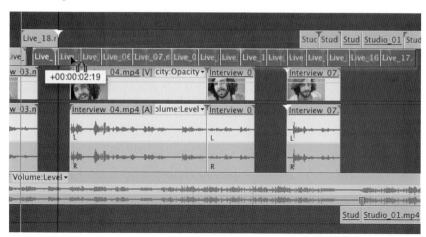

5 Now select Live_18.mp4 in Video 3 and drag it down into Video 2, making sure that you are not also adjusting its timing in the sequence.

Finding a good edit point

Let's find another point in the music track that could motivate a visual edit.

1   Adjust the CTI forward to 0:00:29:06. The music increases tempo right here, which could help motivate another edit in the video.

2   Press the equal (=) key to zoom in so that you can see the clip names in the Timeline.

3   Marquee-select Live_08.mp4 through Live_13.mp4 in Video 2.

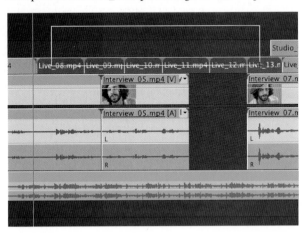

4   Drag these clips to the left until the head of Live_08.mp4 snaps to the CTI.

5   Press Space Bar to play your sequence and review your edit.

Removing clips

Now let's remove some clips in Video 2 that aren't needed. Don't be afraid to make editing decisions that may seem brutal, because in most cases, no matter how good the footage is, you can't use it all.

1   Live_14.mp4 just shows a stage light. It doesn't add anything to the story, so select it and press Delete.

2   Live_15.mp4 is another shot of a turntable. It's redundant because there is already a shot like this. Select Live_15.mp4 and press Delete.

3   Live_16.mp4 is a crowd shot and is mostly in silhouette. Select it and press Delete.

4   Live_17.mp4 is another redundant shot of an instrument. Select it and press Delete.

5   The framing in Live_19.mp4 is off balance, and it only shows Joey's arm. Select it and press Delete.

6 The lighting in Live_20.mp4 is a bit dark. Select it and press Delete.

Removing these clips leaves a large gap in Video 2, but the clips in Video 3 cover the gap.

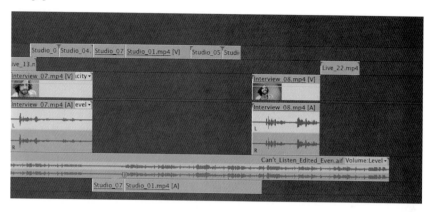

Adding a closing shot

Now you need a closing Live shot to go before the marker at 0:01:01:04. Live_22.mp4 is a well-composed shot from the crowd's point of view, because it shows Joey smiling on stage.

1 Select Live_22.mp4 and drag it to the left until its tail snaps to the marker at 0:01:01:04.

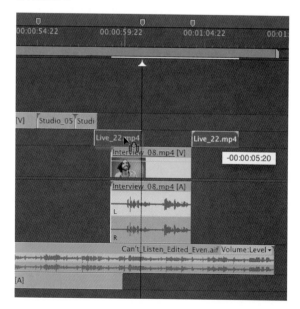

2   Click the Toggle Track Output switch for Video 3 to turn it back on.

3   Press Home to move the CTI to the beginning of your sequence. Press the spacebar to play your rough edit.

This edit will serve as the foundation for what you'll be doing in the remaining lessons in this book.

4   Press Command+S (Ctrl+S) to save your Adobe Premiere Pro project.

Review questions

1 Why are bins important?

2 What is a subclip, and how can it be useful?

3 How do you lock video and audio tracks to prevent them from being adjusted?

4 How do you raise or lower the volume on an Audio track?

5 What makes Dynamic Timeline Trimming effective?

6 What are the advantages of using the Snap feature?

Review answers

1 Bins are where you organize your media, making it easy to find what you're looking for during the editing process.

2 A subclip is a portion of an existing clip. Making subclips allows you to extract sound bites from a long interview clip.

3 Toggling the Lock button on Video and Audio tracks in the Timeline will prevent you from making any unwanted changes on those tracks.

4 In the Audio Mixer you use the Volume fader to raise or lower the volume of an Audio track.

5 Dynamic Timeline Trimming allows you to loop playback of an edit point and trim it in real time. This can help you line up edit points with audio or other visual or aural cues.

6 The Snap feature allows the CTI to easily adjust to edit points in the Timeline. It also allows easy adjustment of the CTI to clip markers and sequence markers.

4 ADVANCED EDITING TECHNIQUES

Lesson overview

In the previous lesson, you created a basic edit with Adobe Premiere Pro CS6. In this lesson, you'll use more advanced editing techniques and learn how to do the following:

- Create simple dissolve transitions between clips in your Timeline
- Apply and modify an effect to clips in your Timeline
- Use an Adjustment Layer to apply multiple effects to multiple clips
- Apply the Ultra Key effect to create a green screen composite
- Create a static title with the Abobe Premiere Pro title tool
- Use the Warp Stabilizer effect to smooth unsteady camera movement in a clip
- Generate a preview render of your Timeline

 This lesson will take approximately 90 minutes to complete.

A video clip that has been chroma keyed in Adobe
Premiere Pro CS6.

Versioning your edit

If you are continuing from the previous lesson, feel free to continue with the Adobe Premiere Pro project you already have open. If you are starting at this lesson, navigate to the Lesson 04 folder on your hard drive and open the Adobe Premiere Pro project Lesson_04 Start.prproj. Save your Adobe Premiere Pro project file in the Lesson 04 folder as **Afrolicious Promo.prproj**.

Because you are continuing with a previous version of this edit, you'll first save a new version of your sequence. This allows you to go back to the original version if need be and is a recommended best practice in the video editing workflow.

1 In the Project panel, twirl open the Sequences bin.

▶ **Tip:** Press Command+C (Ctrl+C) to copy; press Command+V (Ctrl+V) to paste.

2 Click on the Afrolicious Promo Edit 01 sequence to select it. Choose Edit > Copy to copy it to your clipboard. Then choose Edit > Paste.

   This will make a duplicate of this sequence outside of the Sequences folder.

3 To modify the name of the sequence, click on the name of the sequence to select it.

4 Change the name of the sequence to **Afrolicious Promo Edit 02**, press Return (Enter) and drag it into the Sequences folder.

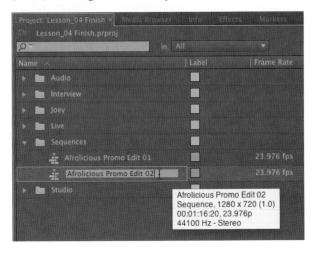

5 Double-click the Afrolicious Promo Edit 02 sequence to load it in your Timeline.

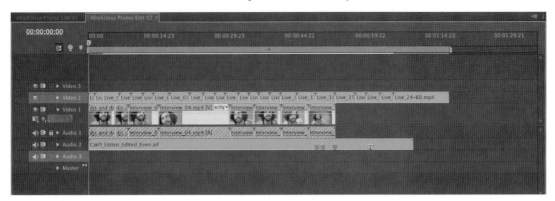

Note that the sequence appears in a new tabbed Timeline panel in front of your original sequence.

Having multiple Timeline panels open simultaneously can be useful in certain situations, but it can also be confusing. For the time being, you'll close the first Timeline to eliminate the possibility of accidentally modifying the wrong sequence.

6 In the Timeline panel, click the Afrolicious Promo Edit 01 tab to select it.

7 Press Command+W (Ctrl+W) to close this sequence. You can also click on the x in the corner of the tab to close it.

The new sequence is now the only one visible in the Timeline, which will ensure that you are working on the most recent iteration.

Adding transitions

In the previous lesson, you created a basic edit containing "hard cuts," meaning that each clip cuts directly into the next. In many instances, you can move between cuts more gracefully with a transition. A transition can serve as a storytelling device to indicate the passage of time or a change of location.

The most commonly used transition is a dissolve, which blends the tail of one clip with the head of the next clip. The term dissolve dates back to traditional film editing where the frames of celluloid were literally dissolved together in a chemical bath to merge them together. With Adobe Premiere Pro, you can add a dissolve simply by clicking and dragging.

Because the first few clips in the edit happen over a calm portion of the music, transitioning between them with dissolves will help give a calmer feeling to that portion of the edit. Let's add those dissolves now.

1 Click on the Timeline panel, and then press the backslash (\) key to zoom your sequence to fit the Timeline panel.

2 Drag the current time indicator (CTI) to the beginning of the sequence, and then play back the first 10 seconds of the edit.

At about 9 seconds, the music track starts to pick up energy, and the existing straight cuts will work well from that point forward. For the edit points before 9 seconds, you'll add a dissolve.

3 Press Shift+7 to open the Effects panel.

4 In the search field, type **dissolve**.

Note that as you type, Adobe Premiere Pro filters out the list to show you only those effects containing the text you are typing. In this case, you'll see the dissolve effects after typing the first few letters; it is not necessary to type the entire word dissolve.

Also, note the yellow square around the icon for Cross Dissolve. This yellow square indicates that this transition is set as the current default Video Transition.

▶ **Tip:** To change the default transition, right-click on a transition in the Effects panel, and then choose Set Selected as Default Transition from the context menu.

5 Make sure that the Track Header for Video 2 is highlighted in the Timeline. If it is not, click it. Doing this will ensure that transitions will be applied to clips in this track when using the Apply Video Transition keyboard shortcut or menu command.

6 In the Timeline, hold down the Shift key and scrub the CTI so it snaps to the first edit point, which is between the clips Live_25-60.mp4 and Live_23-60.mp4.

7 Zoom in by pressing the equal (=) key on your keyboard (not the numeric keypad).

8 Drag and drop the Cross Dissolve effect from the Effects panel onto the edit point on your Timeline. You can also use the Apply Video Transition keyboard shortcut, Command+D (Ctrl+D). Verify that the transition overlaps both clips.

▶ **Tip:** You can zoom in on your Timeline using the equal (=) key. Zoom out by using the minus (–) key.

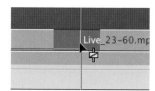

9 Use the Play Around shortcut (Shift+K) to automatically adjust your CTI two seconds before the current frame (or *preroll*), and then play two seconds after the current frame (or *postroll*). This allows you to preview your transition.

Next, you'll add a transition at the beginning of the edit so it fades in from black. This will make for a more graceful start to the piece.

Because you'll be applying a similar transition as before, you can copy that Cross Dissolve that you just made and paste it here.

▶ **Tip:** Change the preroll and postroll values in the Playback preferences to set how many seconds before and after the current frame that Adobe Premiere Pro will play back after pressing Shift+K.

10 Select the transition clip between Live_25-60.mp4 and Live_23-60.mp4. Press Command+C (Ctrl+C).

11 Press Home to adjust your CTI to the beginning of the sequence. Press Command+V (Ctrl+V) to paste the transition.

12 Press Shift+K to play back the first few seconds.

Note that the video in Video 1 is visible during the transition. Because you are only using the audio from Joey's interview, not the video, you'll toggle off the visibility of Video 1.

13 Click the Toggle Track Output button on Video 1.

14 Go to the beginning of the sequence and play back the first few seconds.

Now the video fades in from black. Next, you'll modify the duration of the transition so it lasts one second.

15 In the Timeline, double-click on the transition clip.

Doing this will show the Effect Controls for the transition, which shows the duration is currently 12 frames.

16 Click on the duration value to make it editable. Type **100** and press Return (Enter). Notice that Adobe Premiere Pro translates 100 to 00:00:01:00.

17 Play back your changes to review them.

The most-used transitions

As tempting as it might be to use the video transitions with wild abandon, in terms of style, it's probably not a good idea. Apart from a standard cut transition, only a few video transitions should even be considered unless there are special project-specific circumstances:

- A Cross Dissolve fades out clip A while fading in clip B. Cross Dissolves can also work well at the beginning or end of a clip when you want to fade in or out from black. A Cross Dissolve can indicate passage of time or a change in location to the viewer.

- A Wipe transition replaces clip A with clip B by revealing clip B in a linear or radial fashion. A Wipe is generally used to indicate a change in location.

- An Additive Dissolve functions much like a Cross Dissolve. However, in an Additive Dissolve, the luminance values of clip A and clip B are gradually added together so that at the halfway point of the transition there is a peak of brightness. This makes the transition a bit more noticeable and stylized than a Cross Dissolve.

Creating effects in Adobe Premiere Pro

Adobe Premiere Pro CS6 comes bundled with several dozen effects that enable you to perform simple and complex tasks, such as color correction, blurring and sharpening, audio enhancement, texturing, chroma keying, and a variety of other effects to enhance your edit. Having the ability to apply effects to clips in Adobe Premiere Pro yields efficiency in your workflow, because you don't always have to use another program, such as Adobe After Effects, to create visual effects for your edit.

The most relevant and most important use of effects by far, for most editors, is the ability to adjust contrast and exposure, and make color correction enhancements. The Three-Way Color Corrector effect in Adobe Premiere Pro CS6 has been greatly enhanced and will be covered in Chapter 8.

Let's do a simple exercise that demonstrates some of the general rules about effects in Adobe Premiere Pro CS6. You'll apply multiple effects to a clip to give it an "old film" look, and then save those effects and their settings as a preset.

Applying an effect to a clip

First up is applying a simple effect to a clip. You'll apply the Black & White effect in this exercise.

1 Press Shift+7 to access the Effects panel. You need to find the Black & White effect, which desaturates a clip.

2 In the search field, type the word **black**, which will reveal all effects with that word in their names.

▶ **Tip:** Double-click to apply an effect to a selected clip, or series of selected clips.

3 Select the Black & White effect, and drag it onto the first clip in your sequence, Live_25-60.mp4.

4 Press Shift+5 to access the Effect Controls panel of this selected clip. The Black & White effect is a very basic effect and has no controls.

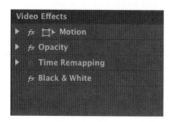

5 Now let's give this clip a bit of sepia tone. In the Effects panel, type **tint** in the search field.

6 Select the Tint effect and drag it onto Live_25-60.mp4.

Change the Tint settings so black is mapped to orange.

7 In the Effect Controls panel, click on the Map Black To color swatch. In the Color Picker, choose a fully saturated bright orange, and then click OK.

8 In the Tint Effect Controls panel, set Amount to Tint to 25%.

The clip should now look sepia toned.

Changing render order of effects

The top-to-bottom stacking order of effects in the Effect Controls panel determines their rendering order. Currently, Black & White is stacked above Tint; therefore, Black & White renders and then Tint renders. You can change the rendering order by adjusting the stacking order of effects.

1 In the Effect Controls panel, select the Tint effect. Drag it above the Black & White effect.

Notice that the clip is no longer sepia toned as before. The reason is that the clip is being tinted, and then the result of that is made black and white.

2 Press Command+Z (Ctrl+Z) to undo this last action.

Copying and pasting effects

You can copy and paste effects between clips in the Timeline. Doing this can ultimately save you time if you need to apply the same effect(s) with the same setting(s) on multiple clips.

1 Select the Black & White effect in the Effect Controls panel. Hold down the Command (Ctrl) key and select the Tint effect. Both are now selected. Press Command+C (Ctrl+C) to copy.

2 In your Timeline, select the Live_23-60.mp4 clip. Press Command+V (Ctrl+V) to paste.

3 Press the Home key, and then press the spacebar to play your sequence from the beginning. The first two clips in your sequence now appear sepia toned.

The first two clips in your sequence have these two effects applied to them. But what if you wanted to apply these effects to all of the clips in your sequence? You could copy and paste these effects to each clip in your sequence. However, if you changed the effect settings on one of the clips to maintain consistency, you would then have to change the settings on all other clips, which would be tedious and time-consuming. There is a better way and that's by using adjustment layers.

Adjustment layers

Adobe Premiere Pro CS6 now features Adjustment Layers, which are special layers that allow you to apply one or more effects to several clips at the same time using the same effect settings. Let's see how these Adjustment Layers work.

1 Press Command+Z (Ctrl+Z) to undo pasting the effects to Live_23-60.mp4.

2 Click the Project panel tab. Make an Adjustment Layer by choosing File > New > Adjustment Layer.

3 In the Adjustment Layer window that appears, make sure that the settings match your sequence settings. The Width should be 1280, the Height should be 720, the Timebase should be 23.976 fps, and Pixel Aspect Ratio should be Square Pixels (1.0). Click OK.

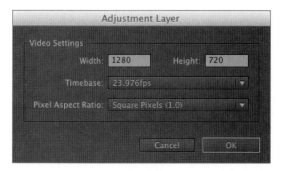

This new Adjustment Layer should appear in your Project panel.

Note: If a bin is selected in your Project panel when you create an Adjustment Layer, the Adjustment Layer will appear inside the selected bin. The Adjustment Layer can then be dragged elsewhere in the Project panel.

4 Select this Adjustment Layer and drag it into your Timeline, on Video 3, so its head snaps to the beginning of the sequence.

5 By itself, the Adjustment Layer is not visible. However, if one or more effects are applied to the Adjustment Layer, those effects are rendered on the clips in the track(s) below the Adjustment Layer.

Now let's apply the Black & White and Tint effects to the Adjustment Layer. You can cut them from the Live_25-60.mp4 layer and paste them onto the Adjustment Layer. In this example, you don't want the effects on the video clip if they will be applied to the Adjustment Layer.

6 Select Live_25-60.mp4 in the Timeline. Press Shift+5 to access its Effect Controls panel.

7 Select the Black & White effect. Hold down the Command (Ctrl) key and select the Tint effect.

8 Press Command+X (Ctrl+X) to cut the effects from the video clip.

In your Program Monitor, notice that the effects are not rendering on Live_25-60.mp4 anymore.

9 In your Timeline, select the Adjustment Layer. Press Command+V (Ctrl+V) to paste the effects.

10 Scrub the CTI in your Timeline to Live_23-60.mp4. Notice that the effects applied to the Adjustment layer render on it because the clip is in a track below the Adjustment Layer.

Now that these two effects are on the Adjustment Layer, you can extend the tail of the Adjustment Layer to render the effects on more clips in Video 2.

11 Show your entire sequence in the Timeline by pressing the backslash (\) key.

12 Select the tail of the Adjustment Layer and drag to the right so the Adjustment Layer covers more clips in Video 2.

13 Scrub your CTI forward in the Timeline to verify that more clips in Video 2 are now sepia toned. Because the Adjustment Layer is a single clip, you need to adjust only its Effect Controls to modify how its effects render on all clips in the track(s) below it.

Saving and exporting presets

Effects and their settings can be saved as a preset, which allows you to easily apply the effects and their settings on clips in your Timeline without having to copy and paste them between layers. Also, because presets can be saved as files on your hard drive, they can be copied between different computers and applied by other users in Adobe Premiere Pro CS6. Let's save and export a preset now.

1 Select the Adjustment Layer in your Timeline. Press Shift+5 to access the Effect Controls panel.

2 Select the Black & White Effect, and then hold down the Command (Ctrl) key and select the Tint effect.

3 Right-click on either of these effects and choose Save Preset.

4 In the Save Preset window that appears, type **Old Film** in the Name field to name the preset. Click OK.

5 To verify that this preset works, press Delete to remove the two selected effects.

6 Press Shift+7 to access the Effects panel. Select any text that may be in the search field and press Delete.

7 Click the disclosure triangle next to the Presets folder to twirl it open. You should see a preset called Old Film.

8 Select this preset, and then drag it onto the Adjustment Layer in the Timeline. The saved effect settings are once again applied to the Adjustment Layer.

> **Note:** Presets can also save settings for Motion and Opacity.

This exercise was just a demonstration. You really don't want to use this old-film look or this Adjustment Layer in your sequence, so let's modify the sequence now.

9   In the Project panel, select the Adjustment Layer, and then press Delete. Click Yes in the warning window that appears to confirm that you want to remove the Adjustment Layer from the project.

The Adjustment Layer should no longer be in your Timeline.

10 Press Shift+7 to access the Effects panel again. Notice that the Old Film preset is still there and could be utilized later if desired.

But it can also be exported and shared with other users.

11 Right-click on the Old Film preset and choose Export Presets.

12 In the Export Presets window, navigate to your Lesson 04 folder. Save the Preset as Old Film and click Save.

Third-party effect plug-ins

In addition to the effects that come bundled with Adobe Premiere Pro, many third-party effect plug-ins can be installed separately. These third-party effect plug-ins are useful because sometimes the features available with native Adobe Premiere Pro effects are insufficient for your project's needs. Third-party effect plug-ins are sometimes available as a free download from the Internet, but there are also some popular effects that are available as a separate purchase. Often, third-party effect plug-ins for Adobe Premiere Pro are also available for Adobe After Effects.

Here is a short list of third-party effect plug-ins that are available for Adobe Premiere Pro CS6:

Red Giant Software (www.redgiantsoftware.com)

• Magic Bullet Suite is a bundle of color-correction effects that enable you to easily color correct and add different grades to your project. The suite also includes Colorista II, a professional color-grading tool, as well as multiple presets for Magic Bullet Looks.

• Trapcode Shine, as the name suggests, enhances the luminance of a clip by creating the visual effect of bursting light. This is useful, for example, in adding style to text or for creating interesting science fiction visual effects.

Digieffects (www.digieffects.com)

• Delirium is a bundle of 45 different effects for generating particles, performing color correction, distorting and displacing, and enhancing Premiere Pro's compositing capabilities.

• Damage is a bundle of various effects for making your clean video footage look degraded and aged.

Boris FX (www.borisfx.com)

• Boris Continuum Complete AE is a bundle of over 200 effects for image restoration, color correction, 3D particle effects, blurs, glows, and more.

For more information on third-party effect plug-ins for Premiere Pro CS6, go to www.adobe.com/products/premiere/extend.displayTab4.html.

Keying and compositing green screen footage

One of the most useful techniques to learn in video postproduction is convincingly inserting a subject recorded in front of a green (or blue) background into a scene, thereby creating the illusion to the viewer that the subject is actually part of that scene. The most common and effective method of achieving this effect is called *chroma keying*.

The typical workflow for chroma keying starts by recording the subject in front of an evenly-lit green or blue background. After importing the footage into Adobe Premiere Pro, you remove the background with a Chroma Key effect (and sometimes a garbage matte), which enables the compositing of the subject with another shot or scene. This technique is used on a range of media—from major motion pictures to the weather report on your local TV news.

How easy or difficult it is to pull a "clean key" (which is essential to achieve a convincing final result) depends on a variety of factors having to do with the quality of the footage:

- **Was the background evenly lit?** Proper lighting while shooting green screen footage is crucial. Chroma Key effects work by sampling the color of the green screen and then making that transparent. If the green screen was not evenly lit, it will appear as more than one shade of green. Therefore, sampling one area of the green screen will not make the whole green screen transparent.

- **Was the footage recorded in a video format optimal for chroma keying?** You should record your green screen footage at the highest resolution possible and with minimal compression, so that the foreground subject has smooth edges and no image artifacts.

- **Was the foreground subject semitransparent?** If your foreground subject has long flowing hair or is wearing semitransparent clothing, the color of the green screen showing through the semitransparency will not be consistent with the unobstructed areas of green screen in frame and will result in more time spent pulling a clean key.

These and other factors will determine whether you can achieve a satisfactory result with a single click, or if you'll need to make some adjustments to get the look you want.

Creating the garbage matte

In some green screen footage, you can remove objects in the shot by simply cropping out that part of the frame. This is known as creating a *garbage matte*.

In the following exercise, you'll include a green screen shot in the edit and apply a Chroma Key effect to it. Then you'll composite another clip in a video track below the Chroma Key clip that will show through the transparency.

1   In the Project panel, twirl open the Joey bin and find the clip Joey_01.mp4. Double-click on this clip to display it in the Source Monitor.

2   Play the entire clip.

Don't use the beginning of the clip when the camera zooms out. Instead, trim the clip to the desired segment.

3   In the Source Monitor, adjust the CTI to 0:00:07:00 and press the I key to set this clip's In point. Adjust the CTI to 0:00:09:23 and press the O key to set this clip's Out point.

4   Click the Drag Video Only icon at the bottom of the Source Monitor, and then drag this trimmed clip into the Timeline on track Video 3 so the head of the clip snaps to the marker at 0:01:01:04. You want to leave a gap in Video 2 directly below.

5   In your Timeline, adjust your CTI to just before this clip. Press the spacebar to play the sequence.

Notice that at the end of the shot the camera pans left, and you see the corner of the wall behind the green screen. You'll remove this extraneous object from the shot by creating a garbage matte.

6 Press Shift+7 to make the Effects panel active.

7 Type **crop** in the search field to quickly locate the Crop effect.

8 Select the clip on the Video 3 track in the Timeline, and then double-click the Crop effect to apply it.

● **Note:** Double-clicking to apply an effect to a selected clip is a new feature in CS6.

9 Press Shift+5 to open the Effect Controls panel.

10 In the Effect Controls panel, click the Crop effect to select it.

Notice that in the Program Monitor you can now see a bounding box around the video frame with handles on the top, bottom, left, and right.

11 In the Timeline, scrub the CTI to the end of the Joey_01.mp4 clip when the wall behind the screen is most visible in the frame.

12 In the Program Monitor, drag the left handle of the bounding box to the right until the wall in the upper-left corner of the frame is no longer visible.

13 In the Effect Controls panel, click in the empty space below the Crop effect to deselect it.

Now let's add a clip to Video 2. Once the green screen in Joey_01.mp4 is chroma keyed and thus transparent, you want to have something that shows through the transparency.

14 In the Project panel, twirl open the Live bin and find the clip Live_26-Lights.mp4. Double-click on the clip to open it in the Source Monitor. Press the spacebar to play the clip. This is what will appear behind Joey.

15 Drag Live_26-Lights.mp4 into the Timeline on track Video 2, directly below Joey_01.mp4 so the head of Live_26-Lights.mp4 snaps to the head of Joey_01.mp4.

16 Click the Selection tool and trim the tail of Live_26-Lights.mp4 so it lines up with the tail of Joey_01.mp4.

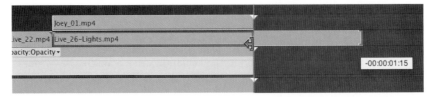

In the Program Monitor, you should see Live_26-Lights.mp4 through the cropped area of Joey_01.mp4.

Next, you'll apply a Chroma Key effect so that the green background of Joey_01.mp4 is transparent.

Using Keylight in Adobe After Effects

For doing basic green screen composites that include a simple video background, the Ultra Key effect in Adobe Premiere Pro CS6 is usually sufficient.

However, for those times when the Chroma Key effects in Adobe Premiere Pro are insufficient for the needs of a challenging green screen composite, you can use the Keylight keying effect in After Effects CS6. In addition to offering more sophisticated control of a clip's alpha channel, it has its own color-correction and edge-cropping controls as well. Also, if you are using After Effects to do chroma keying, you could also use the masks, mattes, and layer modes that make After Effects an industry-standard compositing application.

Applying the Ultra Key

The Ultra Key is a Chroma Key effect that makes it easy to pull a "clean key" from footage shot with a green screen background. You'll first define the background color and then make some minor adjustments that will make Joey appear as if he is part of the background on the Video 2 layer in the Timeline.

1 Select Joey_01.mp4 in the Timeline.

2 Press Shift+7 to make the Effects panel active.

3 Type **ultra** in the Search field to quickly locate the Ultra Key effect.

4 Double-click the Ultra Key effect to apply it.

5 Press Shift 5 to bring up the Effect Controls panel. Locate the Ultra Key effect (it will be on the bottom of the stack) and click the Eyedropper to activate it.

Look at the shot in the Program Monitor and note that the green screen was not lit evenly. The background is lighter on the right side of the frame and gradually gets darker toward the left side of the frame. This is a common scenario that editors have to deal with.

The best approach in this situation is to select a shade of green in the frame that is approximately median luminance so that a maximum area of the green screen background will be made transparent.

6 In the Program Monitor, click on a green value that's halfway between the lightest and darkest areas of green in the frame. In this clip it would be just to the left of Joey's face.

The green background disappears from the frame, and you can see the background clip on Video 1 showing through. However, it's not a "clean key" yet because you can still see some darkness in the background to the left where the green screen was lit darker. Making some minor adjustments will fix this.

7   In the Effect Controls panel, locate the Ultra Key effect and change the Output menu setting from Composite to Alpha Channel.

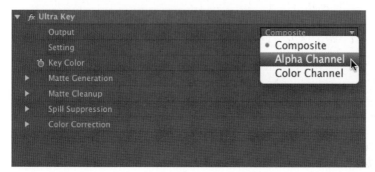

In the Program Monitor, you can now see the alpha channel, or transparency information, of the clip. The black areas are transparent; the white areas are opaque.

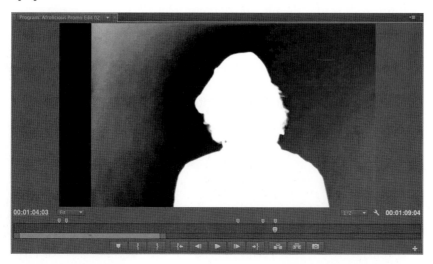

The goal when you are adjusting the controls in the Ultra Key effect is to make the entire background completely black while keeping the subject completely white (with the exceptions of the edges of the subject, which should be halfway between white and black to avoid a "hard edge" on the subject that can make the composite look fake and unconvincing).

8 In the Effect Controls panel, click the disclosure triangle next to Matte Generation in the Ultra Key effect to reveal its properties.

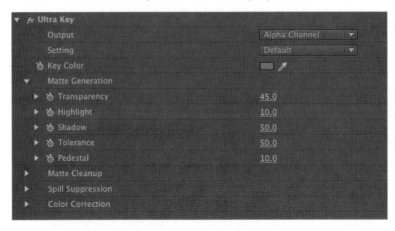

9 Click on the value of the Pedestal property and drag it to the right until its value is 100. As you drag, notice how the background becomes nearly entirely black while the subject remains white.

In this case, adjusting the Pedestal property achieved a threshold for the key, which made most of the green pixels transparent. But you'll still notice an area in the upper-left corner of the background that has not turned completely black. To finish the job, you need to adjust the Shadow property.

10 Click on the value for Shadow and drag it to the left until its value is 25 or until the background area of the frame is completely black. As you drag, notice how the remaining white pixels in the background fade to black.

11 Click on the Output menu and change the setting from Alpha Channel back to Composite.

Notice that the edge of Joey's hat in the frame looks a bit too sharp. Because Joey's head is not actually flat, this edge sharpness looks unconvincing and could use a bit of softening.

12 Twirl open the settings for Matte Cleanup and adjust the value for Soften to 50.

13 In the Timeline, drag the CTI to the beginning of the sequence, and then press the spacebar to play it back.

Joey is now convincingly composited into the background.

Had this clip been shot with an evenly lit green screen, the fine-tuning you just did would likely not have been necessary. The reality in the world of film and video production is that editors have to work with green screen footage recorded in a variety of optimal, and not-so-optimal, situations. The good news is that with the Ultra Key effect, it's usually just a matter of selecting a "middle ground" color when you start the process and then making some minor adjustments (like you just did) to get the desired result.

Adding titles with the Adobe Premiere Pro Title tool

Adobe Premiere Pro gives you the ability to create simple title clips that you can add to your edit. These are typically used as onscreen text to identify a location or someone who is speaking on camera. Although other applications in Adobe CS6 Production Premium, such as Adobe Illustrator or Adobe Photoshop Extended, allow you to create text that you can then import to Adobe Premiere Pro, using the native type engine in Adobe Premiere Pro can save you the trouble of switching back and forth between applications, and having one more media file to keep track of.

The type engine in Adobe Premiere Pro is quite robust and can employ all kinds of different fonts and presets for styles, as well as apply text on a vector path. Titles can either be still or animated.

You'll create a simple static title clip to identify the nightclub that you see in the video.

1   Choose Title > New Title > Default Still. The New Title window appears. Leave the current values for Width, Height, Timebase, and Pixel Aspect Ratio as is. In the Name field, type **Name of Club** and click OK.

The Titler will appear with a collection of panels, all of them related to title design. A Tools panel contains a Selection tool and a Type tool along with Font Family and Font Style fields, Font Size value, type alignment buttons, Spatial Transform properties, and Type Color properties.

Also, a miniature monitor allows you to see how your title will look when superimposed over the current clip in your Timeline. This monitor shows two concentric rectangles that represent the action safe area (the outer rectangle), as well as the title safe area (the inner rectangle). In most cases, you don't want to place titles on the edge of a frame. These rectangles provide a general visual guide to ensure that the titles you create will reliably show in the final video with a sufficient space buffer around them.

2   Click the Type tool in the Tools panel and click once in the Title Monitor. A type field appears. Type **Boku Room** and press Return (Enter) to create a line break. Then type **San Francisco, CA**. Select this second line of type and reduce the Font Size value so that Boku Room is more prominent. Click the Selection tool to commit your changes to the type.

▶ **Tip:** Scrub the CTI in your Timeline when the Title panel is open to show how a title will look over different shots.

Let's apply a few more adjustments to the title.

3   Press Command+A (Ctrl+A) to select all text. Click the Left Align button so the type is left aligned. Set the Fill Type to Solid and set the Fill Color to white.

4   As a general rule, when you're choosing a type font that will appear in a video, choose an easily legible sans serif font. Set the Font Family to Helvetica Neue and the Font Style to Bold. Click the Selection tool to commit the changes to your type.

5   With the Selection tool, click once in the type box and drag it to the bottom left of the title safe area.

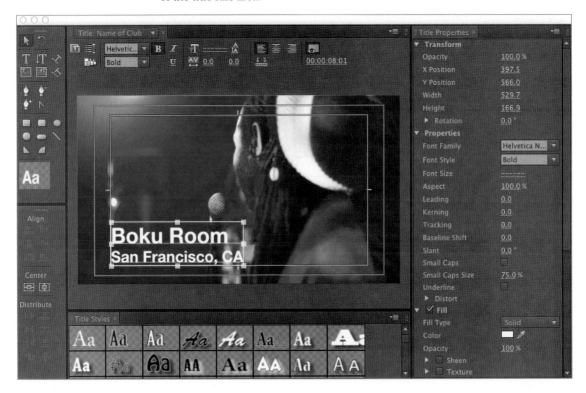

● **Note:** If a bin is selected in your Project panel when you create a title clip, the title clip will appear inside the selected bin. The title clip can then be dragged elsewhere in the Project panel.

6   Close the Titler panels.

7   In the Project panel you should see the Name of Club title clip. Drag this into your Timeline on Video 3 so its head aligns with the In point of Live_02.mp4. With the Selection tool, click on the tail of the title clip and trim it so it aligns with the tail of Live_02.mp4.

8 Adjust the CTI to the beginning of the sequence, and press the spacebar to play. You should see the static title clip composited with the video clip below it in Video 2.

Serif fonts vs. sans serif fonts

A serif is a typographic detail on the ends of some of the strokes that make up letters and numbers. A serif leads the eye to the next letter, but they are only visible at high resolutions, such as in print. When displayed with limited pixels, serif fonts can create visual artifacts in video frames and thus affect legibility.

Sans serif fonts can sometimes look more modern and were developed specifically to be used in electronic media. They feature even spacing between letters and even thickness of the font elements, resulting in legible type onscreen.

Stabilizing footage with the Warp Stabilizer

Now let's look at a technique that will improve the look of your footage instantly. While this may not seem like an "advanced" technique, it's in this section because performing this level of clean up makes your project look even more professional. A common issue that occurs with footage recorded on handheld cameras is that it can be shaky and uneven, making it difficult to watch. The Warp Stabilizer, introduced in Adobe After Effects CS5.5 and now available in Adobe Premiere Pro CS6, is an incredibly advanced stabilization tool that can make this type of footage look as if it was recorded with a sophisticated camera rig.

What makes the Warp Stabilizer easy to use is its automatic analysis of the footage, which allows for minimal customization. The advanced image analysis, which takes place "behind the scenes" in Premiere Pro, does all the heavy lifting for you.

Sometimes, editors will encounter a video clip that is well composed but unsteady and not favorable because the videographer did not hold the camera steady or an isolated bump to the tripod occurred. In such situations, the video clip may still be salvageable by removing the camera shake with the new Warp Stabilizer effect in Adobe Premiere Pro CS6.

The Warp Stabilizer works by analyzing a shaky video clip and automatically applying motion to the clip to counteract the unstable motion in the raw clip.

Let's apply the Warp Stabilizer to a clip in the sequence.

1 Find and select the clip Studio_03.mp4 in Video 3. This is a short clip of Joey sitting at his recording studio workstation as he makes adjustments to an audio recording. Notice that about halfway through the clip is a considerable amount of camera shake, which would ordinarily make this shot unusable.

2 Press Shift+7 to make the Effects panel active.

3 Type **warp** in the Search field to quickly locate the Warp Stabilizer effect.

4 Double-click the Warp Stabilizer effect to apply it to the selected clip.

The Warp Stabilizer effect immediately starts analyzing the clip, and a blue bar across the image in the Program Monitor indicates that the clip is being analyzed.

5 Press Shift+5 to open the Effect Controls panel.

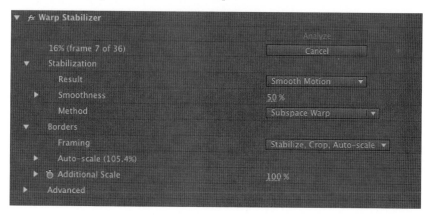

Progress analyzing the clip, in number of frames and percentage, is displayed in the Effect Controls panel. When the analysis process is complete, an orange bar appears across the image, indicating that it is being stabilized.

6 When the stabilization process is complete, play the clip.

Notice how the camera shake is completely gone, and the pan from right to left at the end of the shot is smooth and fluid, as if the camera had been mounted on a tripod with a high-quality head. However, it must be mentioned that the Warp Stabilizer zooms into the clip slightly, which can risk making it appear soft. Scaling of up to 110% is usually acceptable.

In many cases (such as this one), you don't have to change any of the default settings in the Warp Stabilizer effect to get a good result. If necessary, the effect has multiple advanced settings to adjust clips with varying levels of shake.

Rolling Shutter Repair effect

In digital video cameras with CMOS sensors, video is recorded one scan line at a time; therefore, not all video in a given frame is recorded at the same time. This can cause a distortion called *rolling shutter* if the camera is moving quickly while recording or if the recorded subject is moving quickly.

New in Adobe Premiere Pro CS6 is the Rolling Shutter Repair effect, which fixes this distortion.

Rendering your timeline

If you are using Adobe Premiere Pro CS6 on a machine with a GPU that does not support the Mercury Playback Engine, your playback may not be smooth and uninterrupted. Premiere Pro can create preview renders, which are cached video files on your hard drive that allow you to play back your edit in real time if playback is not smooth.

During playback, you may see red and yellow bars at the top of your Timeline with a gray bar above them. What do they mean?

The gray bar is called the Work Area bar. It defines the range of time in your Timeline for which Premiere Pro will create a preview.

The yellow bar(s) indicate source files that are computationally difficult. For example, footage from a DSLR camera may yield a yellow bar in your Timeline. These frames will sometimes play back in real time, but not always. That depends on the speed of your computer.

The red bar(s) indicate clips that have effects applied to them or unrendered clips from Adobe After Effects. These frames will most likely not play back in real time, and need to be rendered.

Let's generate a preview render of your Timeline.

1   Select your Timeline. Press the backslash key (\) to view your entire sequence.

2   Double-click on the Work Area bar so it includes your entire edit.

3   Choose Sequence > Render Entire Work Area.

You'll see a Rendering window with a progress bar indicating how much render time remains.

When the progress bar finishes, the yellow and red bars at the top of your Timeline will be green, indicating frames that have been preview rendered.

4   Press Home and then press the spacebar to play your edit.

5   Press Command+S (Ctrl+S) to save your project.

Open workflows with other applications, such as Final Cut and Media Composer

As you work in Adobe Premiere Pro, you can collaborate more efficiently with colleagues by importing and exporting Apple Final Cut Pro and Avid projects.

Adobe Premiere Pro CS6 allows you to import and export a Final Cut Pro XML project file but with certain limitations. For example, audio keyframes, blur effects, color wipes, and cross dissolves all transfer intact from Final Cut Pro 7 to Adobe Premiere Pro via XML 5.0, but the Three-Way Color Corrector doesn't transfer correctly because Final Cut Pro processes color correction in RGB, whereas the Premiere Pro Three Way Color Corrector processes it in YUV. Additionally, Final Cut Pro text transfers to Adobe Premiere Pro's title tool but loses the formatting. Also, crops in the Final Cut Pro Motion Tab lose their feathering, because the crop filter in Premiere Pro doesn't have soft edges.

It's also possible to import and export an Advanced Authoring Format (AAF) multimedia file between Adobe Premiere Pro and Avid nonlinear editing systems that support AAF files. Exchanging projects to and from Adobe Premiere Pro CS6 and other non-Adobe systems offers the advantage of using the Adobe Suite of applications on projects that did not originate in Premiere Pro.

Exchanging project files between Adobe Premiere Pro and Final Cut Pro or Avid software often requires additional but minor project organization and media management due to the native incompatibility of these systems.

For more information on exchanging project files between Adobe Premiere Pro CS6 and Final Cut Pro or Avid software, go to http://tv.adobe.com/watch/short-and-suite/premiere-pro-cs55-resources-for-professional-editors and http://www.video2brain.com/en/premiere-pro-for-avid-editors.

Review questions

1 How do you apply a Cross Dissolve transition?

2 How do you apply an effect to a clip?

3 What is an Adjustment Layer?

4 How do you create a static title clip in your Timeline?

5 What can you do if a clip in your Timeline shows unsteadiness due to a shaky handheld camera?

Review answers

1 Click the Effects tab, select the Cross Dissolve effect from the Video Transitions folder, and drag it to the Timeline between two clips or at the head or tail of a clip.

2 Select the clip in your Timeline, and then double-click on the effect in the Effects panel. Or, drag the effect from the Effects panel onto the clip in the Timeline.

3 An Adjustment Layer is a clip that renders any effects applied to it onto any clip(s) in the track(s) below it.

4 Choose Title > New Title > Default Still.

5 Apply the Warp Stabilizer effect to the clip.

5 CREATING BASIC MOTION GRAPHICS AND VISUAL EFFECTS

Lesson overview

Production Premium gives you the power to create a wide range of motion graphics and visual effects—from simple animated titles to effects shots for motion pictures. In this lesson, you'll learn how to do the following:

- Use Dynamic Link to integrate work between Adobe Premiere Pro and Adobe After Effects

- Manage your media in After Effects

- Create and modify compositions and layers in After Effects

- Use text animation presets in After Effects

- Import and manipulate layered Adobe Photoshop images in After Effects

- Understand the fundamentals of keyframe-based animation in After Effects

 This lesson will take approximately 90 minutes to complete.

Adding a Lens Flare in Adobe After Effects CS6.

Preserving your rough edit in Adobe Premiere Pro

If you are continuing from the previous lesson, feel free to continue with the Adobe Premiere Pro project you already have open. If you are starting at this lesson, navigate to the Lesson 05 folder on your hard drive and open the Adobe Premiere Pro project Lesson_05 Start.prproj. Save your Adobe Premiere Pro project file in the Lesson 05 folder as **Afrolicious Promo.prproj**.

Because you are continuing with a previous version of this edit, you'll first save a new version of your sequence. This allows you to go back to the previous version if need be and is a recommended best practice in the video editing workflow.

1 In the Project panel, twirl open the Sequences bin.

▶ **Tip:** Press Command+C (Ctrl+C) to copy. Press Command+V (Ctrl+V) to paste.

2 Click on the Afrolicious Promo Edit 02 sequence to select it. Choose Edit > Copy to copy it to your clipboard. Then choose Edit > Paste.

   This will make a duplicate of this sequence outside of the Sequences folder.

3 To modify the name of the sequence, click on the name of the sequence to select it.

4 Change the name of the sequence to **Afrolicious Promo Edit 03,** press Return (Enter), and then drag it into the Sequences folder.

5 Double-click the Afrolicious Promo Edit 03 sequence to load it in your Timeline.

   Note that the sequence appears in a new tabbed Timeline panel in front of your original sequence.

   Having multiple Timeline panels open simultaneously can be useful in certain situations, but it can also be confusing. For the time being, you'll close the first Timeline to eliminate the possibility of accidentally modifying the wrong sequence.

6 In the Timeline panel, click the Afrolicious Promo Edit 02 tab to select it.

7 Press Command+W (Ctrl+W) to close this sequence.

The new sequence is now the only one visible in the Timeline, which will ensure that you are working on the most recent iteration.

8 Press Command+S (Ctrl+S) to save your Adobe Premiere Pro project.

About Adobe After Effects

After Effects is the "Swiss army knife" of motion graphics and effects tools. It has a wide range of uses, from creating simple animated text to creating elaborate title sequences for motion pictures. After Effects is the industry-standard tool for creating motion graphics and compositing visual effects.

The "link" between motion graphic artists and video editors

Note that as a video editor, it is possible to launch Adobe After Effects directly from your Adobe Premiere Pro Timeline by replacing a clip in your sequence with an After Effects composition. As a motion graphic artist, you generally spend more time working in After Effects than in an Adobe Premiere Pro project, and as a result, you would likely begin many projects in After Effects and not Adobe Premiere Pro. For those users who are more familiar with Adobe After Effects but not as familiar with Adobe Premiere Pro, the Dynamic Link workflow between these two applications has allowed motion graphic artists to become better editors and editors to become better motion graphic artists.

In this lesson, you'll learn some of the basic skills you'll need to create basic graphics and effects for your video production projects. This lesson only scratches the surface of the capabilities of After Effects. If motion graphics and/or visual effects are a significant part of your workflow, we strongly recommend obtaining *Adobe After Effects CS6 Classroom in a Book* (Adobe Press, 2012) and *Adobe After Effects CS6 Visual Effects and Compositing,* by Mark Christiansen (Adobe Press, 2013).

Creating a new project in Adobe After Effects CS6

Let's get started in Adobe After Effects!

1 Launch After Effects CS6 and click File > Save As > Save As.

2 Navigate to the Lesson 05 folder (Adobe CS6 Project Assets > Lessons > Lesson 05), type in the project name **Afrolicious_Promo_01**, and click Save.

The concepts of compositing and animation

When you're working in After Effects, you'll be spending most of your time assembling visual elements into a composition and animating them. Put simply, the crafts of compositing and animation can be defined as follows:

- **Compositing** is the merging of multiple images from different sources. For example, your After Effects composition may include video clips, photographs, vector graphics, and text, each with their own unique settings. Sometimes it's necessary to composite layers in a composition so there is a seamless blend between them to create the illusion that multiple layers are a single visible element.

- **Animation** is the rapid display of images to create the illusion of motion. Adobe After Effects allows you to animate the motion of not just visible layers but also the properties of the layers. For example, you could have a text object moving across the frame while a blur effect animates on the text object simultaneously.

Optimizing performance

After Effects is extremely flexible in the ways it can render and display your compositions. The more powerful your hardware, the better After Effects will perform. You can do all the basic tasks in After Effects on modest hardware, but the processing required for more advanced tasks generally means you'll have a better experience by using more powerful hardware.

One important fact about After Effects is that it does not play back your compositions instantly, in real time, like Adobe Premiere Pro can. It needs to render the frames first before playing them back.

After Effects CS6 has made significant strides in making the best use of the hardware you have to render and cache frames in the background while you work.

The main components of your hardware that will affect performance in After Effects are:

- **RAM.** After Effects *loves* RAM, and you simply cannot have enough. The performance of the software, in general, as well as the number of frames you can cache in RAM for previews and playback greatly depends on having a good amount of RAM in your system.

- **Open GL.** After Effects takes advantage of the Open GL graphics language to offload certain rendering tasks to the GPU.

- **Graphics card.** A graphics card with a powerful, Adobe-approved GPU can handle multiple rendering tasks in After Effects, freeing up your CPU to handle other tasks, which results in better performance.

- **Hard drive.** A fast hard drive is especially important if you work with high-resolution, high-bitrate, video formats. The faster your drives can read and write data, the faster your system can render and display frames. Although After Effects can run on a laptop with a single hard drive, for optimum performance, it is recommended that you run After Effects CS6 on a workstation with a separate hard drive for your system drive (with your operating system and applications), another hard drive or a RAID for your media and renders, and a third hard drive for your cache. Ideally, the cache drive would be a solid state drive to achieve the fastest render that would utilize the Global Performance Cache (see the next section, "Global Performance Cache"). Any standard hard disk drive (HDD) in your configuration should operate at 7200 rpm or faster.

● **Note:** For more information on graphics cards that support GPU acceleration in Adobe CS6 Production Premium, go to www.adobe.com/products/premiere/tech-specs.html.

Solid-state drives (SSDs)

Thanks to advances in solid-state memory technologies, it is now possible to obtain a computer or external storage device with a solid-state drive. These have their advantages and disadvantages when compared to standard hard disk drives (HDDs) of similar storage capacity.

Pros of SSDs:

- Faster performance
- Lighter weight
- Smaller form factor
- Silent operation

Cons of SSDs:

- More expensive
- Smaller capacity

Global Performance Cache

New in After Effects CS6 is the Global Performance Cache. This feature greatly speeds up your workflow by taking full advantage of your computer's 64-bit CPU cores, RAM, and hard drive(s). For instance, if you have made a preview render of an animation in After Effects and you then make a change to that animation, you can revert to the previous state of the animation without having to make another preview render of it. Also, the Global Performance Cache will save RAM previews of your After Effects compositions so you can access them the next time you reopen your project. The Global Performance Cache makes your workflow more efficient and allows you more time to be creative.

In order to make the most of the Global Performance Cache, your system needs a supported GPU installed. You can find a list of supported graphics cards at www. adobe.com/products/premiere/tech-specs.html.

Setting preferences for Global Performance Cache

If you have a supported graphics processor, you should optimize some of your After Effects preferences.

1   Choose After Effects > Preferences > Media & Disk Cache (Edit > Preferences > Media & Disk Cache) to view and set your Media & Disk Cache preferences.

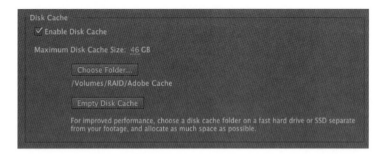

2   Select Enable Disk Cache, and click the Choose Folder button. Navigate to a folder on your system that is on a fast hard drive, preferably an SSD that is separate from your system and your media.

3   Set the Maximum Disk Cache size to as high as your cache drive will allow.

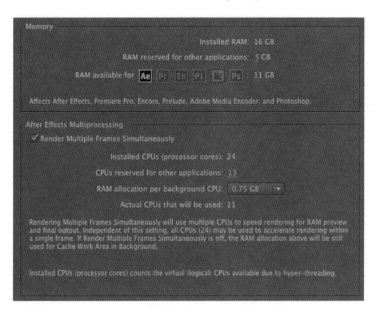

4   Select the Memory and Multiprocessing preferences.

5   Based on your Installed RAM, allocate at least 2 GB for each CPU core on your system.

6   Select Render Multiple Frames Simultaneously. With this feature activated, After Effects will devote the allotted amount of RAM, divided among each CPU core, to dramatically speed up your render times.

7   The Installed CPUs (processor cores) accounts for actual CPU cores as well as virtual CPUs that are available due to hyper-threading. Without getting too technical, you ideally want After Effects to render your frames with actual CPUs, so set "CPUs reserved for other applications" to the number of actual CPUs on your system.

8   Click OK.

For an informative video that explains optimizing After Effects CS6 for the Global Performance Cache, go to
http://tv.adobe.com/watch/digital-video-cs6/
how-to-optimize-after-effects-cs6-for-high-performance/?go=12437.

Understanding the After Effects user interface

When you launch After Effects for the first time, you'll be presented with the default Standard workspace. This workspace is a combination of the most commonly used panels.

To reset the Standard workspace to its default settings, follow these steps.

1   Choose Window > Workspace > Standard.

2   Choose Window > Workspace > Reset "Standard."

3   In the dialog that appears, click Yes.

On the surface of the Standard workspace, seven panels are visible:

- The Project panel is where you store and organize all of your assets, such as footage and compositions.

- The Composition panel is where you view your graphics and make spatial manipulations to layers.

- The Timeline is where you adjust your layer order, layer properties, and time-based animations.

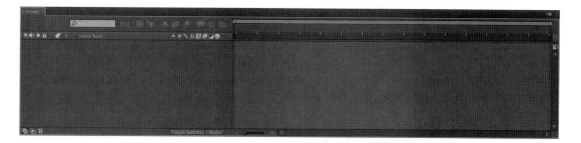

- The Tools panel is where you select different tools used in the animation process.

- The Info panel is where you view data about action, such as spatial coordinates, color values, and numerical changes in layer properties.

- The Preview panel is where you manipulate playback and preview settings for the active composition.

- The Effects & Presets panel is where you access and apply effects and presets to the selected layer or layers.

Notwithstanding the obvious differences, you may notice some similarities between the user interfaces of Adobe Premiere Pro and Adobe After Effects. For instance, both applications have a Project panel, a Timeline, and a Tools panel, all of which serve the same basic respective functions. The Composition panel in After Effects works much like the Program Monitor in Adobe Premiere Pro.

Using Dynamic Link: from Adobe Premiere Pro to After Effects

Adobe Premiere Pro and After Effects are designed to work seamlessly together so that you can bring an element from one to the other without having to do a full render beforehand. For instance, you can bring a clip from Adobe Premiere Pro into After Effects and apply changes to it, and those changes will dynamically update in Adobe Premiere Pro.

For more information about Dynamic Link, refer to Lesson 1.

In this exercise, you'll bring a video clip from your Timeline in Adobe Premiere Pro CS6 into Adobe After Effects CS6 and then apply an effect to it.

1 Switch back to Adobe Premiere Pro by pressing Command+Tab (Alt+Tab).

2 In your Adobe Premiere Pro Timeline, select the clip Live_18.mp4—the clip that shows a point of view from on stage with a bright light shining toward the camera.

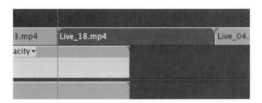

3 Right-click on the clip and choose Replace With After Effects Composition.

In your After Effects project that is already open, a new composition will appear in the Project panel along with the clip Live_18.mp4.

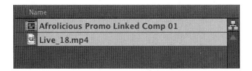

If you switch back to Adobe Premiere Pro, you'll see that the clip in your Timeline has been replaced by a linked After Effects comp.

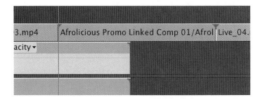

Back in After Effects, look in the new comp that has been created. This video clip shows a stage light shining into the camera.

If a light is shining into a camera lens, the light will refract through the layers of glass in the lens, producing an artifact called a lens flare. Although this type of visual artifact should generally be avoided while shooting video, sometimes adding a visual effect that simulates a lens flare can add an element of subtle (or not-so-subtle) interest for the viewer.

Let's create a lens flare to make the shot look "shinier." To do this, you'll use the Lens Flare effect. Because this composition is Dynamically Linked in your Adobe Premiere Pro project, the Lens Flare effect you apply to it in After Effects will automatically show in the corresponding clip in your Adobe Premiere Pro sequence.

4   Select the Live_18.mp4 layer in your After Effects comp, and then choose Effect > Generate > Lens Flare. The lens flare will appear on the video layer.

Third-party lens flare effect plug-ins

If you want to create lens flares in your After Effects compositions and have a wider array of effect controls for lens type, flare color and brightness, additional lens artifacts, plus a variety of bundled lens flare presets that the native Lens Flare effects do not provide, you may want to look into some of the third-party lens flare effect plug-ins available for Adobe After Effects:

*   Knoll Light Factory from Red Giant Software (www.redgiantsoftware.com/products/all/knoll-light-factory)

*   Optical Flares from Video Copilot (www.videocopilot.net/products/opticalflares)

You should see the Effect Controls panel, which shows the properties for the Lens Flare effect.

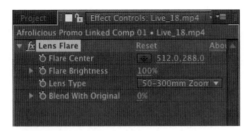

The Lens Flare effect has its own spatial coordinate for Flare Center. Notice that if the name of the effect is selected in the Effect Controls panel, the Flare Center shows as a crosshair in the Composition panel.

You can click on this crosshair and drag it to a new location in the Composition frame.

5   Press the Home key to make sure that your current time indicator (CTI) is at the first frame of your composition.

6   Click on the Flare Center crosshair and drag it to the center of the bright yellow light that shows in Live_18.mp4.

Now you'll animate the Flare Center. If you've never done any kind of animation before, don't panic. This will be simple. Keyframe animation will be covered in more detail later in this lesson.

7 Click the stopwatch icon for Flare Center in your Effect Controls panel. The stopwatch icon will change.

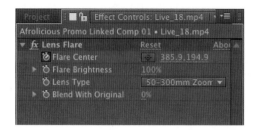

8 Scrub your CTI through the Timeline as you look at the Composition panel. Notice that there is some slight camera movement in the raw clip. The camera moves to the right, but at 0:00:01:21 the camera stops moving.

9 Adjust your CTI to 0:00:01:21 in your Timeline.

10 Select the Lens Flare effect in the Effect Controls panel. In your Composition panel, click and drag the Flare Center crosshair so it's on the bright yellow light, accounting for the slight camera move.

11 Scrub your CTI forward and notice that toward the end of the composition is a quick but slight camera move. The Flare Center should move to follow the yellow light in the shot to maintain the illusion that it was originally in the shot.

12 With the Lens Flare effect still selected in the Effect Controls panel, press the U key. This keyboard shortcut tells After Effects to show all animated properties on the selected layer (or layers).

You should see the Lens Flare effect along with its Flare Center property listed in the Timeline.

▶ **Tip:** To navigate in your After Effects Timeline by single frames, click the Next Frame or Previous Frame button in the Preview panel. You can also press Page Down to move your CTI to the next frame, and press Page Up to move to the previous frame.

The small diamond icons are the keyframes for the Flare Center property. For now, just understand that they hold the values for the Flare Center at certain frames in the layer's duration.

13 Adjust your CTI to 0:00:03:17. Practice using the Page Up and Page Down keys to move your CTI backward and forward one frame.

14 To the left of the Flare Center property name in the Timeline, click once on the empty diamond to add a new keyframe at the current time.

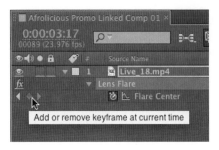

You should see another keyframe icon appear at the current frame.

15 Now press the End key to adjust your CTI to the last frame of the composition.

16 Select the Lens Flare effect in the Effect Controls panel. In your Composition panel, click and drag the Flare Center crosshair so it's on the bright yellow light, accounting for the final slight but sudden camera move.

17 Scrub backward and forward through your timeline to see the Flare Center animate.

Using RAM Preview

Whenever you create anything in After Effects, you should preview your work to make sure it looks the way you intended. In most cases, what you apply in After Effects will not instantly play back in real time unless you render it first. After Effects allows you to render your composition frames and store them in your computer's RAM so you can preview the composition—hence, the term RAM Preview.

Let's do a RAM Preview of your composition so that we can preview the Lens Flare effect on the video clip you brought over from Adobe Premiere Pro. There are a couple of ways of activating a RAM Preview in After Effects: You can either press the 0 key on your numeric keypad, or (if you are using a laptop that doesn't have a numeric keypad) you can go to the Preview panel and click the RAM Preview button.

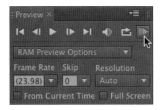

1 Activate a RAM Preview using one of the aforementioned methods.

You'll see a green line creep along the right at the top of your Timeline, which indicates frames that are stored in RAM that can be played back in real time. After Effects will then play back these frames.

2 Press Command+S (Ctrl+S) to save your After Effects project so the changes you applied here will dynamically update in your Adobe Premiere Pro Timeline.

3 Switch back to Adobe Premiere Pro to verify that the Lens Flare effect you applied in After Effects appears on the corresponding clip in your Premiere Pro Timeline.

4 Press Command+S (Ctrl+S) to save your Adobe Premiere Pro project.

Reducing resolution for RAM Previews

In some cases, After Effects will not make a RAM Preview of all of the frames in your composition. This is not a bug. There are a couple factors to consider when doing a RAM Preview. First, because After Effects stores frames in your computer's RAM, you need to determine how much RAM your computer has. Second, you need to determine how much of this RAM is being allocated to other applications currently open.

Although this composition is fairly short, you may end up working with compositions that are longer, and no reasonable amount of RAM on your computer will be enough to preview all of the frames. In such a scenario, you might consider reducing your composition's resolution from Full to Half (or even Third or Quarter) so that, at the expense of RAM Preview image quality, After Effects can render more frames with greater speed.

Working with text and animation presets in After Effects

The title that you created in Adobe Premiere Pro back in Lesson 4 may look fine as a placeholder, but let's create some animated text to replace it. You'll create this text in After Effects, animate it using an animation preset, and then Dynamically Link this text from After Effects to Adobe Premiere Pro.

In your Adobe Premiere Pro project, there should already be a static title graphic that shows the name of the nightclub where Afrolicious was performing.

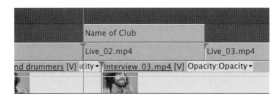

This static text is what you'll be replacing with animated text in After Effects.

1 Switch to After Effects and create a new composition by choosing Composition > New Composition.

2 In the Composition Settings dialog, type in the Composition Name **Text_Name_Of_Club**. With Lock Aspect Ratio unchecked, set the width to 1280 and the height to 720. Set the frame rate to 23.976 fps. Set the Duration to 0:00:05:00. Set Pixel Aspect Ratio to Square Pixels.

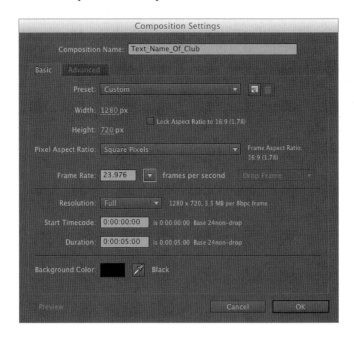

3   Set the background color to black by clicking on the Background Color swatch. Choose black in the color picker. Click OK to close the color picker, and then click OK again to close the Composition Settings dialog.

Adobe applications let you copy and paste text between them with the fonts and formatting intact. Therefore, you can simply copy the text of the static title in Adobe Premiere Pro and paste it into After Effects.

4   Switch back to Adobe Premiere Pro.

5   In your Timeline, double-click on the Name of Club text object.

The Titler window opens showing this text.

6   Double-click in the text field and press Command+A (Ctrl+A) to select all the text.

7   Choose Edit > Copy. Close the Titler window, and then switch back to After Effects.

8   In the Text_Name_Of_Club composition, you need to create a text layer. Do so by choosing Layer > New > Text. Then choose Edit > Paste.

The text you had in Adobe Premiere Pro should now be in your text layer in your After Effects composition with the font and formatting intact.

▶ **Tip:** To make a new text layer in After Effects, press Command+Opt+Shift+T (Ctrl+Alt+Shift+T).

9 Click on a blank area in your Timeline to register your change, or press Enter on your numeric keypad.

Note that when you create a text layer, the Character panel and Paragraph panel appear in the interface. You can change the font and formatting of the text in After Effects by adjusting the settings in these panels.

You should see a text layer in your composition called Boku Room San Francisco, CA. Conveniently, After Effects automatically names text layers based on the content of the layer.

10 In the row of icons and menus at the bottom of the Composition panel, make sure that the Toggle Transparency Grid is deactivated, so that you can see your text against a black background.

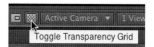

11 Activate the Title/Action Safe guides by clicking the Choose grid and guide options icon and then choosing Title/Action Safe.

12 Select the text layer and press the P key to show the layer's position. Press the V key to activate the Selection tool. In the Composition panel, click on the text once to select it, and then move it so that its bottom-left corner is aligned with the bottom-left corner of the title safe area (the inner rectangle).

Now it's time to animate the text. After Effects comes equipped with a very powerful text-animation engine. The complexities of this text-animation engine can be somewhat daunting. Fortunately, After Effects also comes with animation presets, many of which are designed specifically for text layers and enable you to easily apply complex animation.

13 Press the Home key to make sure that your CTI is at the beginning of your Timeline.

> **Tip:** Toggle the Title/Action Safe guides by pressing the apostrophe (') key.

14 In the Effects & Presets panel, type **Fade Up Characters** in the search field. You should see an animation preset with this name listed below.

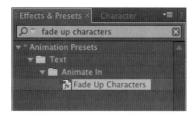

15 Select the Fade Up Characters preset, and drag and drop this preset directly onto the text layer, either in the Composition panel or the Timeline. Select the text layer in the Timeline to register this change.

16 Do a RAM Preview. You should see each character of your text fade in one at a time over a span of two seconds.

Now adjust this animation so that it happens over one second instead of two seconds.

17 Select your text layer and press the U key to show all animated properties and their keyframes in the Timeline.

18 With your Selection tool, draw a marquee around the last of the two Range Selector 1 Start keyframes on your text layer, and adjust your CTI to 0:00:01:00.

▶ **Tip:** To adjust your CTI to a specific timecode in an After Effects composition, click once on the timecode at the top left of the Timeline panel, type the timecode, and then press Return (Enter).

19 Hold down the Shift key and drag the selected keyframe to the left until it snaps to the CTI.

20 Do another RAM Preview and notice that the text animation now happens over one second.

21 Press Command+S (Ctrl+S) to save your After Effects project.

Using Dynamic Link: from After Effects to Adobe Premiere Pro

Just as you can Dynamically Link elements from Adobe Premiere Pro to After Effects, you can also link elements from After Effects to Adobe Premiere Pro.

In this exercise, you'll import your currently open After Effects composition into your Adobe Premiere Pro project and replace the static text clip in your Timeline with the animated text composition that you made in After Effects.

1 Switch back to Adobe Premiere Pro.

2 Choose File > Import, navigate to the Lesson 05 folder (Adobe CS6 Project Assets > Lessons > Lesson 05), select Afrolicious_Promo_01.aep, and click Import.

An Import After Effects Composition panel appears.

3 Select the Text_Name_Of_Club composition and click OK. The composition will appear in your Adobe Premiere Pro Project panel.

Let's replace the original Adobe Premiere Pro text object with this imported After Effects composition with animated text.

4 In your Adobe Premiere Pro Timeline, select the Name of Club clip.

5 Select the imported Text_Name_Of_Club After Effects comp in your Project panel.

6 Hold down the Option (Alt) key, and drag and drop the comp directly onto the Name of Club clip in your Timeline. This will replace the original clip with the new animated text clip.

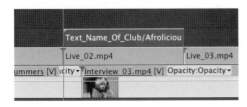

7   In your Adobe Premiere Pro Timeline, adjust your CTI to the head of the Text_Name_Of_Club clip and press the spacebar to play. You should see the text that you created in After Effects animate over your clips in Video 2 of your Premiere Pro Timeline.

8   Press Command+S (Ctrl+S) to save your Adobe Premiere Pro project.

Creating a motion graphic with Adobe After Effects

A motion graphic is, simply, an animated graphic design. It can incorporate abstract graphics, photographs, vector logos, video clips, and text, all of which can be animated separately to convey an overall message.

Motion graphics are used for a variety of purposes, most commonly for titles in motion pictures and television programs; animated graphics in advertisements and corporate presentations; photographic slide shows; and user interfaces for mobile applications.

Adobe After Effects has been available since the 1990s and has established itself as the industry-standard application for creating motion graphics, largely due to its tight integration with Adobe Photoshop Extended and Adobe Illustrator.

In this lesson, you'll create a motion graphic that will go at the end of the Afrolicious promo that you are editing in Adobe Premiere Pro. Because the motion graphic will appear at the end, we'll refer to it as an *outro* (as opposed to an intro, which would go at the beginning). The motion graphic will show the components of the Afrolicious CD cover animate into place.

The first step is to import some footage items to After Effects that you'll be using in the outro.

Importing media files

After Effects enables you to import and work with many different file types and formats of still images, video clips, audio clips, and vector graphics.

▶ **Tip:** To import a file to After Effects, press Command+I (Ctrl+I).

1   Choose File > Import > File and navigate to the Graphics folder (Adobe CS6 Project Assets > Graphics).

2   Select afrolicious_logo.png. Hold down the Command (Ctrl) key, select crowd01.png, and click Open.

3   Press Command+I (Ctrl+I) to import another file. Navigate to the Footage folder (Assets > Footage).

4 Select Live_23-60.mp4. Hold down the Command (Ctrl) key, select Live_25-60.mp4, and click Open.

You should now see all of these imported items listed in your Project panel, including items that have already been imported, namely Live_18.mp4.

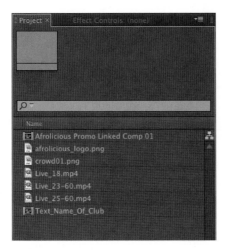

Importing layered Photoshop files into After Effects

One of the convenient aspects of using Photoshop images in After Effects is that After Effects can recognize and maintain the layers built into a Photoshop image. After Effects will let you import any individual layer of a Photoshop image. It will also let you import a layered Photoshop image as a composition, which can greatly speed up your workflow.

1 Choose File > Import > File and navigate to the Graphics folder.

2 Select Afrolicious_cover.psd.

3 Set Import As to Composition-Retain Layer Sizes and click Open.

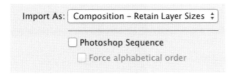

A window appears prompting you to choose whether you want to maintain editable layer styles or merge layer styles into footage. Because no layer styles were used in any of the original Photoshop layers in this image, this doesn't apply. However, if there were layer styles, such as Drop Shadow or Gradient Overlay, in your imported Photoshop document, then you would need to direct After Effects on how to interpret Photoshop layer styles on import.

4 Select Editable Layer Styles, and click OK.

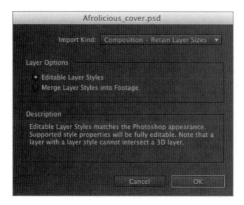

Notice that After Effects has automatically created a new composition named Afrolicious_cover, as well as a folder in the Project panel called Afrolicious_cover Layers.

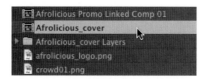

5 Twirl open the Afrolicious_cover Layers folder, and you'll see a list of the original Photoshop layers.

6 To verify that After Effects has indeed imported the PSD file with all layers intact, select any of the layers—bottom_brush_fill, for example—and then choose Edit > Edit Original.

Photoshop Extended CS6 opens the Afrolicious_cover image. Here, you can see all of the original Photoshop layers. Notice how all of the layer names in Photoshop Extended are the same as the imported Photoshop items in After Effects. Keep this image open in Photoshop Extended for later reference.

7 Switch back to After Effects, and in the Project panel, double-click on the composition Afrolicious_cover to open it.

You should see all of the same layers with the same layer names and the same stacking order as in the original Photoshop image.

Organizing the Project panel

So far you've imported multiple graphics and footage items, as well as created a couple of compositions in your After Effects project. It's a good idea to organize your project items as you work so you can easily find what you're looking for later.

You can create folders within the After Effects Project panel that you can place your footage items into.

1   At the bottom of the Project panel, click the Create a New Folder button. A new untitled folder will appear in the Project panel.

2   Replace the default Untitled 1 name with **Footage** and press Return (Enter).

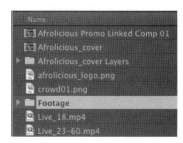

3   Select the footage files Live_18.mp4, Live_23-60.mp4, and Live_25-60.mp4, and
    drag these items onto the Footage folder.

You'll create another folder in the Project panel, but you'll do it a bit differently.

4   Select afrolicious_logo.png, and then hold down the Command (Ctrl) key and
    select crowd01.png so both files are selected.

5   Drag these items directly onto the Create a New Folder button.

    A new untitled folder will automatically be created and contain these two files.

6   Change the default Untitled 1 folder name to **Graphics** and press Return (Enter).

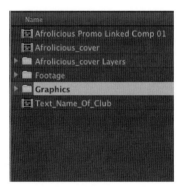

After Effects allows you to organize your footage items further by letting you
place folders within other folders.

7   Select the Afrolicious_cover Layers folder and drag and drop this folder onto
    the Graphics folder.

8 Twirl open the Graphics folder, and you should see the Afrolicious_cover Layers folder as well as afrolicious_logo.png and crowd01.png within it.

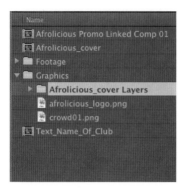

It's also a good idea to create a folder for your compositions.

9 Select the Afrolicious_cover composition item. Hold down the Command (Ctrl) key and select Afrolicious Promo Linked Comp 01 and Text_Name_Of_Club compositions.

10 Drag and drop these compositions onto the Create a New Folder button.

11 Change the default Untitled 1 folder name to **Comps**.

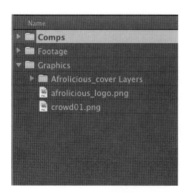

12 Press Command+S (Ctrl+S) to save your project.

Creating a new composition

A composition in Adobe After Effects is analogous to a sequence in Adobe Premiere Pro in that it's your main work interface where you would add layers (still images, video clips, vector graphics, text, etc.) and then manipulate the timing and properties of those layers to create an animation.

In case you hadn't noticed, After Effects allows you to create multiple compositions within the same project.

Let's create a composition that you'll use later. This new composition will serve as the final composition for the animation you'll be creating with the Afrolicious_cover composition later in this lesson.

1 Choose Composition > New Composition.

A Composition Settings dialog appears.

2 Change the Composition Name to **Afrolicious_Outro**.

3 Change the Width setting to **1280** and the Height setting to **720**. You may need to deselect the Lock Aspect Ratio check box to enter the specific settings you want.

4 Set Pixel Aspect Ratio to Square Pixels.

5 Set Frame Rate to 23.976. You can choose this standard frame rate from the "frames per second" drop-down menu.

6 Set Start Timecode to **0:00:00:00** (assuming it isn't already), and set Duration to **0:00:05:00**.

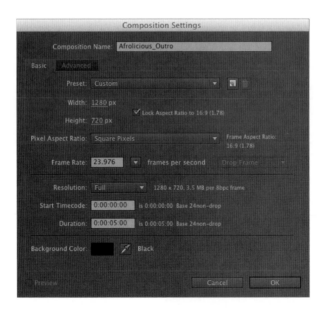

▶ **Tip:** Remember to keep your Project panel organized as you work. Making a habit of this early on will save you time and headaches in the long run.

7 Click OK. The new composition will open.

Because there are currently no layers in it, all you'll see is a blank Composition panel.

In the Project panel, you'll see an Afrolicious_Outro composition item. If your Comps folder was still selected, this new comp will automatically be placed inside it. Otherwise, select this comp, and drag and drop it onto the Comps folder.

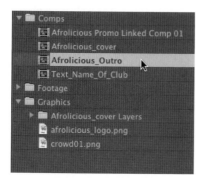

8   Press Command+S (Ctrl+S) to save your project.

Adding video clips to a composition

Now you'll add some video clips to the Afrolicious_Outro composition. These imported media items will be layers that will show in the background of the final outro graphic. These video clips will supplement the look of the final animation with moving video.

1   In the Project panel, in the Graphics folder, select crowd01.png, and drag it into the Timeline of Afrolicious_Outro.

2   In your Footage folder, select the item Live_25-60.mp4, and drag it into the Timeline of Afrolicious_Outro, directly above crowd01.png.

3   In your Footage folder, select the item Live_23-60.mp4, and drag it into the Timeline of Afrolicious_Outro, directly above Live_25-60.mp4.

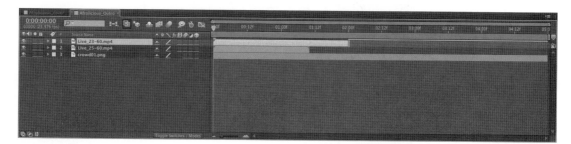

Adding a still image to a composition

You'll return to the Afrolicious_Outro composition shortly. Now add a graphic to the Afrolicious_cover composition. This graphic is the Afrolicious logo that will show prominently in the outro.

1   The Afrolicious_cover composition should still be open. If it isn't, go into your Comps folder and double-click it to open it.

    You should see this composition in the Composition panel as well as all of its layers in the Timeline panel below.

2   Make sure your CTI is at the beginning of the Timeline. If it is not, press the Home key.

3   In your Project panel, in the Graphics folder, select afrolicious_logo.png.

4   Drag and drop this file into the Timeline of the open Afrolicious_cover composition so that it appears in the layer stack directly below the layer called Levels Adjustment. You should also see this graphic in the center of the Composition panel.

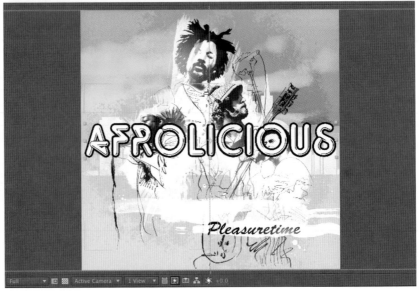

5   Press Command+S (Ctrl+S) to save your project.

Working with layers

Layers can be still images, video, vector graphics, and text. A layer can be an imported graphic created in another program, such as Adobe Photoshop Extended or Adobe Illustrator, or created natively in Adobe After Effects. Most layers contain visual content. However, in some cases, as with Adjustment Layers or Null Objects, they can be used to affect other layers.

As in Photoshop or Illustrator, layers in an After Effects composition can be stacked on top of one another. The top-to-bottom stacking order of layers in a composition generally corresponds to its front-to-back visibility. In other words, if a layer is stacked above another, it will generally appear in front of the other. If you want to change the front-to-back visibility of layers in your composition, you can adjust the stacking order of layers by dragging them up or down in the layer order.

Layers in After Effects not only have spatial visibility to consider, but also temporal visibility, or duration. Each layer has its own duration within the time of the composition that they're in. All layers in a composition don't need to have the same duration within the composition's duration.

You'll animate several of the layers in the Afrolicious_cover composition so that they move into frame and/or appear separately to give the animation a bit of variety. If all of the layers appeared at the same time, that would not be very interesting to the viewer.

Before you animate the layers, you'll adjust their starting times—or In points—in the Timeline.

1   Adjust your CTI to 0:00:02:20, and then select the layer afrolicious_logo.png.

2   Hold down the Shift key and drag the afrolicious_logo.png layer so its In point snaps to the CTI, or press the [key.

▶ **Tip:** To adjust the selected layer's In point to the current time, press the left bracket key ([). To adjust the selected layer's Out point to the current time, press the right bracket key (]).

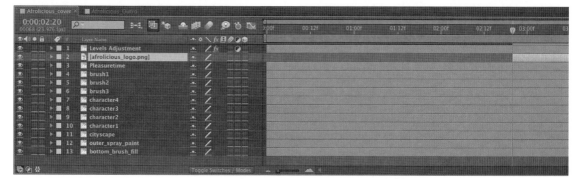

3 Adjust your CTI to 0:00:03:04, and then select the layer Pleasuretime.

▶ **Tip:** Press Shift+Page Up to adjust your CTI back ten frames. Press Shift+Page Down to adjust your CTI forward ten frames.

4 Hold down the Shift key and drag the Pleasuretime layer so that its In point snaps to the CTI, or press the [key.

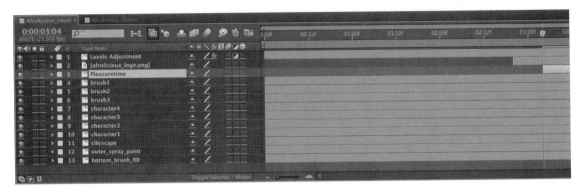

5 Adjust your CTI to 0:00:01:08, and then select the layer brush1.

6 Hold down the Shift key and drag the brush1 layer so that its In point snaps to the CTI, or press the [key.

7 Adjust your CTI to 0:00:01:20, and then select the layer brush2.

▶ **Tip:** Press Command+up arrow (Ctrl+up arrow) to select the layer above the currently selected layer. Press Command+down arrow (Ctrl+down arrow) to select the layer below the currently selected layer.

8 Hold down the Shift key and drag the brush2 layer so that its In point snaps to the CTI, or press the [key.

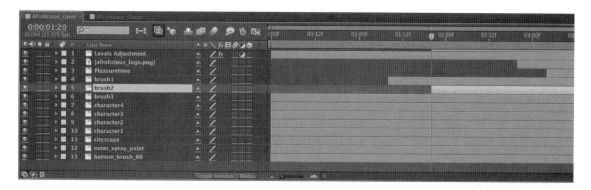

9 Adjust your CTI to 0:00:02:08, and then select the layer brush3.

10 Hold down the Shift key and drag the brush3 layer so that its In point snaps to the CTI, or press the [key.

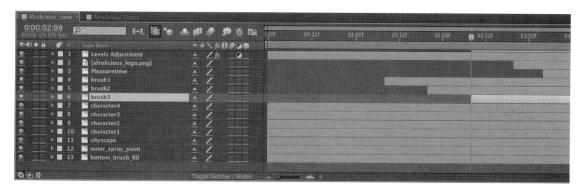

11 Adjust your CTI to 0:00:00:15, and then select the layer character4.

12 Hold down the Shift key and drag the character4 layer so that its In point snaps to the CTI, or press the [key.

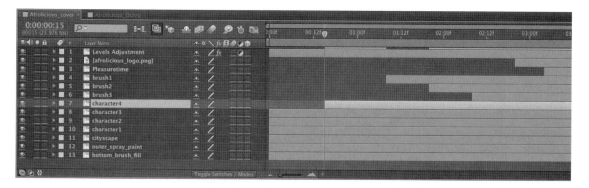

13 Adjust your CTI to 0:00:00:19, and then select the layer character3.

14 Hold down the Shift key and drag the character3 layer so that its In point snaps to the CTI, or press the [key.

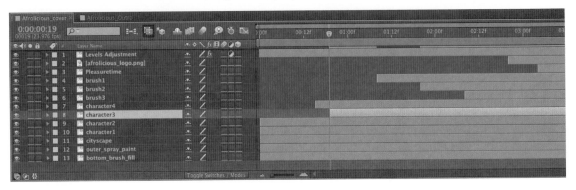

15 Adjust your CTI to 0:00:00:11, and then select the layer character2.

16 Hold down the Shift key and drag the character2 layer so that its In point snaps to the CTI, or press the [key.

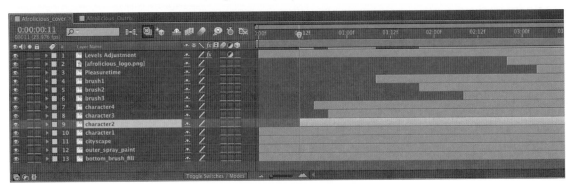

17 Adjust your CTI to 0:00:00:23, and then select the layer character1.

18 Hold down the Shift key and drag the character1 layer so that its In point snaps to the CTI, or press the [key.

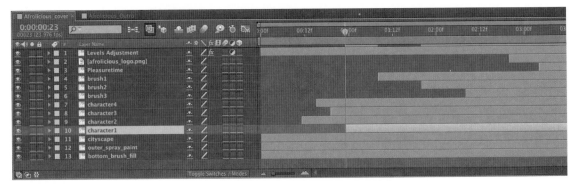

19 Adjust your CTI to 0:00:00:06, and then select the layer cityscape.

20 Hold down the Shift key and drag the cityscape layer so that its In point snaps to the CTI, or press the [key.

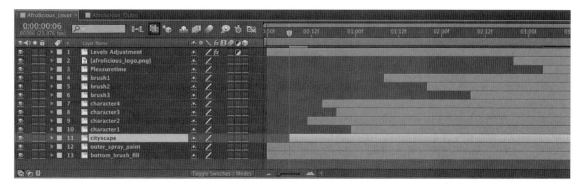

Scrub through your Timeline to see your layers appear at different times.

21 Press Command+S (Ctrl+S) to save your project.

Understanding keyframes

In traditional cel animation, the term *keyframe* refers to a single frame (or drawing) that illustrates key points in an animation. After the keyframes were drawn by a senior animator, the junior animators would draw all of the in-between frames.

In After Effects, keyframes work similarly to their traditional counterparts: A keyframe refers to a fixed property value at any given moment in time. After Effects automatically calculates all of the values in between two or more keyframes.

To create keyframes for a property, you must first activate the stopwatch icon next to the property's name in the Timeline or in the Effect Controls panel.

The stopwatch icon acts as a switch to toggle whether the property is animated or not. When a property's stopwatch is activated, After Effects makes a keyframe at the current time. This keyframe will have the property's current value. Changing the property's value while the CTI is on a frame without a keyframe will create a new keyframe at the current time.

You may change any property's value at any given frame in your composition. Making these changes will automatically add or modify a keyframe for that property at the current time. To put it plain and simple, you would click a property's stopwatch to begin animating a property.

If you are more familiar working with clips in a timeline and not keyframes, this general workflow may not feel intuitive. However, the more you practice with it, the more you will become familiar with this process.

Animating your layers

Now that you have adjusted the In points of many of the layers in Afrolicious_cover, it's time to animate them into place.

Let's start with the Afrolicious logo.

Animating the Afrolicious logo

You'll animate the layer's scale and opacity so that it shrinks down and fades in simultaneously.

1   Select the afrolicious_logo.png layer and press the S key to show the layer's scale.

2   Hold down the Shift key as you press the T key to show the layer's opacity and then the P key to show the layer's position.

3   Press the I key to go to the layer's In point, adjust the Position value to 778.5,1175, and adjust the Opacity value to 0%. Leave the Scale at 100, 100%.

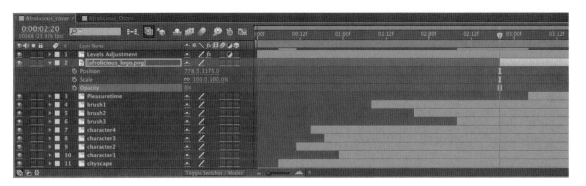

4   Click once on the stopwatch icons for Scale and Opacity to toggle animation for these properties. Notice that Scale and Opacity now have diamond-shaped icons at the current frame. These diamond-shaped icons are keyframes.

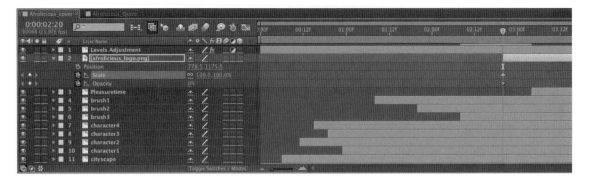

5 Adjust your CTI to 0:00:03:04 and adjust the Opacity to 100%.

Notice that once a property's stopwatch has been activated, any change to the property's value will cause a new keyframe to be created automatically at the current frame.

By animating a layer's Opacity property between 0% and 100%, you are making the layer gradually appear over the span of time between these keyframes.

6 Adjust your CTI to 0:00:03:08 and adjust the Scale value to 70%.

▶ **Tip:** Do not deactivate a property's stopwatch once you have created keyframes. Doing so will automatically delete all of that property's keyframes!

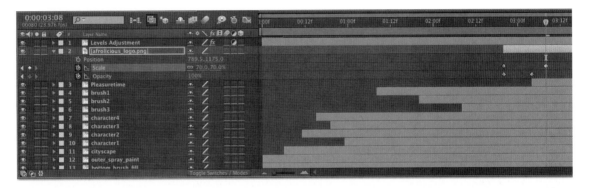

Scrub through your Timeline. Notice how animating Scale causes a layer to grow or shrink in size. Also note that both Scale and Opacity are animated. Indeed, it is possible to animate multiple properties on the same layer.

7 Select the second Scale keyframe icon on the afrolicious_logo.png layer. Then right-click on the keyframe and choose Keyframe Assistant > Easy Ease.

Notice how this keyframe icon is no longer diamond shaped. Anytime a keyframe is not diamond shaped, it means that the speed of animation going into and/or out of that keyframe is not constant.

When Easy Ease is applied to a keyframe, the speed of animation going into the keyframe gradually slows down, and then the speed of animation going out of the keyframe gradually speeds up. Easy Ease lends a bit of realism to animation, because moving objects in the real world typically speed up and slow down gradually rather than move at a constant speed.

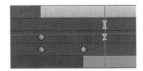

Animating Pleasuretime

Now you will animate the Pleasuretime text object so that it moves and gradually appears, simultaneously.

1 Select the layer Pleasuretime, and press the P key to show the layer's position.

2 Hold down the Shift key and press the T key to show the layer's opacity.

3 Press the I key to go to the layer's In point, adjust the Opacity to 0%, and adjust the Position value to 1289.0,1290.5.

4 Click once on the stopwatch icons for Position and Opacity.

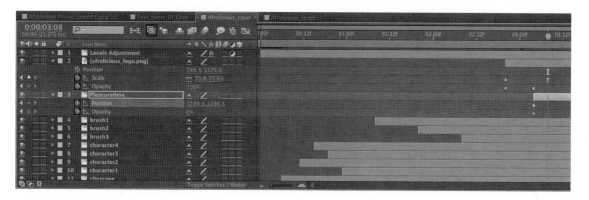

5 Adjust your CTI to 0:00:03:12, adjust the Opacity to 100%, adjust your CTI to 0:00:03:16, and adjust the Position to 1055.0,1290.5.

6 Select this position keyframe icon. Right-click on it, and choose Keyframe Assistant > Easy Ease.

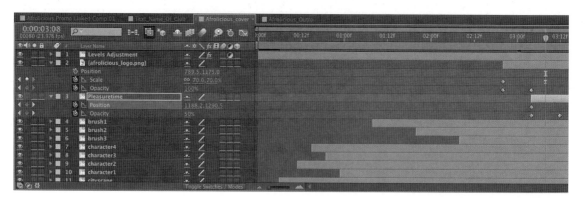

Scrub through your Timeline, and you'll notice that this layer is moving from right to left as it gradually appears.

Animating the character layers

The character layers will all fade in at the same rate but at different times. Because the same animation will be applied to all of them, you can create keyframes for one of them, copy those keyframes, and then paste the keyframes to the rest of the character layers individually.

Let's first apply keyframes to character4.

1   Select the layer character4.

2   Press the T key to show the layer's opacity, press the I key to go to the layer's In point, and adjust the Opacity to 0%.

3   Click once on the stopwatch icon for Opacity.

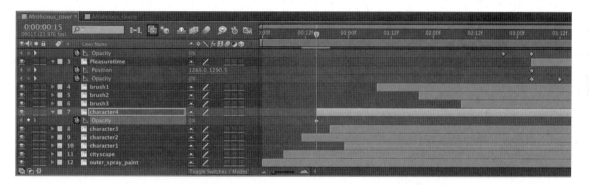

4   Adjust your CTI to 0:00:01:03 and adjust the Opacity to 100%.

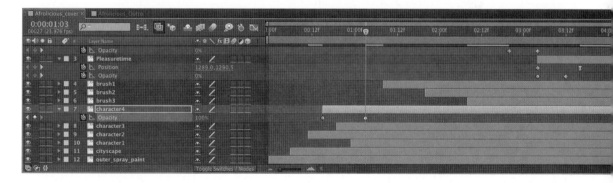

5   With your Selection tool, draw a marquee around these two opacity keyframes.

6   Press Command+C (Ctrl+C) to copy these keyframes.

7   Select the layer character3.

8 Press the I key to go to the layer's In point, and then press Command+V (Ctrl+V) to paste. Press the U key to show all animated properties and their keyframes for character3.

● **Note:** Keyframes will be pasted onto a layer at the current time.

The opacity keyframes that you copied from character4 are now pasted on character3. Note that you didn't have to activate the Opacity stopwatch for character3 because pasting keyframes onto a layer will automatically activate the stopwatch for the property that is getting the keyframes.

Now do the same for character2 and character1.

9 Select the layer character2. Press the I key to go to the layer's In point, and then press Command+V (Ctrl+V) to paste. Press the U key to show all animated properties and their keyframes for character2.

10 Select the layer character1. Press the I key to go to the layer's In point, and then press Command+V (Ctrl+V) to paste. Press the U key to show all animated properties and their keyframes for character1.

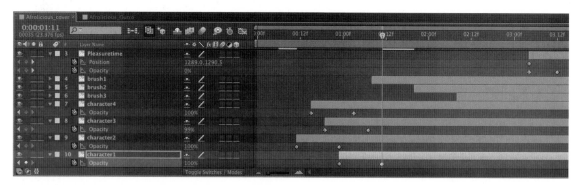

Adjusting an anchor point

You'll animate the cityscape layer so that it appears to grow from the ground, stretching upward and then shrinking back down as if attached to a spring. This will lend a bit of cartoonish motion to your outro.

To do this, you'll need to adjust the cityscape's anchor point. An *anchor point* is the coordinate in a layer's space around which the layer will scale or rotate. To make the cityscape layer appear as if it's growing upward from its bottom, you need to adjust its anchor point to the bottom of the layer.

1 Select the layer cityscape.

2 Press the A key to show the layer's anchor point.

3 Hold down the Shift key and press the P key to show the layer's position, and then press the S key to show the layer's scale.

4 Press the I key to go to the layer's In point.

5 Adjust the anchor point to 789.5,606.0.

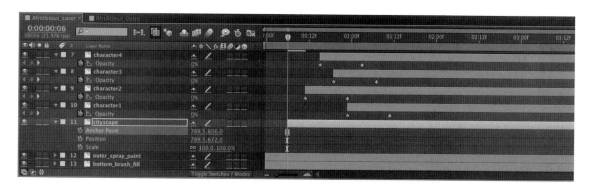

But wait! By adjusting this layer's anchor point, you've shifted it upward in the composition's frame! No problem. This is easily fixed.

6 Adjust the Position to 789.5,975.

Now preview your work.

7 Do a RAM Preview by clicking on the RAM Preview icon in the Preview panel, or by pressing 0 on your numeric keypad.

Deactivating constrained proportions

By default, a layer's width and height scale are linked together. But what if you want to adjust or animate a layer's height and width separately? You can do this easily enough.

On the cityscape layer, click once on the chain link icon next to the Scale value to deactivate constrained proportions.

Animating vertical scale only

Let's make the cityscape layer animate as if it is growing upward, achieving an extended height, and then springing back down to its resting height.

1 Select the cityscape layer and press 1 to adjust your CTI to its In point. Adjust the Scale value to 100.0,0.0%. Click once on the stopwatch icon for Scale.

2 Adjust your CTI to 0:00:00:12 and adjust the Scale to 100.0,120.0%.

3 Select this scale keyframe, right-click on it, and then choose Keyframe Assistant > Easy Ease.

4 Adjust your CTI to 0:00:00:17, adjust the Scale to 100.0,90.0%, adjust your CTI to 0:00:00:21, and adjust the Scale to 100.0,100.0%.

Notice that once a property's keyframe is set to Easy Ease, all keyframes made later in time will automatically be set to Easy Ease.

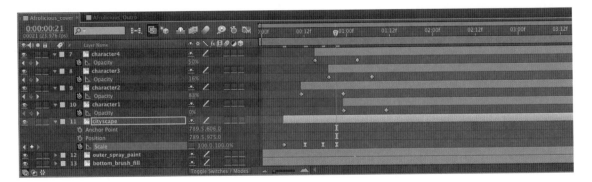

Finishing the outro

Now you'll finish the outro motion graphic that will appear at the end of your edit by employing a few useful techniques in Adobe After Effects.

Using nested compositions

A layer can be an imported footage item, and it can also be another composition! If you create an animation with several layers in one composition and then put that composition into a second composition, the layers of the first composition will be flattened into one layer in the second composition. This is called *nesting a composition*. Nesting compositions in After Effects is a way to group multiple layers, much like creating a folder of layers in Photoshop Extended.

1   In your Timeline, click on the Afrolicious_Outro tab to open that composition.

2   In the Comps folder, in your Project panel, select Afrolicious_cover and drag it into the Timeline of Afrolicious_Outro, directly above Live_23-60.mp4.

3   You'll be animating this composition later. For now, turn off its visibility switch (or eye icon).

Time-stretching

In the Timeline of Afrolicious_Outro, notice how the two video clip layers, Live_23-60.mp4 and Live_25-60.mp4, are not the same duration as this composition. You want to extend their durations, thereby slowing them down in the process, so that these layers don't end abruptly before the animation is done. This is called *time-stretching*.

1 Select the layer Live_25-60.mp4.

2 Activate its solo switch so that all other layers are temporarily made invisible.

3 Choose Layer > Time > Time Stretch. In the Time Stretch dialog, set the New Duration to **0:00:05:00** and click OK.

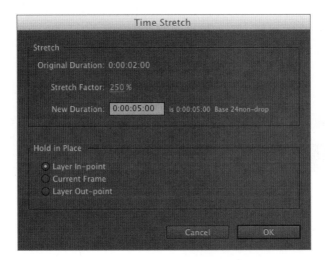

4 Turn off this layer's solo switch.

5 Select the layer Live_23-60.mp4.

6 Choose Layer > Time > Time Stretch. In the Time Stretch dialog, set the New Duration to **0:00:05:00** and click OK.

Finishing touches

Now you'll add the final adjustments and animations to the layers in your final comp. You'll first shrink the two video layers and place them in frame.

1 Select the layer Live_25-60.mp4.

2 Press the P key to show the layer's position. Hold down the Shift key and press the S key to show the layer's scale.

3 Adjust the Position to 320.0,360.0 and adjust the Scale to 50.0,50.0%.

4 Select the layer Live_23-60.mp4.

5 Press the P key to show the layer's position. Hold down the Shift key and press the S key to show the layer's scale.

6 Adjust the Position to 960.0,360.0 and adjust the Scale to 50.0,50.0%.

Now you'll animate the Afrolicious_cover nested comp into place.

1 Press the Home key to make sure your CTI is at the beginning of your comp.

2 Select the layer Afrolicious_cover.

3 Click its eye icon to make it visible again.

4 Press the S key to show the layer's scale and adjust the layer's Scale to 81.0,81.0%.

5 Click once on the stopwatch icon for Scale.

6 Adjust your CTI to 0:00:03:00 and adjust the layer's Scale to 35.0,35.0%.

7 Select this scale keyframe, right-click it, and then choose Keyframe Assistant > Easy Ease.

   Notice that all of the animation in Afrolicious_cover is still visible, and by animating this nested comp, you are compounding the animation.

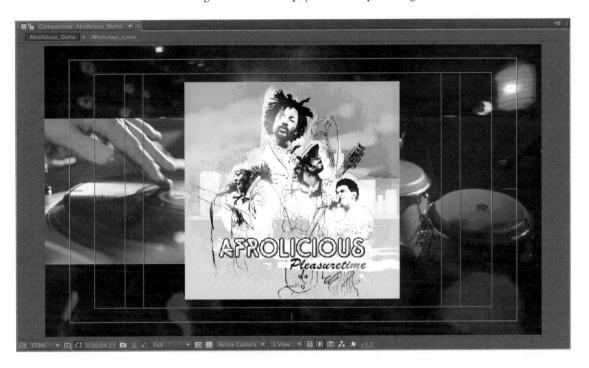

8 Now preview your work. Go to the Preview panel and click the RAM Preview button, or press 0 on your numeric keypad.

9 Press Command+S (Ctrl+S) to save your project.

Review questions

1 What is Dynamic Link, and why is it useful?

2 What does RAM Preview do?

3 How do you modify the timing of a text animation preset?

4 When importing Photoshop files, how do you retain their layers?

5 What is a nested composition?

Review answers

1 Dynamic Link greatly speeds up your workflow by allowing you to work seamlessly with the components of Adobe CS6 Production Premium. It allows you to work on a project in various applications simultaneously without having to render, export, or import your project files between applications.

2 RAM Preview enables real-time playback of cached, rendered frames of your After Effects compositions.

3 You can modify the timing of a text animation preset by modifying its keyframes in the Timeline.

4 When importing a PSD file created in Photoshop, selecting Import as Composition will retain its layers.

5 A nested composition is a composition that is placed in another composition. The nested composition's original layers are grouped as a single layer.

6 ADVANCED STILL AND MOTION GRAPHICS TECHNIQUES

Lesson overview

In the previous lessons, you learned some of the basic compositing, animation, and visual effects techniques that are possible in the components of Production Premium. In this lesson, you'll take your skills a step further and learn how to do the following:

- Create vector image using Adobe Illustrator

- Create a 3D text animation in Adobe After Effects

- Learn how to open a graphic from After Effects in Adobe Photoshop

- Apply Transfer Modes

- Understand and use Motion Blur

- Create static and animated masks

- Apply the wiggle expression to animate layers without keyframes

 This lesson will take approximately 90 minutes to complete.

A completed motion graphic in Adobe After Effects CS6.

Incrementing your After Effects project

If you are continuing from the previous lesson, feel free to continue with the After Effects CS6 project you currently have open. If you are starting at this lesson, you'll open an After Effects project file provided for you.

When working in Adobe After Effects CS6, it's good work practice to regularly save a new version of your project file, especially before making any substantial changes to the project. You can then revert to an earlier version if you need to. Also, if your current project file becomes corrupted, you won't have lost everything. You can restore lost work based on an earlier saved version.

After Effects gives you a simple way to save a new version of your project file by creating an *increment*. An increment is merely a new copy of the current project file with a "2" added to the end of the filename. If your project filename already ends with a number, incrementing your project file will add one to that number. For example, by incrementing Afrolicious_Promo_01, you'll create a new copy called Afrolicious_Promo_02.

1 Launch Adobe After Effects CS6.

2 Choose File > Open Project. Navigate to Lesson 06 (Adobe CS6 Project Assets > Lessons > Lesson 06) on your hard drive.

3 Select Afrolicious_Promo_01.aep and click Open.

4 Choose File > Increment and Save to automatically save the currently open project file as Afrolicious_Promo_02.

   The project file Afrolicious_Promo_01 is still on your hard drive.

Keep this project open in Adobe After Effects for now as you dive into Adobe Illustrator CS6.

About Adobe Illustrator

Adobe Illustrator is the industry-standard application for creating static vector graphics for print, video, and the web. With it, you can create layered images that can be integrated with other layers in Photoshop, Flash, and After Effects.

A great new feature in After Effects CS6 allows you to convert an imported Illustrator image into an editable shape layer, which can then be extruded using After Effects CS6's new Ray-traced 3D Render engine. The following exercises will show you the basics of how to do this.

Creating vector imagery with Image Trace

The motion graphic outro that will appear at the end of the Afrolicious promo video currently displays the Afrolicious logo as a flat graphic. You'll enhance the look of the logo graphic—and with it the motion graphic and the final Afrolicious promo video—by giving it some 3D thickness, or extrusion. An extruded graphic can be more visually interesting than a flat graphic, and with the new extrusion feature in Adobe After Effects CS6, creating an extruded graphic is very easy.

To do this, you must first convert the current raster logo graphic into a vector graphic in Adobe Illustrator CS6 using the Image Trace feature.

Image Trace allows you to easily convert a raster image, such as a photograph or other pixel-based graphic, into a vector graphic. This vector graphic can be brought into Adobe After Effects, which allows vector graphics to be scaled up without getting pixelated artifacts. In addition, using a new feature in After Effects CS6, an imported vector graphic can be converted into an editable shape layer, which means you don't need to return to Adobe Illustrator to make changes to the original vector graphic.

You'll import the Image-traced logo vector graphic to Adobe After Effects CS6 where you'll then convert it into a shape layer, which you'll then extrude.

Raster images vs. vector images

It's important to know the difference between raster images and vector images. Here is a brief explanation of the difference and what they are typically used for.

A **raster image** is made up of a finite grid of pixels. Typically, this would be a digitized photograph, but it could also be a frame from a video clip or a scanned drawing. A raster image can be saved in a variety of different file formats, such as a .jpg, .png, .tiff, or in the native Adobe Photoshop Extended .psd format. Raster images can offer high-resolution photorealistic detail but are limited by their native image size. If a raster image is scaled larger than its native size, the edges in the image will look jagged and pixelated.

A **vector image** is made up of paths; each path is defined by an underlying mathematical formula, which determines how the path is shaped. The paths are assigned colors as strokes on the paths or fills within the paths. A vector image would typically be a logo graphic saved as a .eps file or in the native Adobe Illustrator .ai format. The advantage of vector graphics is that they can be scaled without showing pixelated edges, thus retaining their image quality.

Converting the graphic to a vector image

Let's use the afrolicious_logo.png image in the Graphics folder and convert it into a vector graphic using Illustrator's new Image Trace feature.

1   Open Illustrator CS6.

2   Choose File > Open. Navigate to the Graphics folder, select afrolicious_logo.png, and click Open.

   Notice that many of the tools in Illustrator, such as the Selection tool, are similar to tools that you would see in other Creative Suite applications, and they function the same way.

3   Select the graphic using the Selection tool.

   You want to convert this raster (or pixel-based) image into a vector image that has a transparent background. This is important because the current logo graphic has no background, and you want to maintain consistency in the design of your motion graphic.

4   Click the Image Trace button at the top of the interface.

The image will become a vector graphic with a white background.

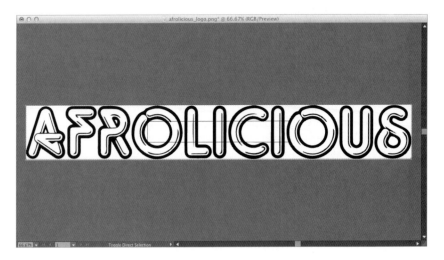

5 Click the Layers panel button on the right side of the interface to open the Layers panel.

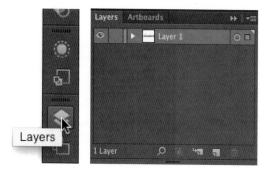

6 Twirl open Layer 1 by clicking the disclosure triangle. You'll notice that the resulting white background cannot be selected and removed.

7 Undo this Image Trace by pressing Command+Z (Ctrl+Z).

8 With the graphic still selected, choose Object > Image Trace > Make and Expand.

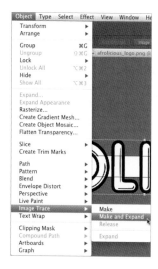

Doing so will not only image trace the bitmap graphic, but it will make every visible element into a separate editable object. This is what you want to do so you can easily remove the white background, thus keeping the background of the resulting vector graphic transparent.

Editing the Image-traced logo

Now you'll do a bit of cleanup to the Image-traced logo graphic.

1   Click the Layers panel button. In the Layers panel within Layer 1, twirl open Group.

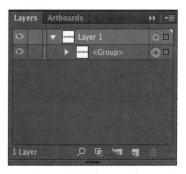

2   Scroll down to the bottom of the Layers panel to find the bottommost object, which is the white background. Turn off this object's visibility switch (or eye icon).

Notice how the graphic no longer has a white box behind the letters.

Also notice how the inner paths of some of the letters—the inner hole of the O, for example—have a white fill. You want to remove those.

3 From the Tools panel, choose the Direct Selection tool, or press the A key.

4 Deselect all by pressing Command+Shift+A (Ctrl+Shift+A), or click on a blank area of the image.

5 Using the Direct Selection tool, click on the inner white fill of the first O to select it, and press Delete to get rid of it.

6 Select the inner white fill of the last O with the Direct Selection tool and press Delete. Do this with the small inner white fills of the A, R, and S.

7 Choose File > Save As, navigate to the Graphics folder (Adobe CS6 Project Assets > Graphics), name this new file **afrolicious_logo.ai**, and click Save.

8 In the Illustrator Options window that appears, click OK.

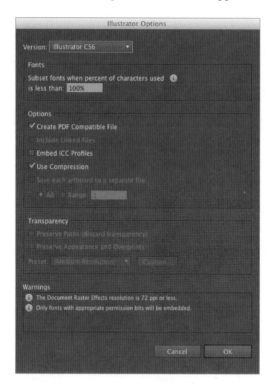

Importing your vector logo to After Effects

Now that the vector logo is cleaned up, you'll take it into After Effects where you will use it to replace a layer that is already in a composition.

▶ **Tip:** Switch between open applications by pressing Command+ Tab (Alt+Tab).

1 Switch to After Effects.

2 Choose File > Import > File, navigate to the Graphics folder, select the afrolicious_logo.ai file that you just made, and click Open.

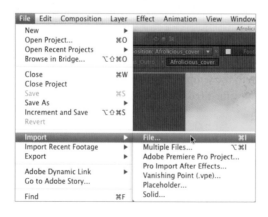

3 The graphic should appear in your Project panel. Double-click on it to display it in the Footage panel.

Here you encounter a slight problem. Notice that you're not seeing the entire graphic! You're only seeing the center section, and the rest of the graphic appears cropped.

● **Note:** Some image formats, such as the Adobe Illustrator native .ai format, .tiff, or .psd contain metadata that determines the size of their artboards when these images are opened in Illustrator. However, other image formats, such as .png or .jpg, do not contain such metadata and the default size of the artboard in Adobe Illustrator CS6 is determined by the size of the last artboard used. Your afrolicious_logo.png graphic may not appear cropped exactly as in the figures shown.

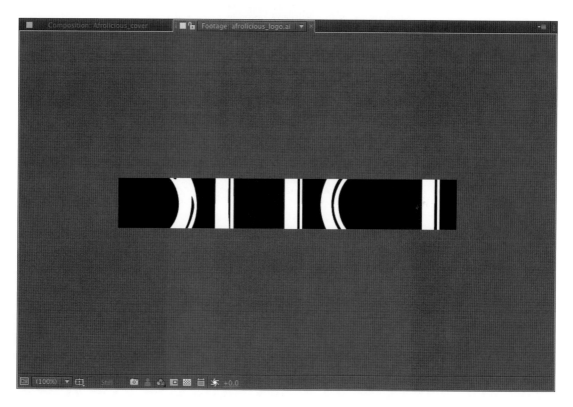

Making motion graphics is rarely a smooth and flawless process, and little problems like this are a typical occurrence. Don't panic! You can fix it.

4 Switch back to Illustrator.

Look closely and you'll see a white rectangle in the background of the graphic. This is called the *Artboard*, and it determines the visible area of this graphic. You'll need to expand the Artboard to the bounds of the graphic, and then resave the file.

▶ **Tip:** Paths from Illustrator can be copied and pasted to After Effects as motion paths, mask paths, or shape paths.

5 Choose Object > Artboards > Fit to Artwork Bounds. The Artboard expands to the outer edges of the entire graphic.

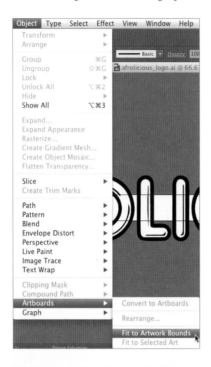

6 Save your file by pressing Command+S (Ctrl+S).

7 Switch back to After Effects.

8 Select the already imported afrolicious_logo.ai footage in your Project panel.

After Effects conveniently gives you the ability to reload an imported graphic to reflect any changes that you have saved to it in another program. You don't need to reimport the graphic and reapply any changes you may have made to it in any compositions.

9 Choose File > Reload Footage.

10 At the bottom of the Footage panel, click the Magnification menu and choose Fit up to 100%. You should see the refreshed changes to the graphic.

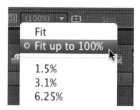

11 Click the Toggle Transparency Grid button to see the graphic against its transparent background.

Swapping a layer with a different media item

Now let's add this graphic to the Afrolicious_cover composition. Recall that you've already applied some animation to the original afrolicious_logo.png layer.

Another convenient feature in After Effects is the ability to swap a layer in a composition with another footage item. You don't have to reapply all of the changes and animations you may have already made to a layer. All of these changes and animations will remain intact when you replace the layer with different footage.

1 In the Afrolicious_cover Timeline, select the afrolicious_logo.png layer.

2 In the Project panel, select the afrolicious_logo.ai graphic.

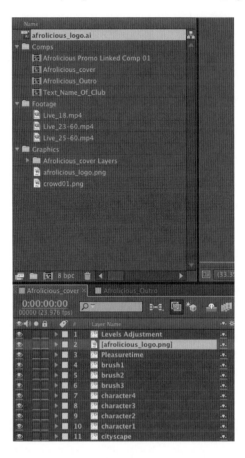

3 Hold down the Option (Alt) key, and drag and drop the afrolicious_logo.ai graphic into the Timeline.

The afrolicious_logo.png layer is replaced by afrolicious_logo.ai.

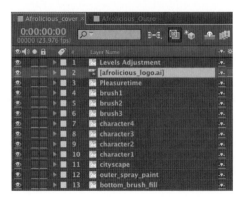

4   Scrub through your Timeline, and you'll notice that everything you had applied to the original afrolicious_logo.png layer remains intact on this new layer.

5   In the Project panel, select the afrolicious_logo.ai graphic, and drag and drop it into the Graphics folder. Try to keep your Project panel organized as you work.

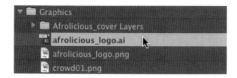

6   Press Command+S (Ctrl+S) to save your After Effects project.

Creating 3D extrusions in After Effects CS6

New in After Effects CS6 is the Ray-traced 3D Renderer, which allows for vector shape layers and text layers to be extruded as well as rendered with reflections and environment maps.

Although it is not required, it is recommended that your system have a supported graphics processor to utilize the increased productivity and speed of GPU rendering.

Note: For a list of supported GPUs for use with the Ray-traced 3D Renderer, go to www.adobe.com/products/aftereffects/tech-specs.html.

Now that you have the vector graphic in the composition, let's convert it into a shape layer and then extrude it.

1   Select the layer afrolicious_logo.ai.

2   Click Layer > Create Shapes from Vector Layer.

You should see a new shape layer in your Timeline called afrolicious_logo Outlines. Also, notice that the afrolicious_logo.ai layer is turned off but is still there. This is convenient because you may end up changing your mind and decide to turn it back on.

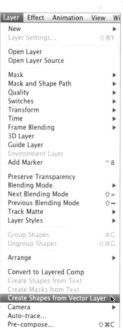

3 Drag this shape layer below the Levels Adjustment layer.

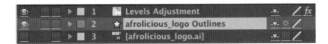

4 To apply an extrusion to this shape layer, you must turn on its 3D switch. Click once on the 3D switch for the afrolicious_logo Outlines layer.

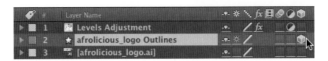

5 The extrusion feature also requires the Ray-traced 3D Renderer to be activated because the Classic 3D Renderer does not support extrusions. Do this by clicking the Classic 3D button at the top right of the composition window (if the Ray-traced 3D Renderer isn't already activated).

The Composition Settings window opens showing the Advanced settings.

3D in After Effects

By default, layers in After Effects CS6 have two-dimensional spatial coordinates. However, you have the option to activate a layer's 3D switch so that the layer has three-dimensional spatial coordinates. A 3D layer can be moved horizontally, vertically, and forward and backward in z-space, and can also be rotated on three separate axes of rotation. Using 3D space in After Effects allows for the use of camera layers and light layers, making your motion graphics more compelling to the viewer.

Ray-traced 3D Renderer

After Effects CS6 introduces a new Ray-traced 3D rendering engine, allowing you to simply and quickly design fully ray-traced, geometric text and shape layers in 3D space. These enhanced 3D capabilities include:

- Beveled and extruded text and shape layers, adding depth to graphic designs without compromising animations

- Bending of footage and composition layers, adding dimension and yielding more interesting lighting effects for otherwise flat content

- Environment map support for photorealistic reflections of virtual imagery in addition to the layers included in a composition

- Additional material options, including reflection, transparency, and index of refraction to mimic light traveling through glass and other translucent materials

The Ray-traced 3D Renderer works best on systems that have a supported graphics processor. Systems without a supported GPU will rely on CPU rendering and the new Ray-traced 3D features will render much more slowly.

For more information on which graphics processors support the new Ray-traced 3D rendering in Adobe After Effects CS6, go to www.adobe.com/products/aftereffects/tech-specs.html.

6 From the Renderer drop-down menu, choose Ray-traced 3D, and click OK at the bottom of this window.

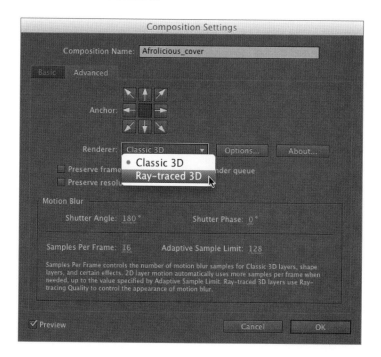

7 Adjust your current time indicator (CTI) to 0:00:03:04.

8 Twirl open the afrolicious_logo Outlines layer to reveal the Geometry Options and set the Extrusion Depth value to **200**.

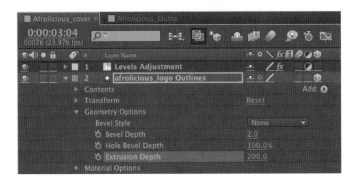

Note: Unless your system has a supported GPU, using the Ray-traced 3D Renderer in After Effects uses your system's CPU cores and can result in slow previewing and final rendering.

Notice how this shape layer has a thickness to it, as if the logo is not just a flat part of the CD cover but is a 3D object extending toward the viewer.

9 Press Command+S (Ctrl+S) to save your project.

Shape layers in After Effects

Adobe After Effects features a versatile type of layer called a *shape layer*. These are vector layers that enable you to create vector graphics natively in After Effects. With these, you don't need to create all of your vector graphics in Adobe Illustrator and import them to After Effects.

Shape layers continuously rasterize, which means that they can be scaled at any size without suffering from jagged pixelated edges.

Shape layers have their own set of effects that allow you to:

- Generate simple and complex shape paths
- Apply solid or gradient stroke colors
- Apply solid or gradient fill colors
- Animate strokes along paths
- Distort and merge paths
- Create repetitions of shapes
- Create groups of different paths and properties on the same layer

About Adobe Photoshop Extended

Adobe Photoshop Extended is the industry-standard application for creating still-image composites and for doing photographic color corrections and manipulations. It is used by graphic designers, web designers, motion graphic designers, and video editors, and it can play an essential role in your workflow when you're using other applications in the Adobe Creative Suite, including After Effects, Flash, InDesign, and Adobe Premiere Pro.

Useful features in Photoshop CS6 Extended

Adobe Photoshop CS6 Extended includes several new features that can enhance the workflow of video editors and motion graphic artists. These include:

- **Mercury Graphics Engine**, which uses the processing power of your graphics card to greatly speed up your image editing tasks.

- **3D controls**, which allow you to create and even animate 3D artwork, such as extruded text.

- **New Blur Gallery**, which gives you more options to apply blurs to your still images and video frames. Create tilt-shift blur effects, manipulate versatile blur focal points, and more.

- **Reflections and draggable shadows**, which enable you to add 3D realism to your images. 3D objects can reflect on the ground plane in your images, and shadows can be realistically manipulated as you adjust virtual light sources.

Using Liquify in Photoshop

Let's take a close look at the design of the Afrolicious_cover graphic and see if there's anything in it that could use a little touching up in Photoshop. Notice that there is a slightly repetitive brush stroke on the far right of the image on the bottom_brush_fill layer.

In this exercise, you'll perform retouching to the Afrolicious_cover graphic using the Liquify effect in Adobe Photoshop CS6 Extended.

Although this layered Photoshop image has already been imported to After Effects and has been used as a layer in a composition, you have the ability to edit any of the original layers in Photoshop and easily refresh your changes in After Effects.

If a graphic has been imported to After Effects, you can access the original file and open it in its native application without having to first find the file on your hard drive.

1 In the Afrolicious_cover composition, select the bottom_brush_fill layer.

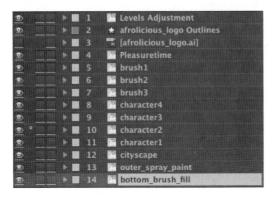

▶ **Tip:** Press
Command+E (Ctrl+E) to
edit a selected footage
item or layer in a
supported application.

2 Choose Edit > Edit Original. Photoshop Extended opens the original Afrolicious_cover image.

3 Select the bottom_brush_fill layer, hold down the Option (Alt) key, and click on this layer's visibility switch to make it the only visible layer. This will prevent any accidental edits to the other layers.

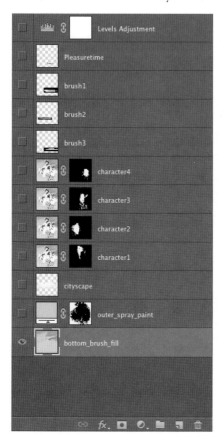

Now let's focus on the brush stroke on this layer that you want to fix.

You'll smooth out this brush stroke using the Liquify filter. Photoshop CS6 Extended takes advantage of the Mercury Graphics Engine, which accesses the power of your computer's GPU to calculate complex image manipulations with great speed. Using this engine, the Liquify filter can make visible changes in real time.

4 Choose Filter > Liquify to activate the Liquify filter.

The filter window appears, and you'll see a brush icon that resembles a circular crosshair.

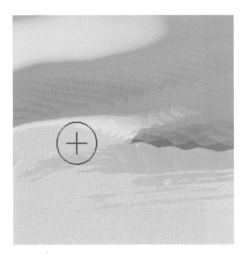

5 With this brush, click and drag across the layer until the repetitive brush stroke is smoothed over. Repeat as you deem necessary.

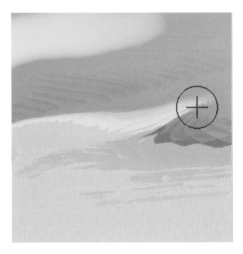

6 When you're done, click OK.

The filter window will close, bringing you back to the main Photoshop interface.

7 In the Layers panel, hold down the Option (Alt) key and click on the visibility switch for the bottom_brush_fill layer to make all the layers visible again.

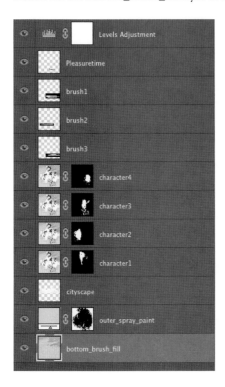

8 Press Command+S (Ctrl+S) to save your Photoshop image.

9 Switch back to After Effects.

10 In the Project panel, open the Graphics folder, and then open the Afrolicious_cover Layers folder within it.

11 Select the file bottom_brush_fill/Afrolicious_cover.psd.

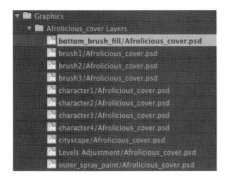

12 Choose File > Reload Footage. You can also right-click on this item and choose Reload Footage.

13 Press Command+S (Ctrl+S) to save your After Effects project.

Using Transfer Modes in After Effects

After Effects gives you many different ways of compositing layers to achieve desired results. For instance, it offers different ways of blending layers through the use of layer opacity (with masks, for example, which you'll explore later). Another way that you can composite layers is through the use of Transfer Modes, which are very effective at removing the white or black areas of grayscale layers.

Transfer Modes work by blending color values of layers, including color brightness, hue, or saturation.

Let's take a look at some of the layers in the Afrolicious_cover composition and determine how Transfer Modes are being utilized.

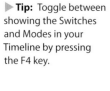

Tip: Toggle between showing the Switches and Modes in your Timeline by pressing the F4 key.

1 Click the Toggles Switches/Modes button at the bottom of the Timeline.

Notice how some layers are set to the default Normal mode, and others are set to Screen or Soft Light. How did these settings get there?

This is another example of how well Photoshop Extended and After Effects integrate seamlessly. If a layer in a Photoshop image has a Blend Mode applied to it and that Photoshop image is imported to After Effects as a composition (as you have done), the Blend Mode remains intact in the corresponding After Effects layer as a Transfer Mode.

● **Note:** Blend Modes in Photoshop Extended are analogous to Transfer Modes in After Effects.

2   Click on the solo switch for the brush1 layer.

▶ **Tip:** Toggling solo switches on layers in Adobe After Effects allows you to make all other layers invisible in the same composition.

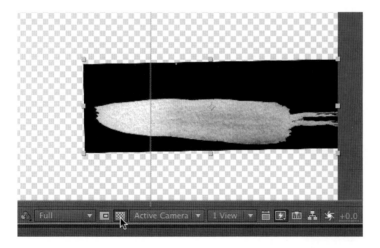

3   At the bottom of the Composition panel, click the Toggle Transparency Grid button to activate it.

Notice that the brush1 layer is now the only layer visible (because its solo switch is on). But more important, notice that this layer has its own black background along with the light-gray brush stroke. Why didn't you see this black area on the layer before?

The Screen mode applied to the layer uses the layer's color brightness and blends it with the visible layers below it. The Screen mode is a form of additive blending whereby darker colors approach transparent while brighter colors are retained. Modes such as Add, Lighten, and Color Dodge will yield similar results with different subtleties. So although the layer has a rectangular black background, instead of masking or keying the black region, all you need to do is apply the Screen mode and the black background disappears.

4   Deactivate the solo switch for the brush1 layer to confirm that, indeed, the Screen mode is causing the black background to disappear.

Understanding and applying Motion Blur

Motion blur is a visual artifact that occurs in varying degrees based on the speed of a camera's shutter. Objects in motion will appear blurry, especially at lower shutter speeds.

After Effects can easily simulate this visual effect on a layer in motion. Let's apply Motion Blur to some of the layers in the Afrolicious_cover composition as well as the Afrolicious_Outro composition to give these moving layers a subtle touch of realism.

1   In After Effects, Open the Afrolicious_cover composition, and click the Toggle Switches/Modes button at the bottom of the Timeline so that the Switches are visible.

Notice the three columns of switches that appear as empty boxes. The left column, underneath an icon of a ball in motion, is the Motion Blur switch. To activate Motion Blur for a layer, click inside its Motion Blur switch.

2 Turn on Motion Blur for *all* of the layers in this comp except for Levels
   Adjustment and afrolicious_logo.ai (because these layers are not visible).

▶ **Tip:** To activate the
Motion Blur switch—or
any other switch—for
multiple layers in the
Timeline, click one
switch and then drag
up or down along the
same switch for other
layers in the layer stack.

3 To see motion blur in your RAM Preview, you must also click the large Motion
   Blur button at the top of the Timeline to activate it.

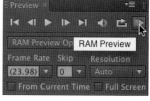

4 Do a RAM Preview by clicking the RAM Preview button in the Preview panel
   or by pressing the 0 key on your numeric keypad.

Watch your RAM Preview and notice how the layers appear slightly blurred
while they are moving.

5 As a comparison, turn off the Motion Blur switch for the Pleasuretime layer and do another RAM Preview.

6 Reactivate the Motion Blur switch for the Pleasuretime layer.

7 Open the Afrolicious_Outro composition, and activate the Motion Blur switch for the Afrolicious_cover layer.

It should be noted that because you did a RAM Preview of the Afrolicious_cover composition, After Effects would render the Afrolicious_Outro composition more quickly because it does not need to recalculate the preview for the nested Afrolicious_cover composition.

▶ **Tip:** The amount of motion blur that renders on a layer is determined by the Shutter Angle property in the Advanced tab in Composition Settings.

8 Press Command+S (Ctrl+S) to save your project.

Simply by activating the Motion Blur switches on layers that are moving, your final motion graphic will have an added subtle touch of realism.

A word of warning; although motion blur will yield a more realistic and visually attractive result, having motion blur turned on will also significantly increase your render time. On the other hand, using motion blur is less time-consuming than hand keyframing a blur on each layer. There is no reason to activate motion blur for layers that are not in motion.

The most-used effects

Although Adobe After Effects ships with dozens of effects for doing color correction, blurring and sharpening, texturing, and shape generation, chances are that you won't use all of these effects. However, you'll probably use a handful of these effects on a regular basis. Your mileage may vary, but the following effects are generally accepted as the most-used because they can be applied to projects for motion graphics, visual effects compositing, and video editing:

- **Levels.** This is a general purpose effect for adjusting brightness and contrast on discrete Red, Green, and Blue color channels, or all color channels combined. This effect has a histogram control that functions like that of the Levels image adjustment in Adobe Photoshop Extended.

- **Fast Blur.** This is a Gaussian Blur effect with very simple controls that can be used to soften the details of a layer to reduce video noise or grain, create a "dreamy" look, or make a layer look like it's far away and out of focus.

- **Hue/Saturation.** This effect is used for adjusting the hue and saturation color properties of a layer. This has a multitude of uses, including applying a duotone look to a layer, enhancing or reducing the saturation of a layer's colors, and remapping the hues of a layer's colors to different hues.

- **Drop Shadow.** This effect is used to create the illusion of depth on a 2D layer to make what appears to be a shadow being cast behind the layer. This is very useful to create a subtle separation between a layer in the foreground and layers behind it.

- **Ramp.** This creates a two-colored gradient on a layer that can be a linear gradient or a radial gradient. The Ramp effect is useful for making simple gradients for a background layer.

Adding and animating effects with After Effects

After Effects comes with hundreds of effects—analogous to filters in Photoshop—that can be applied to layers to perform a multitude of operations, such as color correction, blurring and sharpening, texturing, and image distortion. Don't be daunted by the sheer number of effects, because you'll probably use only a dozen or so on a regular basis.

Let's apply a Blur effect to some layers in the Afrolicious_Outro composition. This is a simple way of making layers in the background appear out of focus and far away, lending an illusion of depth to your composition.

1 Open the Afrolicious_Outro composition, and press the End key to adjust your CTI to the last frame in the Timeline.

2 Select the crowd01.png layer.

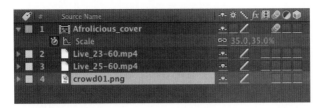

3 Choose Effect > Blur & Sharpen > Fast Blur.

▶ Tip: To show all effects on a layer, select the layer and press E.

4 Twirl open the crowd01.png layer to reveal the Fast Blur Effect and all of its controls.

5 Adjust the Blurriness value to 5, and change Repeat Edge Pixels to On. This setting ensures that the edges of an applied layer do not appear softened, and that layers below do not show through the blurred layer's edges.

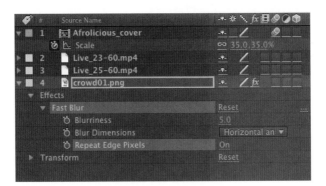

In your Composition panel, notice how the crowd01.png layer in the background now appears slightly blurred.

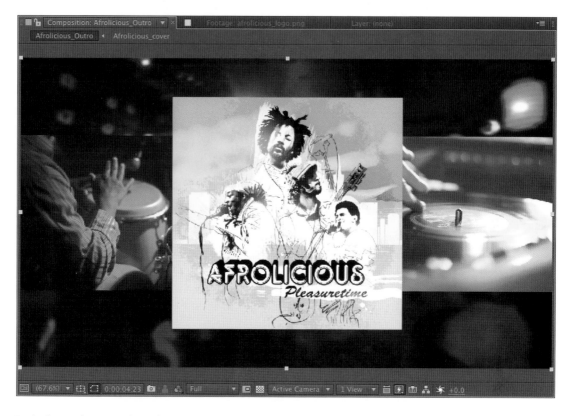

Let's also apply a Fast Blur effect to the layers Live_23-60.mp4 and Live_25-60.mp4. You could apply the Fast Blur effect to these layers separately, but there's an easier way to apply one effect to multiple layers: You use an Adjustment Layer, which is a special type of layer. When one or more effects is applied to an Adjustment Layer, those effects are rendered on all visible layers stacked below the Adjustment Layer.

6 Create an Adjustment Layer by choosing Layer > New > Adjustment Layer.

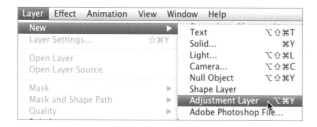

A new Adjustment Layer 1 appears at the top of the layer stack in your Timeline.

7 With your Selection tool, drag this layer so that it is below the Afrolicious_cover layer but above the Live_23-60.mp4 layer.

Incidentally, you may notice that the Adjustment Layer is not a visible object in your composition window.

▶ **Tip:** To apply the last effect used, press Command+ Option+Shift+E (Ctrl+Alt+Shift+E).

8 With the Adjustment Layer still selected, choose Effect > Blur & Sharpen > Fast Blur.

The Fast Blur effect will be applied to the Adjustment Layer.

9 Twirl open the Adjustment Layer in your Timeline to reveal the Fast Blur effect and all of its controls.

10 Adjust the Blurriness value to 5, and change Repeat Edge Pixels to On.

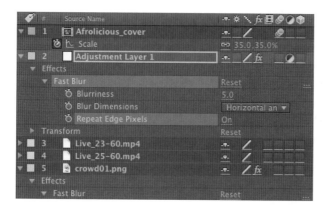

Notice that the layers Live_23-60.mp4 and Live_25-60.mp4 now appear slightly blurred, but the Afrolicious_cover layer does not. The reason is that the effects applied to an Adjustment Layer will only render on the visible layers stacked below it.

Also notice that the file crowd01.png appears slightly more blurred than before. Again, the reason is that it has a Fast Blur effect already applied to it, but it is also stacked below the Adjustment Layer with its own Fast Blur effect.

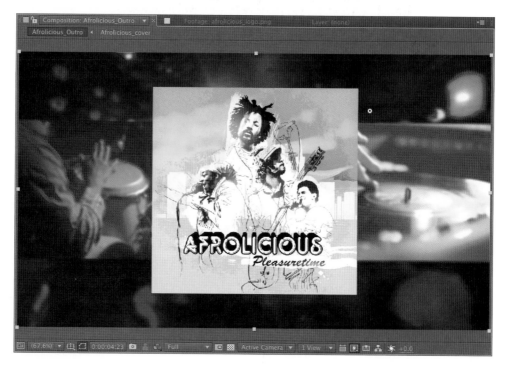

11 Press Command+S (Ctrl+S) to save your project.

Creating static and animated masks in After Effects

A *mask* is a vector shape that you can draw on a layer so that the layer is visible or invisible based on the area of the layer that is masked. This is an operation that is available in Photoshop. However, in After Effects, a mask can either be static or animated.

Using masks in After Effects gives you more control over visibility for each layer. For instance, you can crop out areas of a layer that you don't want the viewers to see. In addition, by using an animated mask, you have a customizable method of making a layer appear or disappear over time, so that a layer does not have to be revealed all at once or animated from offscreen. In its simplest form, this can look like a Wipe transition.

▶ **Tip:** Adjust your CTI one frame backward by pressing the Page Up key or one frame forward by pressing the Page Down key. Adjust your CTI ten frames backward by pressing Shift+Page Up or ten frames forward by pressing Shift+ Page Down.

Let's apply masks to some of the layers in the Afrolicious_cover composition and animate these masks by keyframing the Mask Shape property to gradually reveal these layers along the horizontal axis.

1 Open the Afrolicious_cover composition.

2 Select the brush1 layer, and activate its solo switch.

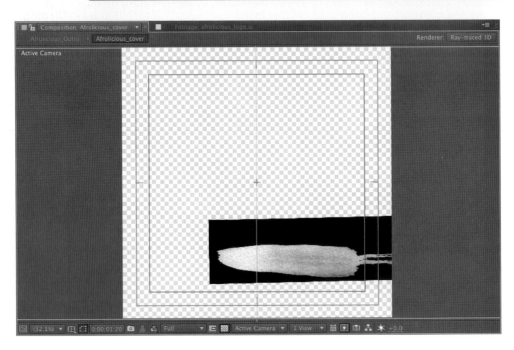

3   Making sure your layer is selected, press the I key to adjust the CTI to the layer's
    In point. Press Shift+Page Down to move ten frames ahead, and then press
    Page Down twice to move ahead two more frames for a total of 12 frames or a
    half second.

4   In the Tools panel, click the Rectangle tool.

5   Starting at the top left of the brush1 layer in the Composition panel, click and
    drag with the Rectangle tool down and to the right so that the resulting mask
    encloses the visible, gray brush stroke. Try to make your mask slightly larger
    than the layer.

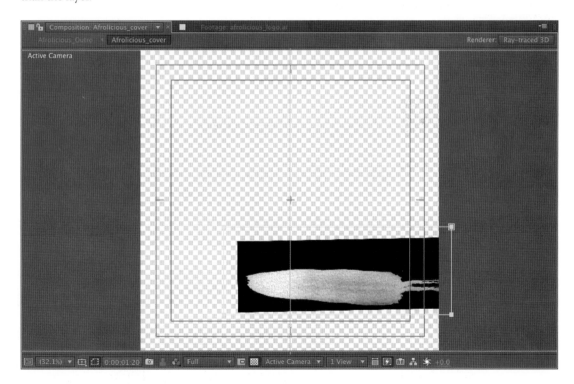

6 Press MM (two Ms quickly) to reveal the mask properties.

7 Click the chain link icon next to the Mask Feather values to unconstrain their proportions.

8 Set the horizontal Mask Feather value to 20 to soften the edges of the mask.

9 Click the stopwatch icon for Mask Path.

10 With the brush1 layer selected, press the I key to go to its In point.

11 With the Mask Path property still selected, press Command+T (Ctrl+T) to activate the mask's free transform bounding box.

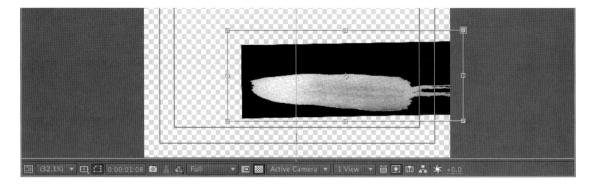

12 Press the V key to activate the Selection tool.

13 Hold down the Shift key and drag the free transform bounding box to the right until it is outside of the composition frame. Holding down Shift while you move a mask constrains the movement to either the horizontal or vertical axis.

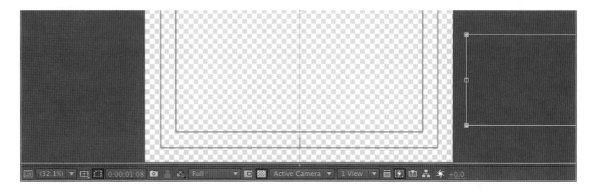

14 Select the second Mask Path keyframe on brush1, right-click on it, and choose Keyframe Assistant > Easy Ease.

Now that you've animated a mask on one of the brush layers, you can save some time by copying and pasting its mask properties to the other brush layers.

15 With the Mask 1 properties visible on brush1 in the Timeline, along with the keyframes for Mask Path, use the Selection tool to draw a marquee around the Mask Path and Mask Feather properties. Note that by selecting Mask Path you're also selecting its keyframes.

16 Press Command+C (Ctrl+C) to copy these settings and keyframes. Turn off the solo switch for brush1.

Now it's just a matter of pasting this animated mask onto the remaining two brush layers.

17 Select the brush2 layer. Turn on its solo switch and press the I key to adjust your CTI to its In point.

18 Press Command+V (Ctrl+V) to paste the animated mask.

19 Scrub your CTI through the Timeline to confirm that the animation looks fine on brush2. Turn off its solo switch.

20 Select the brush3 layer. Turn on its solo switch and press the I key to adjust your CTI to its In point.

21 Press Command+V (Ctrl+V) to paste the animated mask.

22 Scrub your CTI through the Timeline to confirm that the animation looks fine on brush3. Turn off its solo switch.

23 Do a RAM Preview by clicking the RAM Preview icon in the Preview panel or by pressing the 0 key on your numeric keypad.

You should see all of the brush layers animate along with the animation of the other layers in this composition.

24 Press Command+S (Ctrl+S) to save your project.

Finishing the outro motion graphic

The final graphics you'll create for your outro will appear to be stage lights roaming through the frame. These will enhance the look and feel of the video clips in the background of the outro that show a live performance in progress.

Using shape layers

To create the stage lights, you'll use yellow circles on shape layers. These layers will animate their positions horizontally back and forth across the frame.

Let's create a shape layer in the Afrolicious_Outro composition.

1   Your Afrolicious_Outro composition should still be open. Click on its tab in the Timeline to reveal its layers.

2   Click on the visibility switch (eye icon) for the Afrolicious_cover layer so you can see your work.

3   Create a new shape layer by choosing Layer > New > Shape Layer.

    This empty shape layer will appear in the Timeline at the top of the layer stack.

4   Click and drag this shape layer directly below the Adjustment Layer.

5   Twirl open the shape layer in the Timeline to reveal the Add button.

6   Click on the Add button and a context menu will appear. This context menu lists all of the objects and various shape effects that can be added to the shape layer.

7   From this list, choose Ellipse.

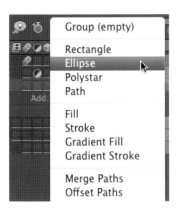

An Ellipse Path property will now be listed under the Contents of the shape layer. Twirl open Ellipse Path.

You should see the property for Size, which determines the width and height of the Ellipse Path 1. By default, these values are constrained, so adjusting one will adjust the other to maintain a constant aspect ratio.

8 Adjust the Ellipse Path Size to 720 pixels.

In the Composition panel—with the shape layer still selected—you should see that the Ellipse Path is the same height as the composition frame.

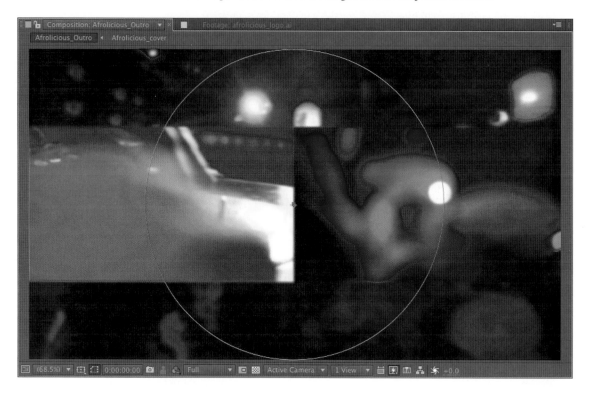

Now you'll give the elliptical shape a yellow fill color.

9 In the Timeline, click once again on the shape layer's Add button, and then choose Fill from the list.

Your shape layer now has a solid fill color. By default, the fill color for a shape layer is red. You'll change this to white.

10 Under the shape layer Contents, twirl open the Fill properties. Click on the Color swatch.

11 A Color window appears. Choose a pale yellow, and then click OK on the Color window.

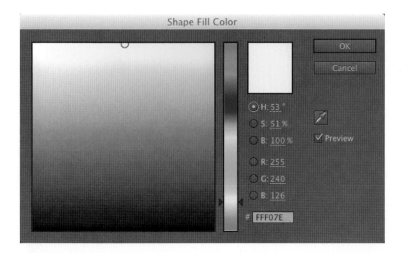

Your circle now has a yellow fill color.

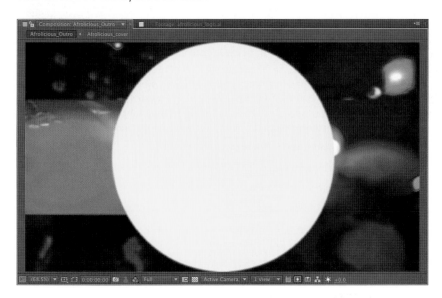

Because this shape is supposed to resemble a spotlight landing on a surface, let's give it a bit of blur to soften its edges.

12 With your shape layer selected in the Timeline, choose Effect > Blur & Sharpen > Fast Blur.

13 In the Effect Controls panel, under the Fast Blur properties, set Blurriness to 50.

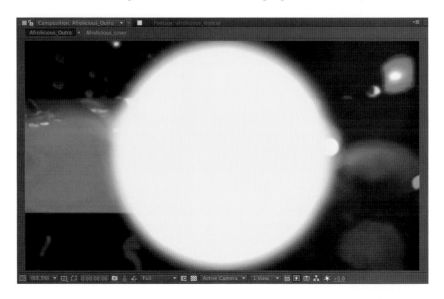

Expressions explained

An expression is a script that you can apply to a layer's property to manipulate the property's underlying numerical value. Expressions use a scripting language that is based on JavaScript. Expressions can have many different functions, ranging from the very simple to the incredibly complex, including but not limited to:

- Assigning a static value to a property

- Generating a random value for a property

- Linking one property's value to another property's value

- Translating one range of values into a different range of values

- Performing Boolean operations (e.g., if x=1 then y=2)

- Analyzing the content of a text layer

- Using the value of the current time to apply an ever-increasing numerical value to a property

- Using layers' stacking order in the Timeline to apply incremental values to the layers

Using the wiggle expression

You won't animate the shape layer with keyframes. Instead, you'll create the animation with an expression.

An *expression* is a script that manipulates the underlying numerical value of a property to perform various operations. One such operation—using a *wiggle* expression—allows you to animate a property by adding randomly generated interpolating values to its current value at set intervals of time.

1   In the Timeline, select the shape layer and press P to show its Position property. Because you only want to animate the horizontal position, you'll need to separate the Position property into separate properties for horizontal and vertical position.

2   Right-click on the Position property and choose Separate Dimensions.

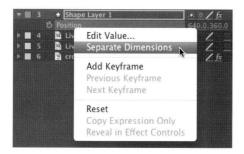

You should now see separate properties for X Position and Y Position.

To apply an expression to a property, hold down the Option (Alt) key and click once on the property's stopwatch icon.

3   Press Command+Shift+A (Ctrl+Shift+A) to de-select all. Hold down the Option (Alt) key and click the stopwatch icon for X Position. This will change the Timeline interface slightly. A text field will appear next to X Position that has a default script in it.

4   Click once in this field to select the entire script. Using lowercase letters, type **wiggle(.5,1000)**.

Translated to English, this means *Every .5 seconds interpolate this property's value within a range of plus or minus 1000 pixels.*

5 Press Enter on your numeric keypad, or click on a blank area in the Timeline panel, to register the expression.

6 Do a RAM Preview by pressing 0 on the numeric keypad, or click the RAM Preview icon in the Preview window. You'll see the yellow circle move back and forth randomly across the frame. Note that this animation was achieved without applying keyframes.

Adding Motion Blur

Now you'll add motion blur to the shape layer.

1 Click on the shape layer's Motion Blur switch.

2 Do a RAM Preview. Notice that the shape layer doesn't appear to have motion blur. The reason is that you need to activate the switch at the top of the Timeline to enable Motion Blur for all layers with the Motion Blur switch set.

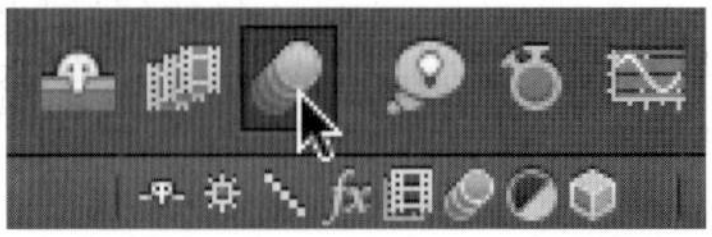

Note: Remember that motion blur can significantly increase your render times.

3 Do another RAM Preview; the shape layer should now have motion blur.

Applying a Transfer Mode

Because you're supposed to be simulating a stage light, you don't want it to look like a solid yellow circle. You can use a Transfer Mode to blend the yellow fill with the layers stacked below.

1 Click the Toggle Switches/Modes button. Click the Modes menu to the right of Shape Layer 1 and choose the Add mode.

The Add mode blends the colors of a layer with the visible layers below it, resulting in brighter colors than on any contributing layer. By applying the Add mode to a bright yellow shape, the result resembles a bright, yellow light shining on other colored areas.

2 With the shape layer selected, press the T key to reveal its Opacity setting.

3 To decrease the brightness of this layer, adjust the Opacity value to 20%.

Duplicating layers

Now you'll make more of the stage light shape layers. Fortunately, you won't have to go through all of the previous steps again. You can duplicate After Effects layers, and any properties and their values (and animations) will be duplicated with them.

If a layer with a wiggle expression applied to it is duplicated, After Effects will call on a different set of random values for the duplicate's wiggle expression. In other words, if you duplicate your shape layer, the duplicate will not wiggle in synch with the original, and you'll end up with several shape layers that move differently. All of these shape layers will be made by simply duplicating the one you now have.

1 With your shape layer selected, press Command+D (Ctrl+D) four times to make four duplicates. You should now have five of these wiggling shape layers.

2 Turn the Afrolicious_cover layer back on by clicking once on its visibility switch.

3 Do a RAM Preview and watch your composition play in real time.

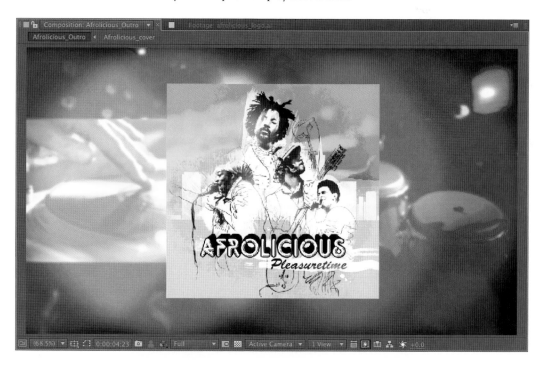

4 Press Command+S (Ctrl+S) to save your After Effects project.

Integrating your After Effects composition into your Adobe Premiere Pro Timeline

If you're continuing from the previous lesson, you should still have your project open in Adobe Premiere Pro. If you started at this lesson, navigate to the Lesson 06 folder on your hard drive and open the Adobe Premiere Pro project Lesson_06 Start.prproj. Save your Adobe Premiere Pro project file in the Lesson 06 folder as **Afrolicious Promo.prproj**.

In your Adobe Premiere Pro CS6 project, you'll need to import your outro motion graphic that you created in Adobe After Effects CS6. Then you'll add your outro to the end of your edit.

Adobe Premiere Pro and Adobe After Effects can work seamlessly together thanks to a feature called Dynamic Link (see Lesson 5 for more details), which allows you to import a composition from After Effects into Adobe Premiere Pro without having to do any intermediate rendering beforehand. Once your After Effects composition is brought into your Adobe Premiere Pro project, any changes you make to the composition in After Effects will automatically refresh in your Adobe Premiere Pro project.

1   In Adobe Premiere Pro, choose File > Import, or press Command+I (Ctrl+I). In the Import window, navigate to your Lesson 06 folder and select your After Effects project file Afrolicious_Promo_02.aep. Click Import.

2   An Import After Effects Composition window appears. Click the disclosure triangle next to the Comps folder to twirl it open. Select the Afrolicious_Outro composition, and then click OK.

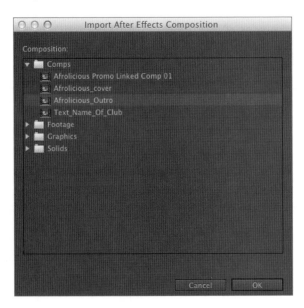

Your imported After Effects composition will appear in the Adobe Premiere Pro Project panel.

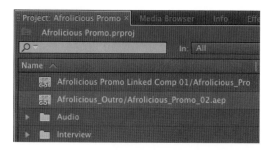

3 Double-click on the imported composition to open it in the Source Monitor.

4 At the bottom of the Source Monitor, click the Drag Video Only icon, and then drag it to track Video 3 in your Timeline at the end of the sequence.

5 Make sure that the head of this clip snaps to the marker at 00:01:04:04.

6 Press Home to adjust your CTI to the beginning of your sequence. Press the spacebar to play your sequence.

Let's do a bit of cleaning up in the Project panel.

7   Select the imported Afrolicious_Outro composition. Hold down the Command (Ctrl) key, and select Afrolicious Promo Linked Comp 01 and Text_Name_Of_Club.

8   Drag these items onto the New Bin icon at the bottom of the Project panel to make a new bin in the Project panel with these compositions in it.

9   Name this new bin **After Effects Comps** and press Return (Enter) or click on a blank area in the Project panel.

10 Save your Adobe Premiere Pro project by pressing Command+S (Ctrl+S).

Review questions

1 What is the difference between raster and vector artwork?

2 What is the Adobe Illustrator feature that converts raster artwork to vector artwork?

3 What is the menu command to send a graphic from After Effects to Photoshop?

4 Why is Motion Blur important?

5 How many masks can you have on a layer?

Review answers

1 Raster artwork is made up of pixels, and if you scale up your artwork in size, it will degrade in image quality. Vector artwork is made up of coordinates and can scale up and down to infinite proportions.

2 Image Trace is the Illustrator feature that converts raster artwork to vector artwork.

3 To open a graphic from After Effects in Photoshop, select the graphic in the Project panel, and then choose Edit > Edit Original.

4 Motion Blur is important because it simulates the blur that would occur when the shutter opens and closes in a real camera lens. Applying Motion Blur in After Effects can make computer-generated animation look more realistic.

5 You can have an unlimited number of masks on an individual layer.

7 WORKING WITH AUDIO

Lesson overview

In the previous lessons, you learned some of the basics of video editing using Adobe Premiere Pro, as well as some of the basics of motion graphics using Adobe After Effects. Creating engaging audio is essential in video production, because it produces an emotional context through music and sound design, and moves the story forward through dialogue and natural audio. In this lesson, you'll take your skills a step further and learn how to do the following:

- Understand the difference between audio clip editing and audio track editing

- Keyframe the relative loudness of an audio clip in Adobe Premiere Pro

- Send audio clips between Adobe Premiere Pro and Adobe Audition

- Apply noise reduction to audio clips in Audition

- Create and export a final audio mixdown in Audition

- Add a final audio mixdown to a sequence in Adobe Premiere Pro

 This lesson will take approximately 90 minutes to complete.

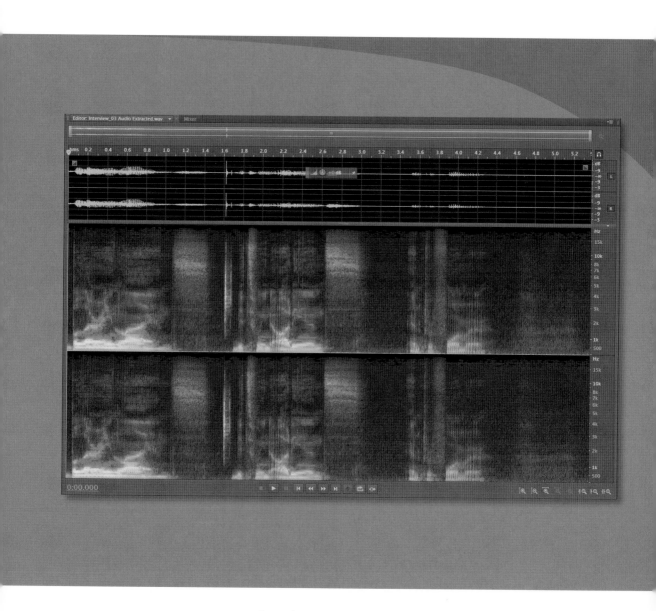

Spectral Frequency Display in Adobe Audition CS6.

Making your final edit sequence in Premiere Pro

If you are continuing from the previous lesson, feel free to continue with the Adobe Premiere Pro project you already have open. If you are starting at this lesson, navigate to the Lesson 07 folder on your hard drive and open the Adobe Premiere Pro project Lesson_07 Start.prproj. Save your Adobe Premiere Pro project file in the Lesson 07 folder as **Afrolicious Promo.prproj**.

Because you are continuing with a previous version of this edit, you'll first save a new version of your sequence. This allows you to go back to the previous version if need be and is a recommended best practice in the video editing workflow.

1 In the Project panel, twirl open the Sequences bin.

▶ **Tip:** Use Command + C (Ctrl + C) to copy. Use Command + V (Ctrl + V) to paste.

2 Click on the Afrolicious Promo Edit 03 sequence to select it. Choose Edit > Copy to copy it to your clipboard. Then choose Edit > Paste.

This will make a duplicate of this sequence outside of the Sequences folder.

3 To modify the name of the sequence, click on the name of the sequence to select it.

4 Change the name of the sequence to **Afrolicious Promo Edit 04**, press Return (Enter), and drag it into the Sequences folder.

5 Double-click the Afrolicious Promo Edit 04 sequence to load it in your Timeline.

Note that the sequence appears in a new tabbed Timeline panel in front of your original sequence.

Having multiple Timeline panels open simultaneously can be useful in certain situations, but it can also be confusing. For the time being, you'll close the first Timeline to eliminate the possibility of accidentally modifying the wrong sequence.

6 In the Timeline panel, click the Afrolicious Promo Edit 03 tab to select it.

7 Press Command+W (Ctrl+W) to close this sequence.

The new sequence is now the only one visible in the Timeline, which will ensure that you are working on the most recent iteration.

8 Press Command+S (Ctrl+S) to save your Adobe Premiere Pro project.

Monitoring audio

If you're editing audio with the Adobe Creative suite of applications, it's important to use recommended methods and quality equipment. You should make sure that the audio in your Timeline is not too loud or too soft, and that there isn't any unwanted noise. A simple way to determine if your Timeline audio is too soft is to listen to your playback and compare it to another mastered audio source, for example, a video playing on a website or music playing in an MP3 application. If, by comparison, your Timeline audio is too soft, consider adjusting your Timeline audio settings to a higher level. To determine if your Timeline audio is too loud, play your Timeline while listening closely with headphones on and pay close attention to your Audio Meters panel (covered in the next section of this lesson). If you hear distortion or if your Audio Meters peak continually into the red indicators, your audio is too loud. If this is the case, adjust your Timeline audio settings to a higher level.

You also want to ensure that what you are hearing in your Timeline is what end users will experience when they hear the finished content. To do this, you must work with quality studio monitors (or speakers) and studio headphones to guarantee that your audio sounds the way you want it to under optimal conditions.

Bear in mind that end users may not be using the best equipment, so you should also listen to your audio using equipment that is not of the highest quality. For example, monitor your audio with inexpensive earbuds that come with an MP3 player, or perhaps use the internal speakers of a laptop. Consider who your listeners are and anticipate their listening environment.

Above all, trust your ears! If you're hearing anomalies or artifacts, such as distortion or unwanted noise, end users will probably hear them, too. Consider making the appropriate adjustments.

Understanding the Audio Tools in Adobe Premiere Pro and Audition

Adobe Premiere Pro CS6 and Adobe Audition CS6 offer optimal tools for editing audio, including:

- A redesigned Audio Mixer in Adobe Premiere Pro that gets its new look and functionality from Adobe Audition

- An enhanced Audio Meters panel in Adobe Premiere Pro

- Easy transfer of audio clips between Adobe Premiere Pro and Audition

- Noise-removal effects in Audition

Before you do anything in Adobe Premiere Pro, you need to change your workspace, set your preferences, and open the Audio Mixer.

Changing your workspace in Adobe Premiere Pro

Your workspace is an assortment of panels that displays a graphical representation of your controls. Adobe Premiere Pro CS6 comes with a set of preset workspaces that were designed to maximize productivity based on certain tasks.

Up until now you've been using the workspace for editing. Because you'll be working with audio in this lesson, it's best to change your workspace in Adobe Premiere Pro to help streamline your work. To change your workspace, follow these steps.

1 Choose Window > Workspace > Audio.

2 Choose Window > Workspace > Reset Current Workspace. Click Yes in the window that appears.

Notice that by doing this your user interface has changed slightly. Most notably, the Audio Mixer panel is now prominent. You'll explore the Audio Mixer later in this lesson.

Let's add another panel to your workspace.

3 Choose Window > Audio Meters. The Audio Meters panel appears in the workspace.

4 Hover your cursor between the Timeline panel and the Audio Meters panel until the cursor changes shape. Drag to the left to stretch the Audio Meters panel horizontally.

5 Now scrub your current time indicator (CTI) across the Timeline. Notice that if the Audio Meters panel is stretched wider than its height, the green meters bounce horizontally, whereas if the height of the Audio Meters panel is longer than its width, the meters bounce vertically. This feature allows for very precise readings on audio levels.

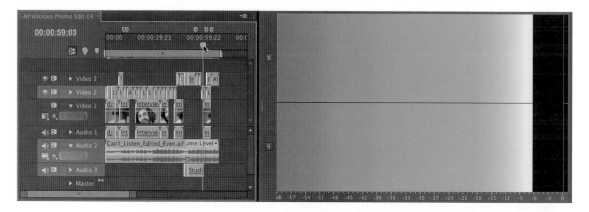

If you want to adjust the scale of units to yield even more precise measurement of volume, right-click on the Auto Meters panel to select from a list of options.

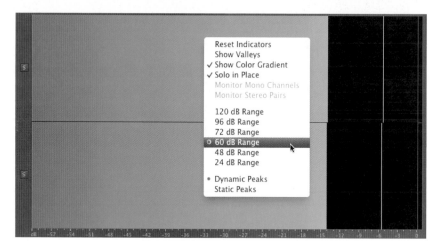

6 Stretch your Audio Meters panel so its height is longer than its width.

Verifying your preferences

Your audio monitoring may already be configured properly. However, you should verify your preferences to make sure you can hear your audio output from Premiere Pro.

Regardless of whether you're listening to your computer's sound through studio monitors or headphones (or earbuds!), set a preference in Adobe Premiere Pro that will use your operating system audio output setting.

1   Choose Premiere Pro > Preferences > Audio Hardware to select your audio monitoring device.

2   Choose your Default Device and click OK.

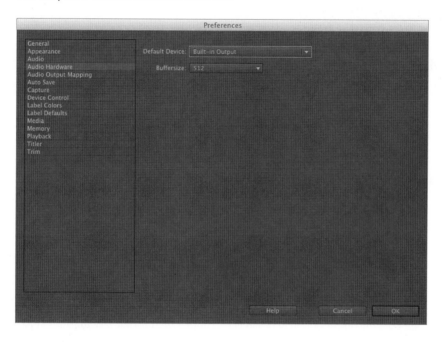

Viewing audio waveforms

An *audio waveform* is a graphical representation of the frequency and volume of an audio clip. Generally, where the graphic is thin, the volume is low, and when the graphic is thick, the volume is high. If you play your movie and listen carefully as you watch your CTI move across the audio waveform, you can get an idea of when sounds occur just by looking at the waveform.

1 In the Timeline, click the disclosure triangle next to Audio 1 and Audio 2 to twirl them open and see the audio waveforms.

▶ **Tip:** You can zoom in on your Timeline pressing the equal (=) key. Zoom out by pressing the minus (–) key.

2 Zoom in by pressing the equal (=) key on your keyboard (not the numeric keypad).

3 Play the sequence by pressing the spacebar.

This blocky graphic becomes a line that moves up and down over time. This is a visual representation of the vibration on the capsule of a microphone when recording audio, as well as the vibration of a speaker when playing back audio.

Opening the Audio Mixer

The Audio Mixer panel in Adobe Premiere Pro CS6 has a sleek new look that provides fast, accurate visual feedback about your audio signal levels and includes revamped Mute, Solo, and Record buttons and pan controls, as well as an improved channel strip layout. Now, double-clicking a fader returns it to 0dB, and the Mixer includes separate decibel level scales for the meters and faders. In addition, right-clicking on the Audio Mixer reveals context menus that provide a number of options, including the ability to reset the peak level indicators, show valleys at low amplitude points, change the displayed decibel range, and choose between dynamic peak indicators that update every three seconds or static peak indicators that hold the loudest peak until reset or playback is restarted. And—when signal is present— peak levels are displayed numerically below each meter, giving you precise visual feedback about your audio signal levels. Let's open the Audio Mixer.

1 Press Shift+6 to show your Audio Mixer panel.

2 In your Timeline, click on the CTI and drag it to the right to scrub through your sequence.

You'll see a green line in the audio meters moving up and down at varying degrees based on the level of the audio on a given track.

Reset your fader

In a previous lesson, you adjusted the Audio Mixer to temporarily compensate for the music audio levels. Later in this lesson, in the section "Audio Clip Editing in Premiere Pro," you'll perform audio editing operations on track Audio 2 in your Timeline

1 Press Shift+6 to show your Audio Mixer panel.

2 Option-click (Alt-click) on the fader icon for Audio 2 to reset it to 0.

Adobe Premiere Pro effects

Just as Adobe Premiere Pro offers many effects for video, it also offers many effects for audio. Audio effects can be applied to audio clips in the same way that video effects can be applied to video clips in your Timeline, as demonstrated in Lesson 4. You can apply the following effects and more:

- **Dynamics effect.** Provides a set of controls that allow you to adjust audio, including Limiter, Compressor, and Expander settings. The dynamics effect is a good way to fix problems with audio levels that vary too much.

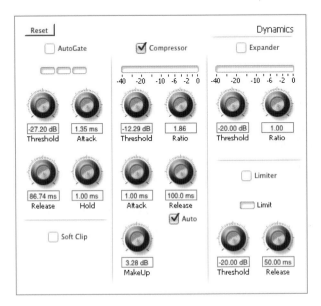

- **Parametric Equalization effect.** Allows you to adjust frequencies in relation to a Center frequency. This can be used to simulate a more expensive microphone or reduce an unwanted hiss from a high frequency.

- **Reverb effect.** Can apply a simulation of the acoustics of audio playing in a room.

- **Delay effect.** Creates an echo of an audio clip's sound. This can be useful to simulate the sound of an audio clip as if it were played in a cavernous space.

These audio effects, and others, are located in the Effects panel within the Audio Effects category.

Track-based effects when applied affect entire tracks and are accessed via the Effects and Sends menu in the upper region of the Audio Mixer panel.

Clip editing vs. track editing

There are two general ways of editing audio during postproduction: clip editing and track editing.

Clip editing entails making changes to the audio of a specific audio clip by adjusting its volume, adding an effect, or performing some other operation. You use clip editing when you want to make changes to a certain clip and not necessarily to any others. Clip editing is common when one clip has a lower or higher volume than the other clips on the given track. It can also be useful when noise is present in one clip but not others. Adjustments made on the clip level are applied only to the clip's instance on the Timeline and will not affect the master clip. Therefore, by moving an instance of a modified clip in the Timeline, any changes applied to it will move with it.

Track editing entails making changes to an entire track, which applies a secondary adjustment to the signal flow of the given track. For instance, by adjusting the volume of an audio track, the output level is the compounded volume of the clip(s) and then of the track.

When applying automation (i.e., keyframing volume changes over time) to a clip, the time-based changes to a clip are attached to the clip regardless of which track or where in time the clip exists. Whereas automation applied to a track is independent of clips and is fixed to that track regardless of which clips are on that given track. Although you can apply keyframes to a clip manually, Automation Modes apply keyframes to the track rather than the clip.

Audio clip editing in Adobe Premiere Pro

Editing audio clips in Adobe Premiere Pro CS6 is just as simple and intuitive as editing video. Clip volume and duration can be adjusted in the Source Monitor as well as in the Timeline.

Now let's dive into clip editing. You'll be automating the volume of the music clip so that as Joey—the interview subject—speaks, the music volume is reduced but is raised when he is not speaking.

In your Afrolicious Promo Edit 04 Timeline, look closely at the Audio 1 track. All of the clips in that track have a yellow horizontal line, which indicates a clip's current volume level.

1 Press the Home key to set your CTI to the beginning of your edit.

2 With the Selection tool, click on the yellow line for the music clip in Audio 2, and drag downward until your tool tip reads between −3 and −4dB. Notice that it's challenging to achieve a precise result making this adjustment on the Timeline.

Audio Gain

The term "gain" refers to the input level of a clip or clips, whereas volume refers to the output level. You can adjust the gain of a clip using the Audio Gain command, which is accessible by selecting one or more audio clips in the Timeline and then right-clicking on a clip and choosing Audio Gain from the context menu. By adjusting gain, you are compounding this adjustment with the volume of the clip and the track volume. Here are some of the adjustments you can make:

- **Set Gain to** allows you to set the gain of a clip or clips to a specific value.

- **Adjust Gain by** allows you to adjust the gain of a clip or clips by a relative amount.

- **Normalize Max Peak to** allows you to adjust the peak amplitude of a clip or clips to a value below 0dB and all other peaks in the audio will adjust by an amount relative to that.

- **Normalize All Peaks to** allows you to adjust all peaks in the amplitude of a clip or clips to a value below 0dB.

- **Peak Amplitude** indicates the selected clip's highest dB level.

3   With the music clip in Audio 2 selected, press Shift+5 to open the Effect Controls panel and notice the corresponding volume adjustment for the Level property. Here you can set precise values for your volume adjustments. Change the Volume Level to –3.0dB. By making this adjustment in the Effect Controls panel, Adobe Premiere Pro makes a new keyframe at the current time.

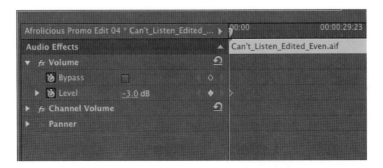

Notice the stopwatch icon next to Level. This is activated by default. If you deactivated it, Adobe Premiere Pro would not automatically create new keyframes.

You'll continue to add keyframes to the Volume Level of the music clip on Audio 2 in this fashion. By automating the music clip, you can set different adjustments at different points in time so the music doesn't overpower the interview and the music is prominent when there is no interview audio.

4   Advance your CTI to approximately 00:00:01:12. Adjust the Volume Level in the Effect Controls panel to –12dB.

5   Play your Timeline from the beginning, listening carefully and noticing that the music level is louder at the beginning than it is for the remainder of the clip. Also, listen to the interview audio. Stop right after you hear Joey say, "blurring lines between audience and performer."

6   Keep the music clip selected. Go to the Effect Controls panel and set a value of –12 for Level by clicking the Add/Remove Keyframe icon.

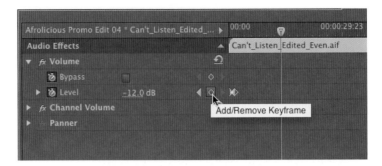

You could also click the corresponding Add/Remove Keyframe icon in the Timeline.

7   Adjust your CTI one second ahead when there is no interview audio and only music. Adjust the Level to −3dB. This will make another keyframe at the current time.

8   Play back your sequence from the beginning. The music gets louder as Joey finishes saying, "audience and performer."

9   Scrub your CTI to the right until it snaps to the head of the next interview audio clip in which Joey says, "Afrolicious began five years ago." Adjust your CTI backward 12 frames.

Let's make the music softer as Joey begins speaking again.

10 With the music clip selected, click the Add/Remove Keyframe icon next to the Level value. Again, this makes a new keyframe using the current value, which should be −3dB.

11 Move your CTI forward one second. Adjust the Level to −12, making another keyframe with this value.

12 Play back the sequence to hear the music get louder and then softer again. As you work through making these volume adjustments, be sure to play back your audio and make any adjustments needed to create a seamless audio edit. This could mean overlapping volume changes to the music track during the beginning and end of the interview segments.

13 Do the next edit on your own so that the music gets louder during the next break in the interview audio. Keyframe your music Level between −12dB and −3dB over one second to make it louder and then between −3dB and −12dB over one second to make it softer.

14 Find the point in your Timeline when the singer at the studio microphone sings the line "I can't listen." From here, keyframe your music Level from −12 to −3 over a span of one second.

▶ **Tip:** Press Shift+right arrow to adjust your CTI forward five frames. Press Shift+left arrow to adjust your CTI backward five frames.

15 Advance your CTI forward. Right before Joey says, "My confidence comes from the music," keyframe the music Level over one second between −3dB and −12dB. Then as Joey finishes saying, "with that music behind us," keyframe the music Level over one second between −12dB and −3db.

16 Twirl open Audio 3, and select Studio_01.mp4. Move your CTI back to when the singer finishes singing "when they tell me." Go to the Effect Controls panel and set a Volume Level keyframe for 0dB at this frame. Advance your CTI forward to right before he sings "I can't make it...." Adjust the Volume Level to the lowest possible value, making a keyframe with this value, so that the audio for this clip dips down as the music gets louder, thus blending with the music track.

17 Press Home to jump to the beginning of your sequence. Press Shift+6 to show the Audio Mixer so that you can see the meters. Press the spacebar to play your sequence. Notice that the green meters for Audio 2 get higher and lower as the Level keyframes for this clip automate upward and downward.

18 Press Command+S (Ctrl+S) to save your project.

Audio clip editing in Adobe Audition

Adobe Audition is a cross-platform, high-performance multitrack audio editor with a versatile arsenal of sound-restoration and editing tools, strong integration with Adobe Premiere Pro, and dozens of new features, such as real-time clip stretching, parameter automation, and automatic speech alignment, that increase your efficiency and control.

Although you can use Adobe Premiere Pro in the clip editing and finishing stages of audio production, you'll be using Adobe Audition for its more robust and efficient tools to resolve issues such as clicks and background noise.

Examining clips for distractions

Let's closely examine the interview and natural audio track to determine what needs to be fixed in the sequence Afrolicious Promo Edit 04.

1   In your Adobe Premiere Pro Timeline, mute Audio 2 by clicking its Toggle Track Output switch, so that you can listen closely to the interview audio in Audio 1 and the natural audio in Audio 3. Click Play.

2   Listen closely to when Joey says, "blurring lines." Immediately after he says that is an audible click sound. This is distracting and should be removed.

3   Toward the end of the video is a clip of Joey and the singer sitting in the studio (Studio_07-Dialogue.mp4). As Joey says, "We should lay down that vocal," notice that there is an audible low-frequency hum produced by a poorly grounded microphone or cable. This noise should also be removed.

For this lesson, you'll use Adobe Audition to remove the click sound from Interview_03.mp4 and the low-frequency hum from Studio_07-Dialogue.mp4.

Sending audio clips from Adobe Premiere Pro to Audition for cleanup

Adobe Premiere Pro allows you to easily send an audio clip to Adobe Audition.

Let's first work with the Interview_03.mp4 clip. Select that audio clip in your Timeline. Right-click on it, and then choose Edit Clip In Adobe Audition.

Adobe Premiere Pro automatically renders this as a .wav file and replaces the original audio clip within the Timeline. This new .wav file, Interview_03 Audio Extracted.wav, will open in Adobe Audition.

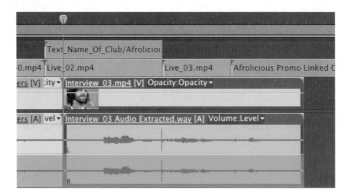

Any changes applied to Interview_03 Audio Extracted.wav in Audition will automatically update in your Adobe Premiere Pro sequence.

Understanding the Spectral Frequency Display

In Adobe Audition, Interview_03 Audio Extracted.wav will appear in the Editor panel. At the top of the Editor panel you'll see a stereo waveform. Below the waveform is the Spectral Frequency Display. It offers a different way of visualizing frequencies and volume in the left and right channels of the clip.

▶ **Tip:** If you are seeing the waveform but not the Spectral Frequency Display, click the small triangle icon at the bottom right of the Editor panel, just above the zoom tools, to reveal the horizontal interface divider, which you can then drag upward.

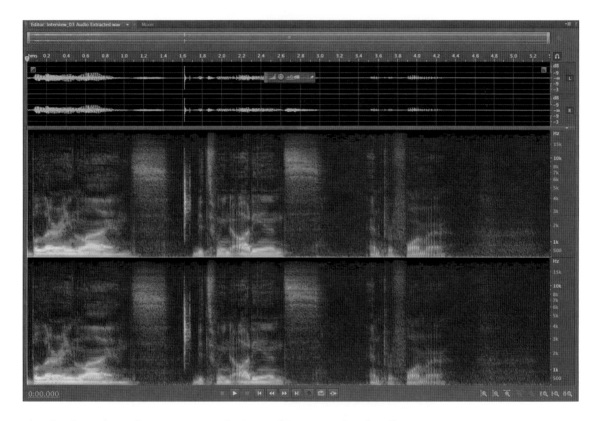

Play the clip and pay close attention to the Spectral Frequency Display. There are separate (but in this case, largely identical) spectra for the left and right audio channels. Frequency is represented on the vertical axis, whereas amplitude is represented by a range of colors and brightness. Notice the range of frequencies displayed on the right side of the Spectral Frequency Display. Also, notice that louder sounds are represented by yellow and orange areas, whereas softer sounds appear red and purple.

As you play the clip a few times, watch the CTI and pay close attention to which areas of the spectrum correspond to the sounds you hear. Try to visually isolate where the click sound is in the spectrum.

Removing transient sounds using the Spectral Frequency Display

The click noise that should be removed from Interview_03.mp4 is visible in the Spectral Frequency Display as a narrow vertical orange area. You'll remove it using the Lasso tool.

1 From the Tools panel at the top, select the Lasso tool.

2 Adjust your CTI to just before the click sound. Zoom in to the spectrum by pressing the equal (=) key several times.

3 Using the Lasso tool, draw around the click sound in the spectrum. Try to isolate it without selecting any spectrum of the audio of Joey speaking.

4 Press the Delete key.

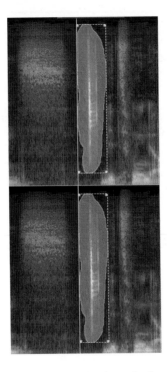

Play back the clip from the beginning and verify that the click sound is gone and the audible voice frequencies or natural noise floor is still intact.

▶ **Tip:** To switch between open applications, press Command+Tab (Alt+Tab).

5 Save your .wav file in Audition by pressing Command+S (Ctrl+S). Then switch back to Adobe Premiere Pro.

6   Play your sequence and notice that the changes you saved in Audition are
    indeed applied, and that the click sound has been removed.

Removing background noise from your audio

You need to edit one more audio clip in Adobe Audition. Studio_07-Dialogue.mp4
has a low-frequency hum. This time you can't simply select and delete an unwanted
bit of audio. The low-frequency hum is audible throughout and is interlaced with
frequencies that are essential to keeping the quality of dialogue. To remove it, you
must select a region of the audio spectrum that represents the room tone, or the
background noise only, which captures a snapshot of these unwanted frequencies.
Then you'll use a noise-removal effect in Adobe Audition. The background noise
will be removed from the whole clip, leaving the dialogue audio intact.

Based on the edit you currently have in the Timeline, Studio_07-Dialogue.mp4 has
been tightly trimmed to Joey saying, "Let's lay down that vocal." To sample some room
tone from this clip, you need to temporarily extend the In point of this audio clip.

1   In the Adobe Premiere Pro Timeline, you need to extend the head of the audio
    but not the video of Studio_07-Dialogue.mp4. To do this, hold down the Option
    (Alt) key, and with the Selection tool, click and drag the head of this clip in
    Audio 3 to the left 12 frames.

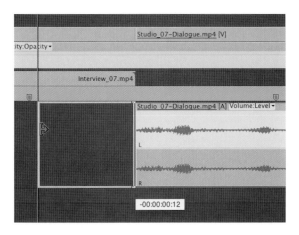

2   Now select that audio clip. Right-click on it, and then choose Edit Clip In Adobe Audition. Again, you should see its replacement audio clip, Studio_07-Dialogue Audio Extracted.wav, open in Adobe Audition.

3   Listen to the audio and find a region of time at the beginning of the clip that is only room tone and nobody speaking.

4   You can define your region of selection by setting In and Out points. Adjust your CTI to 0.082 seconds and press I to set the In point. Adjust your CTI to 0.191 seconds and press O to set the Out point.

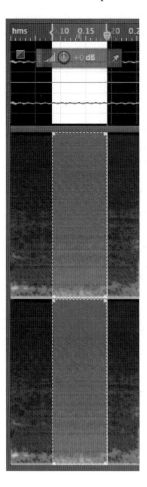

5   Choose Effect - Noise Reduction Process > Noise Reduction / Restoration > Noise Reduction Process.

6   In the Noise Reduction Process window, click the Capture Noise Print button to sample the room tone.

7   Now click the Select Entire File button so that any changes you make with the sampled room tone will apply to the entire file.

8 Click the Play button at the bottom of the Effect - Noise Reduction window to hear the audio with the noise removed.

The Noise Reduction slider controls the percentage of noise reduction in the output signal. Fine-tune this setting while previewing audio to achieve maximum noise reduction with minimum artifacts. Reduce By determines the amplitude reduction of detected noise.

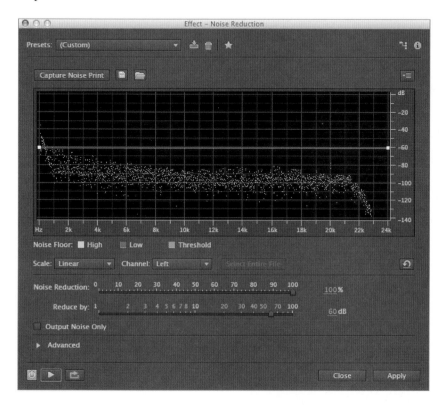

Noise Reduction is a frequency value, whereas Reduce By is a decibel value. Basically, you want to capture the frequencies you want to remove while maintaining integrity of the frequencies that are integral to the sounds you'd like to preserve. It helps to try increasing the Noise Reduction value to the point at which the sound degrades. Listen for destructive qualities to the sound you're trying to preserve, and then ease back the value to a nominal threshold that sounds good to your ears. Use the Reduce By value to reduce the selected frequencies more or less. It is recommended to use the Noise Reduction and Reduce By values in an inverse fashion.

Remember that the goal here is not to reduce noise completely, but to reduce it so that the speaker is clearer and still sounds natural. There is a balance between clarity and overprocessed audio.

9 Once the noise reduction sounds satisfactory, click Apply.

The Noise Reduction effect offers many capabilities to refine your noise reduction, but in most cases you'll only need to slightly adjust the Noise Reduction and Reduce By properties. Again, trust your ears as you identify the optimal balance between destructive and effective changes.

10 Press Command+S (Ctrl+S) to save your .wav file, and then switch back to Adobe Premiere Pro.

11 Now you need to re-trim this audio clip in your Timeline. Hold down the Option (Alt) key, and click and drag the In point forward 12 frames, back to its original state.

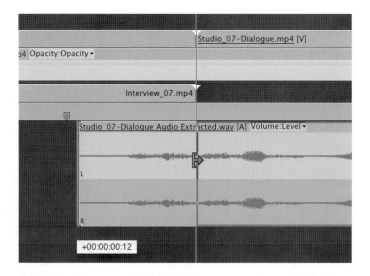

12 Press Command+S (Ctrl+S) to save your Adobe Premiere Pro project.

Real-time track mixing in Adobe Premiere Pro and Audition

Just as you have keyframed volume changes to clips over time, audio tracks can also be keyframed as well as receive real-time automation, so that the volume of an overall track can be increased or decreased regardless of which clip or clips are on the Timeline.

Much like other DAWs (digital audio workstations), the Audio Mixer in Adobe Premiere Pro and the Mixer in Adobe Audition offer a unique feature to allow users to make these volume changes in real time during playback by dragging the fader icon up and down. Although this is a great feature and is useful in some cases, this records precise keyframes to the track, yielding a large number of keyframes, which you can manage in the Adobe Premiere Pro Audio Preferences under Automation Keyframe Optimization.

To do this, you'll need to adjust the mode of the track you want to keyframe from Read to Latch, Touch, or Write based on the nature of the track automation you want to perform. For music producers and audio engineers, this tool works the same as other DAWs. You would play your sequence and adjust an Audio Mixer slider in real time to generate track keyframes. An audio track in the Timeline can show track keyframes instead of clip keyframes simply by clicking the Show Keyframes icon in the audio track and then choosing Show Track Keyframes from the context menu.

Multitrack mixing and finishing in Adobe Audition

At the point in postproduction when your picture is locked—that is, when the edit is complete and no further adjustments to timing will be made—it is standard procedure to finish the audio mix by balancing levels between tracks and maximizing overall amplitude without introducing distortion.

You'll finish the audio mix in Adobe Audition using its multitrack mixing features. You'll also add a sound effect to the final mix. Then you'll export a final stereo mixdown from Audition and replace the original clip audio with the final stereo mixdown in the current Adobe Premiere Pro Timeline.

Let's send the entire sequence into Audition.

1 In your Adobe Premiere Pro sequence, make sure that all of your audio tracks are turned on.

2 In the Project panel, in the Sequences folder, select Afrolicious Promo Edit 04.

3 Choose Edit > Edit in Adobe Audition > Sequence.

4 In the window that appears, select the Export Preview Video check box and match the rest of the settings in the following figure. Click OK.

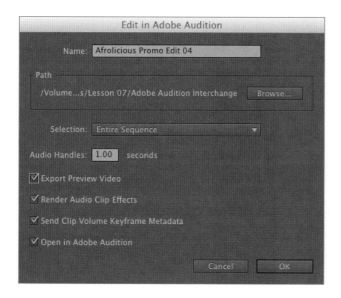

You are exporting preview video with your audio mix so that in Audition you'll have a visual cue for when to insert a sound effect.

Adobe Premiere Pro exports the video and Audition opens showing all of your tracks and clips from your Timeline.

Note that a few operations happened automatically. The video track is exported as a single video clip that is only for reference in Audition. All audio clips are exported as .wav files. These are then brought into an Audition multitrack project with all automation keyframes intact and all effects rendered in the copied audio clips. All original media remains on your computer and will not be affected.

5 Change your Audition workspace to show the video preview. Choose Window > Workspace > Edit Audio to Video. Then reset the workspace by choosing Window > Workspace > Reset "Edit Audio to Video." Click Yes.

You'll first add a sound effect to the final audio mix in Adobe Audition. Then you'll add the sound of a crowd cheering toward the end of the video.

Note: Exporting preview video when sending a sequence to Adobe Audition may result in a long render time.

6 Choose File > Import > File. Navigate to the Audio folder in the Adobe CS6 Project Assets folder. Select Large Crowd Applause 02.wav and click Open. You'll see this clip in your Files panel.

7 You need to add a new track for the sound effect, so click Multitrack > Track > Add New Stereo Audio Track. This new track appears in the Editor panel below Audio 3.

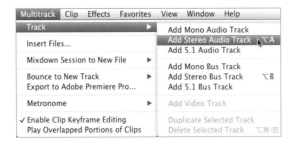

8 Click the Video tab near the top left of the interface. This allows you to see the edit of the video so that you can synch sounds with visual cues.

9 Adjust the CTI to 00:00:58:13 to when you see Joey on stage smiling at the crowd. This moment would be good for the crowd applause to be heard.

10 Drag the file Large Crowd Applause 02.wav into the Editor panel in the new audio track. Press V to activate the Move tool. Click on the Large Crowd Applause 02 clip in the Editor panel so that its head snaps to the CTI.

11 Now you'll need to trim the tail of the sound effect clip. Adjust your CTI to 00:01:07:15, right before the last four bass notes in the music. With the Move tool, click and drag the bottom-right corner of the Large Crowd Applause 02 clip until the tail of the clip snaps to the CTI.

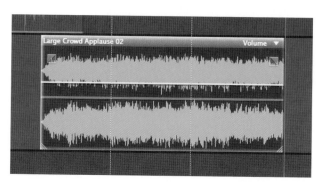

12 A yellow horizontal line indicates this clip's volume. With the Move tool, click and drag this yellow line to −12dB.

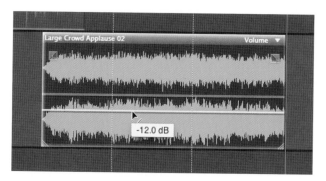

The Zoom tools at the bottom of the Editor panel can be used to expand the tracks horizontally or vertically, making it easier to adjust volume or make time-based edits.

13 Now let's fade the clip in and out. Select the clip and choose Clip > Fade In > Fade In. Choose Clip > Fade Out > Fade Out.

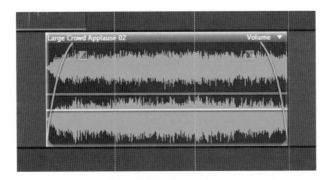

14 Press Command+S (Ctrl+S) to save your Audition session. Name your file **Afrolicious Promo Final Audio Mix.sesx** and save it in the default location. Click OK.

Dynamic and condenser microphones

There are two basic types of microphones: dynamic and condensor.

Dynamic microphones are typically used on stage or in noisy environments. Dynamic microphones are more durable and usually cheaper than condenser microphones and do not require their own power source.

Condensor microphones are of higher quality and more expensive. They are often used for voice-over and music recording in controlled, noise-proof environments. They are highly sensitive and thus susceptible to background noise, or other noises like breathing or nearby traffic. Condensor microphones require their own power source.

Recording and Editing a Voice-over

Dialogue can come from many different sources, including on-camera interviews and candid moments captured between subjects. It's common in cases like these for the quality of the audio to be compromised in favor of capturing good video. If you don't intend to use video and only need a voice track to move the story forward, Adobe Premiere Pro and Audition can be used to capture a voice-over.

To do this, you'll need a microphone with a digital connection to your host system. This could be as simple as a USB microphone and a laptop, or as complex as a multichannel audio interface with analog microphone pre-amps and analog-to-digital converters. It's best to use a cardioid condensor microphone. You'll also need a set of headphones to monitor while recording and a quiet space. Configure your audio device in the audio hardware preferences in Adobe Premiere Pro or Audition. You may also have to adjust settings in the audio preferences for your computer's audio hardware. For example, a Mac user may have to select the specified audio device in the input and output settings in the System Preferences for sound. Once you've configured your device, add a new empty audio track in your sequence and record-enable the selected track in the Audio Mixer. Then click the Record button in the Transport controls of the Audio Mixer.

You can edit voice-over in either Adobe Premiere Pro or Audition, depending on your needs for sophisticated editing tools and effects. Editing a voice-over in Adobe Premiere Pro is performed in much the same way as editing a video clip, and edits can be made in the Timeline or Source panels.

Audio track editing in Adobe Audition

Now it's time to do the final multitrack mix. To reiterate, applying changes to a track affects the entire audio output of that track. You'll apply an effect to the music track as well as to the interview track. Then you'll apply an effect to the Master track, which will affect the output of all tracks.

1 Select track Audio 2. Choose Effects > Filter and EQ > Parametric Equalizer to open the Rack Effect window. Set Presets to Loudness Maximizer. This preset will boost the low and high frequencies, leaving the midrange frequencies between 100 Hz and 4 kHz (the frequency range of the human voice) unchanged.

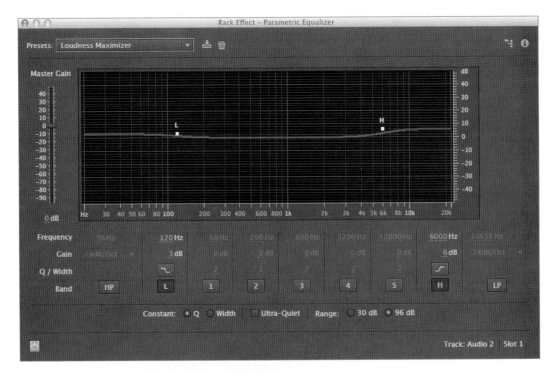

2 Close the Parametric Equalizer window.

3 Select track Audio 1. Rather than use the menu, this time click the Effects Rack panel tab to access it.

You'll see several empty rows with a number on the left and triangle icons on the right. These rows represent slots where audio effects would appear as a list.

4 Click the first triangle icon and a menu will appear. From the menu choose Filter and EQ > Parametric Equalizer. It will show as the first effect in the rack.

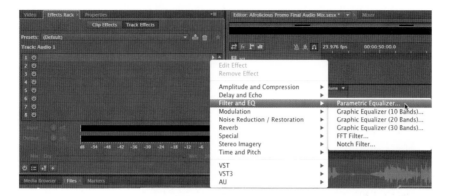

5 In the Rack Effect – Parametric Equalizer window that appears, set the Preset to Vocal Enhancer. This preset enhances the vocal range of audio frequencies by making a subtle increase to frequencies associated with the human voice while reducing unwanted frequencies so that the resulting vocal sounds are audible and clear. Close the Parametric Equalizer window.

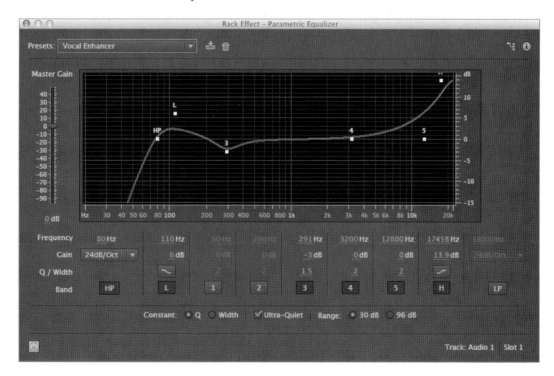

Note: Limiting refers to setting a maximum audio output threshold. With limiting applied, no clip in a track can be louder than this set volume.

6 Select the Master track in the Editor panel. Choose Effects > Amplitude and Compression > Hard Limiter. In the Rack Effect window, set the Preset to Limit to –.1dB to ensure that audio in the entire mix is at maximum loudness without clipping or distortion. Close this window.

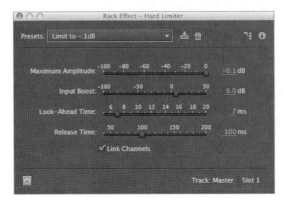

7 Press Command+S (Ctrl+S) to save your Audition session.

Creating the final audio mix

The final task you want to do in Audition is export the final audio mix.

1 Choose File > Export > Multitrack Mixdown > Entire Session.

2 In the Export Multitrack Mixdown window, name your file name **Afrolicious Promo Final Audio Mix_mixdown.wav**. Set Location to the Lesson 07 folder.

3 You'll need to change the Sample Type so that your sample rate is 48 kHz, the standard for audio and video production. Click the Change button to the right of the Sample Type values.

4 In the Convert Sample Type window, click the Presets menu and choose Resample to 48000 Hz.

5 Click OK to close the Convert Sample Type window. Click OK again to close the Export Multitrack Mixdown window.

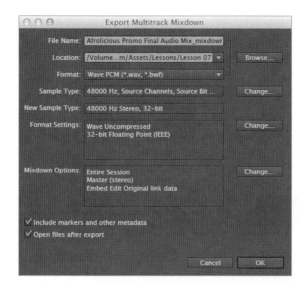

6   Switch back to Adobe Premiere Pro. In the Project panel, in the Sequences folder, select Afrolicious Promo Edit 04. Choose Edit > Duplicate. Select the resulting Afrolicious Promo Edit 04 Copy, click on it once to make its name editable, and then change it to **Afrolicious Promo Final Audio Mix**. Double-click on this to open it. Close the tab for Afrolicious Promo Edit 04 in the Timeline panel to avoid confusion.

Now import the final audio mix that you made in Audition.

7   Choose File > Import. Navigate to your Lesson 07 folder and select Afrolicious Promo Final Audio Mix_mixdown.wav. Click Import and drag the file into the Audio folder.

8   In the Timeline for Afrolicious Promo Final Audio Mix, hold down the Option (Alt) key as you draw a marquee around all of the audio clips in Audio 1, Audio 2, and Audio 3 to select them. Once they are selected, press Delete.

▶ **Tip:** Press the backslash key (\) to show your entire sequence in the Timeline panel.

9 Drag Afrolicious Promo Final Audio Mix_mixdown.wav from the Audio folder in the Project panel into the now-empty track Audio 1. Make sure that its In point is at the very beginning of the sequence.

10 Play back your entire sequence and monitor the audio. Pay close attention to ensure that the audio is still synched properly with the video. You should now have a finished audio mix with optimum amplitude and balancing between tracks.

11 Press Command+S (Ctrl+S) to save your Adobe Premiere Pro project.

Review questions

1 What is the difference between clip editing and track editing?

2 How do you make the volume of an audio clip change over time in a sequence?

3 What new feature in Adobe Premiere Pro CS6 allows for precise readout of sequence volume viewable as both horizontal and vertical meters?

4 How do you send a clip from a sequence in Adobe Premiere Pro CS6 to Audition CS6?

5 What is the name of the user interface feature in Audition that shows an audio clip represented by a range of colors and brightness, and simplifies selection and removal of unwanted noise?

6 What audio effect in Audition allows for capturing a sample of background noise that can then be removed from an entire clip?

Review answers

1 Clip editing entails making changes to the audio of a specific clip by adjusting its volume, adding an effect, or performing some other operation. Track editing entails making changes to an entire track.

2 You make the volume of an audio clip change over time in a sequence by applying Volume Level keyframes to the clip in the Effect Controls panel.

3 The Audio Meters panel to the right of the Timeline panel can show volume readout both horizontally and vertically.

4 Select the audio clip in the Adobe Premiere Pro Timeline, right-click on it, and choose Edit Clip In Audition.

5 The user interface feature is the Spectral Frequency Display.

6 The audio effect is the Noise Reduction Process effect.

8 FINISHING, RENDERING, AND OUTPUTTING

Lesson overview

In previous lessons, you learned how to add motion graphics created in Adobe After Effects CS6 to your edit and how to use Adobe Audition CS6 to create a final audio mix. The final stage of a video project involves just as much work, but the applications in the Adobe CS6 Production Premium Suite can be your guides. In this lesson, you'll learn how to do the following:

- Perform color-correcting tasks in Adobe Premiere Pro

- Apply color grading presets in Adobe SpeedGrade

- Export a sequence as a movie file in Adobe Premiere Pro

- Apply encoding presets in Adobe Media Encoder

- Render a composition from Adobe After Effects

- Perform batch rendering tasks in Adobe Media Encoder

 This lesson will take approximately 60 minutes to complete.

Export settings in Adobe Media Encoder.

Preserving your final audio edit in Adobe Premiere Pro

If you are continuing from the previous lesson, feel free to continue with the Adobe Premiere Pro project you already have open. If you are starting at this lesson, navigate to the Lesson 08 folder on your hard drive and open the Adobe Premiere Pro project Lesson_08 Start.prproj. Save your Adobe Premiere Pro project file in the Lesson 08 folder as **Afrolicious Promo.prproj**.

Because you are continuing with a previous version of this edit, you'll first save a new version of your sequence. This allows you to go back to the previous version if need be and is a recommended best practice in the video editing workflow.

1   In the Project panel, twirl open the Sequences bin.

▶ **Tip:** Press Command+C (Ctrl+C) to copy. Press Command+V (Ctrl+V) to paste.

2   Click on the Afrolicious Promo Final Audio Mix sequence to select it. Choose Edit > Copy to copy it to your clipboard. Then choose Edit > Paste.

This will make a duplicate of this sequence outside of the Sequences folder.

3   To modify the name of the sequence, click on the name of the sequence to select it.

4   Change the name of the sequence to **Afrolicious Promo Final Color Correction,** press Return (Enter), and drag it into the Sequences folder.

5   Double-click the **Afrolicious Promo Final Color Correction** sequence to load it in your Timeline.

Note that the sequence appears in a new tabbed Timeline panel in front of your original sequence.

Having multiple Timeline panels open simultaneously can be useful in certain situations, but it can also be confusing. For the time being, you'll close the first Timeline to eliminate the possibility of accidentally modifying the wrong sequence.

6   In the Timeline panel, click the Afrolicious Promo Final Audio Mix tab to select it.

7   Press Command+W (Ctrl+W) to close this sequence.

The new sequence is now the only one visible in the Timeline, which will ensure that you are working on the most recent iteration.

8   Press Command+S (Ctrl+S) to save your Adobe Premiere Pro project.

The basics of color correction

Before rendering and outputting a final movie, it is standard procedure to spend some time adjusting the color in your video. You should do this to ensure that all video clips in a given sequence are consistent in terms of hue, saturation, and brightness.

Color correction is also a very important step in meeting broadcast standards. Color correction may involve a variety of processes. The most common is white balancing. *White balancing* is the process of adjusting the hue of a video so that any object in a shot that appears white in reality also appears white in the video. This is often necessary if lighting exposure was miscalculated during production. Many color-correcting tools include white balancing controls as well as saturation and contrast controls.

Similar tools for color correction may be used in the process of color grading to achieve stylistic adjustments to hue, saturation, and brightness.

Color grading entails selectively adjusting the color of a video using masks and color-correcting tools to enhance the colors that were captured in-camera. This is done to draw attention to specific subjects in frame and further evoke the desired emotional tone of a story.

For example, color grading can be used to colorize a sequence to make it appear as though it was shot on old film stock or to make a scene that was shot during the day appear to take place during twilight. Color grading can be a simple process driven by presets, or it can be a complex set of operations that is artistic and highly technical.

Using color-correction techniques in Adobe Premiere Pro

Adobe Premiere Pro comes equipped with a variety of color-correction tools and effects that will serve the needs of most projects.

In this exercise, you'll learn the basics of using the YC Waveform monitor in Adobe Premiere Pro CS6 as well as how to perform simple color correcting with the Three-Way Color Corrector effect.

Before you start color-correcting the clips in Adobe Premiere Pro, it is recommended that you change your workspace so the related panels are showing in your Adobe Premiere Pro interface.

Setting up for color correction

Adobe Premiere Pro, along with the other applications in Adobe CS6 Production Premium, comes with preset workspaces so that you can quickly change your user interface without having to open all of the relevant panels manually. By enabling a workspace, the relevant panels are placed for you automatically.

There are workspaces in Adobe Premiere Pro for various tasks, including one for color correction.

1 Change your Adobe Premiere Pro workspace by choosing Window > Workspace > Color Correction.

   You want your user interface to correspond to the instructions in this lesson, so you'll reset your Color Correction workspace to its default setting in case the workspace had been modified on your system.

2   Reset this workspace by choosing Window > Workspace > Reset Current
    Workspace, and then click Yes.

3   At the bottom right of the interface, you should see a Reference panel. You want
    to bring up the YC Waveform monitor in this panel. Click the wrench icon at
    the top right of the Reference panel and choose YC Waveform from the menu.

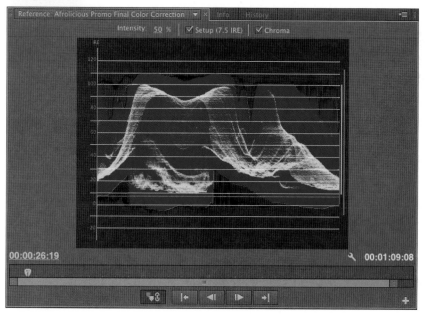

Using the YC Waveform

The YC Waveform displays a graph showing the signal intensity in the video clip.
The horizontal axis of the graph corresponds to the video image (from left to
right), and the vertical axis is the signal intensity in units called IRE (named for the
Institute of Radio Engineers).

The YC Waveform displays luminance information as a green waveform. Bright
objects produce a waveform pattern (bright green areas) near the top of the graph;
darker objects produce a waveform toward the bottom. Generally, luminance and
chroma values should be about the same and distributed evenly across the 7.5 to
100 IRE range.

The YC Waveform also displays chrominance information as a blue waveform.
The chrominance information is overlaid on the luminance waveform.

When you scrub through your Timeline, you should see that the luminance of all of the shots fall within this broadcast-safe range. In projects that use raw media with extended dynamic range, the footage may not be broadcast safe and the editor would need to spend considerable time color correcting it. However, in this lesson you'll be using the YC Waveform monitor to make sure that any color corrections that you apply to the clips do not cause the luminance of these clips to fall outside the broadcast-safe range.

Using scopes to monitor color information

Several different scopes are built into Adobe Premiere Pro, aside from the YC Waveform. Among them are the RGB Parade, YCbCr Parade, and Vectorscope. Each one has a different way of displaying color information, and each has a different usage. Like the YC Waveform, the RGB Parade and YCbCr Parade scopes display a rectangular grid with waveform information, whereas the Vectorscope is characterized by a circular chart:

- **RGB Parade.** In this chart the distribution of the three cardinal colors of light is represented by three respective waveforms. The red, green, and blue patterns indicate the levels of each color channel that make up the image. Ascending on the vertical axis is the value of the color, and the horizontal axis corresponds to the position on the image. You use this scope to visualize the presence of each color from left to right. For example, an image that is grayscale will show all three charts with the same waveform pattern, because in the absence of color all RGB patterns are identical.

- **YCbCr Parade.** This chart displays three distinct waveforms, each indicating a different relationship between color and luminance levels. The first of the three is a cyan graph that simply tracks the overall luminance in the image. The middle chart in magenta represents the blue minus luma, and the yellow chart on the right indicates the red minus luma.

- **Vectorscope.** This scope displays the distribution of chrominance in an image. The positions of each point on the scope are determined by two variables: hue and saturation. The saturation of the color is displayed on the Vectorscope by the distance of a point from the center, and the direction, or angle, of the point indicates the hue on the color wheel. An image populated by vibrant colors will produce a pattern farther out from the center, whereas more bleak colors will appear closer to the center of the chart.

Note that the YC Waveform is the only scope that indicates the broadcast-safe threshold for luminance. The horizontal dotted line positioned at 7.5 IRE is the lower limit, meaning that if any part of an image falls below that line, it is too dark for broadcast and should be adjusted accordingly. If an image peaks above the 100 IRE mark, it also must be corrected before it can be broadcasted as it was intended to be viewed.

Warm and cool colors

Common light sources—for example, household incandescent bulbs, candlelight, halogen, tungsten, and direct sunlight—all have different color temperatures on a spectrum from "warm" to "cool." Lower color temperatures like 2800 Kelvin (K) appear warm, or contain more oranges and reds, whereas higher temperatures like 5800K appear cool with a higher concentration of blue tones. In the event that a video wasn't properly white balanced at the time of recording, the colors in the image might appear different from how they would look naturally—either too warm or too cool—and what you would naturally perceive as gray instead appears orange or blue, respectively.

Unfortunately, due to the fact that almost all video systems record compressed video (with the rare exception of raw file formats, such as R3D), attempts to perform white balance color correction in postproduction will not yield perfect results 100 percent of the time. However, tools like the Three-Way Color Corrector effect can make a phenomenal improvement to clips that have an unpleasant color cast over the scene.

Using the Three-Way Color Corrector

Next, you'll do some white balancing to the video clips of the inside of Joey's recording studio because these shots appear a bit too warm—that is, the hue of the colors in the shot is a bit too orange/yellow—and could use a bit of overall brightening. Select the second of these shots, Studio_04.mp4. The clip shows Joey's hands on a synthesizer keyboard.

> **Tip:** Press the equal (=) key to zoom in on your Timeline. Press the minus (–) key to zoom out of your Timeline. Press the backslash (\) key to show your entire sequence in your Timeline.

1   Press Shift+7 to access the Effects panel. In the Effects panel search field, type **three** to find the effect called Three-Way Color Corrector. Double-click on the effect to apply it to the selected clip in your Timeline.

2 Press Shift+5 to access the Effect Controls panel and look at the controls for the Three-Way Color Corrector.

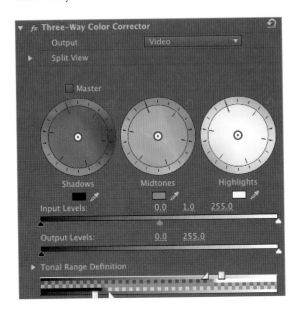

The Three-Way Color Corrector effect

The redesigned Three-Way Color Corrector effect in Adobe Premiere Pro CS6 makes precise color work directly inside Adobe Premiere Pro CS6 easier than it's ever been. Key elements in the effect's interface have been enhanced and repositioned, exposing essential controls the moment you apply the Three-Way Color Corrector to a clip and open the Effect Controls panel.

The Three-Way Color Corrector effect is also GPU-accelerated, so when you have a supported NVIDIA or AMD graphics card in your system, you can view results in real time as you work. And thanks to the enhanced Mercury Playback Engine, the new Uninterrupted Playback feature lets you make color corrections while your footage plays. Although this can be used on even the most challenging of color-correction jobs, you'll use it for some subtle and simple changes.

3   Adjust your CTI to Studio_04.mp4. This clip just needs a bit of brightening. In the Three-Way Color Corrector effect controls, you'll see a slider for Input Levels, which has a black slider handle on the left, a white slider handle on the right, and a gray slider handle in the middle. Adjust the white slider to the right, keeping an eye on the Program Monitor to see the changes. You should notice that the clip now appears brighter overall. While making the adjustments, also look at the YC Waveform monitor to make sure that the luminance peak doesn't go higher than 100 IRE.

When color correcting, it's also important to maintain consistency and continuity in your edit. If you're color correcting a clip that shows the same location or intended lighting conditions as other clips in your edit, make sure that the color correcting you do doesn't make the shots look different in terms of brightness, contrast, and color hue.

4   Adjust your current time indicator (CTI) to show the previous shot, Studio_03.mp4. Is there color consistency between these two shots? Adjust the input sliders on the Three-Way Color Corrector effect on Studio_04.mp4 until the lighting of the shots match.

5   When you're done, scrub the CTI in your Timeline ahead to clip Studio_06.mp4, and select the clip. Notice how this shot is a bit warmer in hue than the previous studio shots. You can use the Three-Way Color Corrector effect again but this time to apply white balancing.

6   Press Shift+7 to access the Effects panel. Your previous search results should still be visible. If not, type **three** in the Effects panel search field to find the Three-Way Color Corrector effect. Double-click on the effect to apply it to the selected clip in your Timeline.

7   Press Shift+5 to access the Effect Controls panel. Notice the three color wheels in the Three-Way Color Corrector: one for Shadows, one for Midtones, and one for Highlights. Each has its own eyedropper color sampler. You can achieve white balance in a clip with this effect by using the Highlights eyedropper to sample an area in frame that is pure white or close to pure white. White balancing can be enhanced by using the Shadows eyedropper to sample an area in frame that is pure black or close to pure black.

8   Use the Highlights eyedropper to sample an area in Studio_06.mp4 that is close to pure white, such as a white area on the computer monitor. Use the Shadows eyedropper to sample an area in frame that is close to pure black, such as the black outer frame of the computer monitor or the black speaker hanging on the wall in the background of the shot. Use the Midtones eyedropper to sample an area in frame that is of medium luminance, such as the singer's beige shirt. Adjust the middle slider under Input Levels to the right to brighten the shot a bit and match the other Studio clips in the sequence.

9 To see the subtle changes that you've made to this shot, click the "Toggle the effect on or off" button for the Three-Way Color Corrector in the Effect Controls panel. Make sure that this button is left on after reviewing.

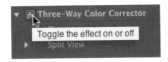

10 Press Command+S (Ctrl+S) to save your project.

Color Finesse in Adobe After Effects

There may be instances when you'll be working primarily in After Effects, not Adobe Premiere Pro, in which case it might suit your workflow to do your color correcting in After Effects. The Synthetic Aperture Color Finesse plug-in included with After Effects has excellent color-correction tools, including waveform and vectorscope monitors, histograms, tone curves, and levels adjustments. Even if they are working predominantly in Adobe Premiere Pro, many editors prefer this self-contained, color-correction tool, because it is accompanied by the host of tools in After Effects and offers some advantages over the color-correction effects in Adobe Premiere Pro.

For instance, Color Finesse has its own separate full interface with built-in vectorscopes and waveform monitors. Color Finesse can measure and control colors with Hue/Saturation/Lightness settings, Red/Green/Blue settings, and even Cyan/Magenta/Yellow settings for easy conversion of print color values to video color values. Histogram and curves controls are also in Color Finesse, giving users options between color controls they may already be familiar with from working in Photoshop Extended. In fact, Color Finesse even allows users to import curve color control presets from Photoshop Extended to allow their video colors to maintain consistency with colors in their still images, which the RGB Curves effect in Adobe Premiere Pro cannot do.

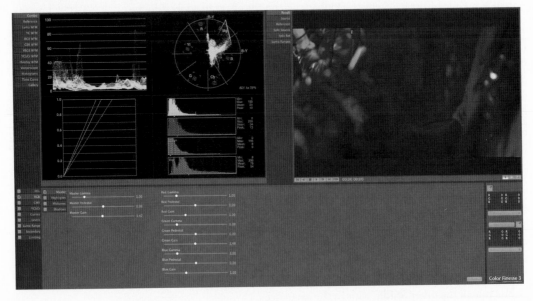

32-bit color

Many of the color-correction effects in CS6 are able to take advantage of ultra high precision 32-bit color. A huge step up from 24-bit "true color," 32-bit "deep color" is capable of producing over a billion different colors as compared to true color's roughly 16 million. In the Color Correction window (Effects > Color Correction) you'll notice that several effects display an icon with the number 32 to the right. This means that Adobe Premiere Pro processes an incredibly very rich color depth while performing the specified effect, allowing editors to feel confident that their color correction is not hurting the original image or creating unwanted artifacts.

About SpeedGrade

Adobe SpeedGrade is a high-end, color-grading application that is a recent addition to the Adobe Creative Suite of applications. Adobe SpeedGrade lets you handle technical grading tasks like matching shots and creating consistent color across a scene. The GPU-accelerated, 64-bit LumetriTM Deep Color Engine delivers real-time playback as you grade footage regardless of its resolution or frame size. SpeedGrade supports file-based workflows and includes support for raw and high dynamic range (HDR) footage. HDR support retains the bit-depth of your image files, whereas the ability to work directly with raw images—recorded straight from the camera sensor—lets you pull details from blacks and highlights that might otherwise have been crushed or blown out.

Adobe SpeedGrade does not yet Dynamically Link with other Adobe applications, but it will in future releases.

Using color-correction presets in SpeedGrade

Color grading is a specialized skill that requires knowledge of advanced color-compositing techniques. This book will not explore SpeedGrade's more advanced features, but we'll briefly cover how to take advantage of one of its simpler features, applying a Look preset to a clip. Get ready to do that now!

1   In your Adobe Premiere Pro Project panel, in the Live folder, find the clip Live_06.mp4. Double-click this clip to display it in the Viewer. Play the clip to see how it looks without a color correction adjustment.

2   With this clip selected, go back to the Project panel and choose File > Send to Adobe SpeedGrade. A file navigation window opens.

3   Navigate to the Lesson 08 folder, and then click Save.

A progress bar window appears as Adobe Premiere Pro renders out all of the frames in this clip as .dpx image files. SpeedGrade will open automatically.

4   Once in SpeedGrade, you'll encounter a user interface that looks different when compared to the other applications in the Adobe Creative Suite. Click the Monitor tab at the top of the interface to see the clip you'll be working on.

Below the Monitor is a row of Transport buttons, a Timeline, and a row of tabs that allow you to view and apply various settings.

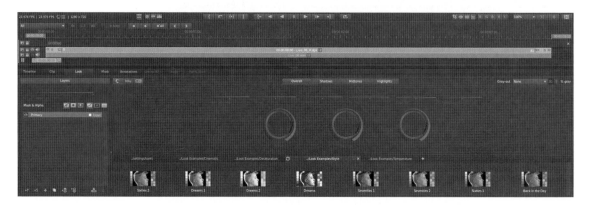

5   In the Timeline, click on the gray bar that represents the video clip.

● **Note:** Luminance values of any video frame can be broken down to three categories. Darkest regions are shadow areas, brightest are highlights, and everything in between is midtone range.

6   Click the Look tab. You should see a row of buttons labeled Overall, Shadows, Midtones, and Highlights. Choosing one of these buttons determines which range of color luminance you want to affect. Leave Overall highlighted.

At the bottom of the Look panel is a row of tabs for preset Look Examples that includes Cinematic, Desaturation, Style, and Temperature.

7   Choose any one of the preset Look Examples, and then select any preset within. To apply the chosen preset, you must press Return (Enter).

These presets are a series of color correction adjustments saved into presets and can be applied to a shot to achieve a specific look. Using presets saves you time and you don't need to make multiple adjustments manually.

Now you need to output your clip from SpeedGrade. You'll also need to do an intermediate render, because SpeedGrade does not yet Dynamically Link objects in its Timeline with Adobe Premiere Pro or After Effects.

8 At the top right of the interface, click the Output tab to see all of the Output settings.

9 You need to tell SpeedGrade where to save your rendered frames. In the Folder settings, click the arrow to the right of the Desktop icon to show a folder navigation menu that will list the hard drives on your system. Choose the hard drive where your Adobe CS6 Project Assets folder is, and then continue clicking the arrow icons to the right as you navigate deeper into your system's folder structure until you reach the folder Live_06 Media in the Lesson 08 folder.

10 Name the file **Live_06_cc**, and set the Format & Options to TGA (no alpha).

11 Click Render to render a new .tga image sequence. Doing this will render a .tga image file for every frame in the clip, and you'll end up with many .tga images, all numbered chronologically according to their order of appearance in the clip.

Using a clip from SpeedGrade in Adobe Premiere Pro

● **Note:** Do not get confused between an image sequence and an edited sequence in your Premiere Pro project. This lesson uses the term "sequence" to refer to both, but they are not the same.

▶ **Tip:** Press Command+Tab (Alt+ Tab) to switch between open applications.

Next, you'll import your rendered .tga image sequence to Adobe Premiere Pro and perform a couple of simple operations so that you can use it to replace a clip that's in your Timeline.

Importing and interpreting an image sequence

To begin, follow these steps to import the sequence:

1 Switch back to Adobe Premiere Pro. Choose File > Import. Navigate to the Live_06 Media folder, and select the first frame that you rendered from SpeedGrade, Live_06_cc0000.tga. At the bottom of the Import window, select the Image Sequence check box and click Import.

2 The new clip appears in your Project panel. If you had any item in the Live bin selected, this .tga sequence will be put in the Live bin.

For any clip that you import to your Adobe Premiere Pro project, you want to make sure that its native frame rate matches the frame rate of the sequence that you would put it in.

Look at the Frame Rate column in the Project panel to confirm that, indeed, the imported .tga sequence has a frame rate of 29.97 fps.

3 Your edited sequence, however, has a frame rate of 23.976 fps. Confirm this by selecting your Timeline panel and then choosing Sequence > Sequence Settings.

4   In the Sequence Settings window, confirm your sequence's frame rate at the top.

5   Click OK at the bottom of the Sequence Settings window to close it.

6   For your imported .tga sequence to conform to the different frame rate on your edit, you must modify it so that Adobe Premiere Pro interprets its frame rate as some rate different from its actual frame rate. Right-click on it in your Project panel, and then choose Modify > Interpret Footage.

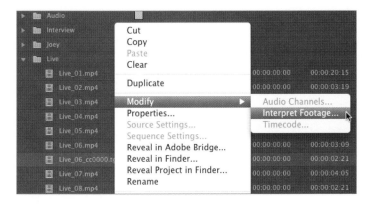

7   In the Modify Clip dialog, select "Assume this frame rate," and then enter **23.976** in the field next to it. Click OK.

Replacing a clip in your Timeline with a different source

Using a simple shortcut, you can replace a clip in your Timeline with a different clip in your Project panel. Any effects that are applied to the original clip are retained on the replacement clip.

1   Double-click Live_06_cc0000.tga in your Project panel to open it in the Viewer, and then play it to verify that the Look preset in SpeedGrade was rendered properly. Next, you'll replace a clip in your Timeline with this clip.

2   Scrub through your timeline and find the clip Live_06.mp4 on track Video 2. Select this clip.

3   Hold down the Option (Alt) key as you click on the video frame in the Source Monitor, and then drag into your Timeline.

This exercise was intended as a brief exposure to applying a preset to a clip in SpeedGrade. Because the color graded clip may not match the look and feel of the rest of your edited sequence, let's remove it.

4   Press Command+Z (Ctrl+Z) to undo the clip replacement. Then select Live_06_cc0000.tga in your Project panel and press Delete.

Sending a sequence from Adobe Premiere Pro to SpeedGrade

It's possible to send an entire sequence to SpeedGrade by clicking a sequence icon in the Project panel and choosing File > Send to Adobe SpeedGrade. This command first exports a .dpx sequence for all of the source media found in the selected sequence and then shows all clips in a corresponding Timeline in SpeedGrade. Using this method creates a new copy of the media, which occupies hard drive space. Alternatively, SpeedGrade supports the import of edit decision lists (EDLs) and thus allows you to apply color grading to instances of the original media without doing an intermediate render.

To create an EDL, select the sequence in your Project panel, and then choose File > Export > EDL. To import this EDL to SpeedGrade, click the Open SpeedGrade project icon at the top left of the interface, change the session type from Composition files to EDL Conform files, navigate to where your EDL file is, select it, and then click Open.

Understanding compression and other factors for exporting files

When exporting a sequence, it is important to bear in mind the way you intend to share or broadcast the media, for example, whether you want to upload it to a streaming website or burn it to a DVD or Blu-ray Disc. The codec used to compress the video, the frame rate, and file size are all factors that need to be accounted for when exporting.

Compression

An infinite number of colors exist in light, but only so many can be captured by video cameras and represented on monitors. Because light carries such an incredibly unwieldy amount of visual information, it will always need to be compressed before it is practical for viewing and distributing as digital media content. To that effect, the highest quality that a video file can be is the quality of the initially captured and compressed source file. To understand video compression, you'll focus on the exporting stage of media: from the editing platform to a self-contained media file. Through an understanding of how and why compression works, you can control the balance between the quality and size of your media, and also avoid unwanted outcomes in the process of exporting. Video compression is the process of compacting sound and image information, whether compressing it as a lossless file (no loss of quality from original) or a lossy file (some loss of image and sound quality).

During the process of editing footage in applications such as Adobe Premiere Pro and After Effects, the video does not undergo any compression in addition to the compression that inevitably occurred in-camera. Compression only occurs when the video is rendered or exported. When you export a video using lossless compression, the file experiences only "data compression," a process of analyzing and eliminating redundancies on the binary level. It does not experience "image compression," or a visible deterioration from the original quality. A lossless export yields a very large file size that is unwieldy for web sharing, yet is an essential part of rendering a master copy for screening, or for subsequent stages of compression in a variety of formats. It is important to note that you cannot improve the original quality of footage (create information) by any conventional methods; however, you can create information by adding graphics and effects.

Lossy compression, on the other hand, squeezes the sound and image information for more practical file sizes. When you export a video using H.264 or MPEG-4, you lose a certain amount of information but in varying degrees depending on the settings. Lossy, like lossless, puts the source files through routine data compression to conform the video to a self-contained file. Unlike lossless, however, lossy compression is also characterized by image compression. For example, a lossless image will store information for each pixel of each frame uniquely, whereas a lossy video export (depending on the amount that it is compressed) might lump clusters of color data together to make them easier to store and thus allow for a smaller file size. For example, instead of saving a multitude of different magenta hues as separate pieces of information, it may analyze them and decide to attribute them to the same color value, forever discarding the subtle differences between the unique colors to reduce the amount of memory needed to store the information. Depending on the codec, it may also compress across time, meaning that certain regions of the frame retain the same information over a series of frames. During lossy compression, the video codec analyzes the frame and compacts the information for playback and sharing convenience.

Note: When evaluating the best settings to use when performing a lossy export, it is good practice to consider the file format at which it was captured to minimize unnecessary compression.

Format

As the demand increases for higher-quality video at quicker loading speeds, industries develop video format standards to continuously improve the way that digital video is viewed and shared. Different codecs and file formats use different methods to store color and light information. A standard video compression is H.264, which is used for web streaming on sites such as YouTube and Vimeo. It is the standard compression used in Blu-ray media and is the format that many HD video cameras natively record to, such as several of the latest DSLR models. In most cases, exporting in H.264 is ideal because of its versatility and quality in relation to its file size.

Frame rates

A video's frame rate is indicative of the number of frames that are displayed sequentially during one second. For example, at a typical frame rate of 30 fps, 30 still images are projected in rapid succession in the duration of one second. Thirty frames per second has become the standard NTSC speed for video in DVD and online media, which was changed to 29.97 fps, because of a slight change in broadcast frequency to account for FM interference. The typical frame rate used in film cameras is 24 fps, which is the frame rate that many videographers choose to shoot at to emulate the consistency of film. When exporting video it is important to note the frame rate at which the video was originally shot, or else the export might have choppy playback.

File size

When exporting a video, one of the most important variables you want to control is the file size of the exported file. For instance, a normal DVD is capable of storing only 4.7 GB of information, and YouTube recommends a file size of 2 GB or less. If you want your video to load quickly, it needs to be relatively smaller than either of these examples. An easy way of controlling the size of the video file is to manually set the bitrate of the export in the Video tab at the bottom right side of the Adobe Media Encoder Export Settings interface. It's important to note the duration of the video in proportion to your target file size when evaluating the best bitrate to use.

Exporting the final output with Adobe Premiere Pro

After editing your video, creating a motion graphic, finalizing your audio mix, and doing some color correcting, you're ready to export your sequence as a movie file. Before you dive into the finer details of rendering, you'll export the sequence directly from Adobe Premiere Pro using simple presets.

1 With the Afrolicious Promo Final Color Correction sequence in the Timeline panel, choose File > Export > Media to open the Export Settings window.

▶ **Tip:** Press Command+M (Ctrl+M) to export media from Premiere Pro.

As its name suggests, this window allows you to apply settings to export your sequence in a range of file formats, frame rates, frame sizes, and video and audio compression settings. You can configure all of these settings manually, or you could choose from a list of presets. Let's use presets for this simple render.

2 At the top right under Export Settings, choose H.264 from the list of presets in the Format menu. Choose HD 720p 23.976 from the Preset menu. Click on the filename next to Output Name, and name your output **Afrolicious Promo Final**. Navigate to the Exports folder (Adobe CS6 Project Assets > Exports) and click Save.

● **Note:** See Lesson 1 for more details on H.264.

3 Without changing anything else, click Export at the bottom of the Export Settings window.

An Encoding window appears with a progress bar that shows how much time remains for the render to finish.

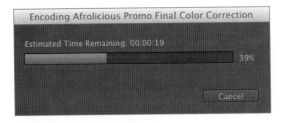

Because the movie is just over one minute in duration, this render shouldn't take very long. That said, render times will vary depending on the speed of your computer's processor(s), how much RAM is installed in your computer, and whether or not your computer has a supported graphics card for the Mercury Graphics Engine, among other factors.

When your render is finished, you'll find the Afrolicious Promo Final.mp4 movie file in the Exports folder on your computer's hard drive. You should be able to open this file with the Apple QuickTime player or other supported media player software.

This movie file was rendered using a preset for web video compression. But what if you wanted to render your Adobe Premiere Pro sequence as an archival quality copy plus other versions using different export settings without having to render them one at a time directly from Adobe Premiere Pro? That's when you'd use Adobe Media Encoder CS6.

The .mp4 file type

The .mp4 video format is a cross-platform standard that can be played back on nearly every type of device, from Mac to Windows and Linux operating systems, streaming websites, and even among an array of mobile and multimedia devices. An integral component of the widespread H.264 format, .mp4 is ideal for many types of usage.

About Adobe Media Encoder

Adobe Media Encoder (AME) CS6 is a separate, 64-bit software application that saves you time by automating the process of creating multiple encoded versions of source files, Adobe Premiere Pro sequences, and After Effects compositions. The new Preset Browser, improved batch-encoding performance, more new presets, and user interface enhancements in Adobe Media Encoder CS6 make outputting your work to multiple formats and devices a faster, more intuitive process.

Adobe Media Encoder CS6 has a new yet familiar "panelized" user interface like that of Adobe Premiere Pro and other Adobe Creative Suite applications. For example, you can group panels in frames; position, size, and float panels and frames to your liking; and save workspace configurations.

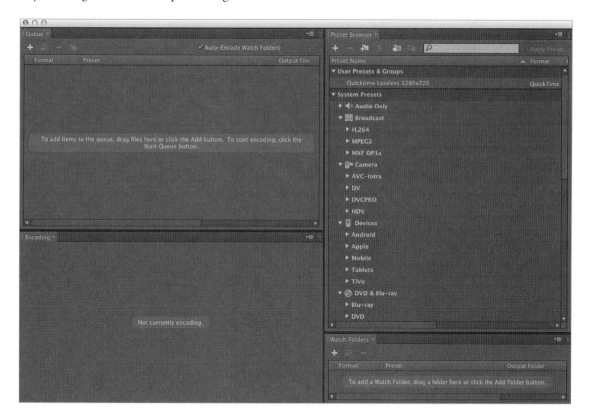

Using AME across the suite

AME is the central encoding tool used in the Adobe CS6 Production Premium Suite. You'll discover that it is very helpful for video editing tasks, such as:

- Exporting final sequences
- Batch transcoding of raw clips
- Batch compression of master files
- Encoding files that are put in a predesignated watch folder which is a directory that's specified to be polled periodically by an encoding platform for new content. When new content arrives, the system will pull the file and convert it to the type of video you have requested.
- Uploading an exported file to an FTP server

Rendering master files

It's a good idea as an editor to have a final export of your edit that could serve as the master file that other copies can be made from. Simply by copying this master file, you can easily and quickly make other copies without having to do all of the raw rendering for each, particularly if your sequence requires a long render.

Therefore, your master file should be of the highest possible quality, because a master file cannot make copies that are of higher image quality than itself. Once image quality of a movie file is lost as a result of data compression or reduction in frame size, it cannot be regained. And, in a worst-case scenario, if your raw project files get lost or corrupted, you would at least have your master movie file.

In this exercise, you'll render a master file of your final Adobe Premiere Pro sequence, but this time you'll use Adobe Media Encoder CS6. You'll also render other versions of your movie—one for mobile devices and one for the web—using AME.

1   In Adobe Premiere Pro, with the Afrolicious Promo Final Color Correction sequence in the Timeline, choose File > Export > Media. The Export Settings window appears. Let's create a preset for minimal data and image compression, and no audio compression.

● **Note:** If you want to export using QuickTime for Windows, you'll need to purchase the Pro version of QuickTime.

2   Under Export Settings, choose QuickTime from the Format menu. QuickTime is an industry-standard movie file format that is compatible with most nonlinear editing systems, including Adobe Premiere Pro CS6.

If you are using a Windows system, you must have the QuickTime Player installed to export QuickTime files from AME. To download the QuickTime Player go to http://support.apple.com/downloads/#quicktime.

3 In the Video tab below Export Settings, set Video Codec to Animation.

The Animation codec applies minimal compression to the movie's file size and to its image quality, thereby making it suitable for yielding a master file. Be warned, however, that because of minimal compression, the output file size will be huge.

4 Under Basic Video Settings, uncheck the box next to the Width and Height dimensions to unlock their proportions. Set Width to **1280** and Height to **720**. These dimensions denote the frame size of the rendered movie, which you want to be no smaller than your sequence frame size in Adobe Premiere Pro.

5 Set Frame Rate to 23.976. Again, this was the frame rate in your Adobe Premiere Pro sequence, and you want to maintain that.

6 Set Aspect to Square Pixels (1.0). This refers to whether or not the pixels would be stretched horizontally to meet certain video broadcast standards.

7 Click the Audio tab to access all of the Audio Export settings. Set Audio Codec to Uncompressed. Set Sample Rate to 48000 Hz, Channels to Stereo, and Sample Size to 16bit. These are all standard settings for audio in a movie file that yields optimum quality.

Aspect ratios

The aspect ratio of an image refers to the proportion between the width and the height of the frame. Standard aspect ratios used in video are 4:3 and 16:9, which are referred to as "fullscreen" and "widescreen," respectively. Fullscreen is the standard frame size for television broadcast and also the increasingly obsolete Standard Definition digital video (DV). The standard HDTV aspect ratio, also known as Full HD, has a frame size of 1920 by 1080 pixels and is composed of square pixels at the standard widescreen aspect ratio of 16:9. With the growing popularity of HD video sizes, such as 720p and 1080p, the widescreen ratio has become a preference over the older fullscreen ratio.

Because different cameras record at different sizes and have varying ways of capturing pixels in an image, it is critical to input the correct aspect ratio settings when exporting your media, or else your image may appear stretched or have an unwanted crop. Some cameras that capture to tape tend to record pixels slightly stretched to conform a fullscreen image to a widescreen image. However, for the purposes of displaying video on the web, it is optimal to use Square Pixels, because this is the standard used on the majority of computer video monitor and mobile device. If your final video is stretched, make note of the size of the frame and the pixel size selected in the Export Settings.

Saving a preset

Now let's save all of the settings we configured as a preset that can be used again later.

1   At the top of the Export Settings window, for Output Name, save this movie as **Afrolicious Promo Final Master** in the Exports folder (Adobe CS6 Project Assets > Exports). Next to the Preset menu, click the Save Preset button.

2   In the Choose Name window that appears, name this preset **QuickTime Lossless 1280x720**. Click OK.

3 At the bottom of the Export Settings window, next to the Export button, click the Queue button to open Adobe Media Encoder CS6.

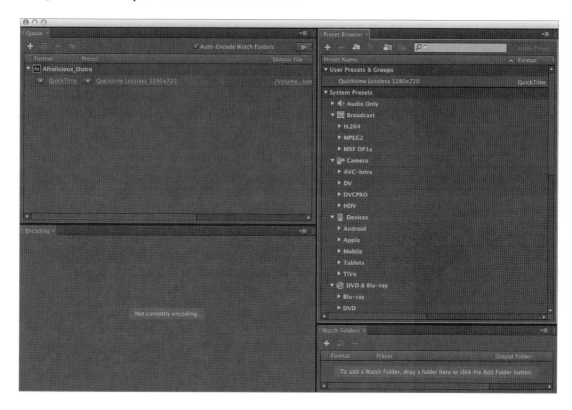

A Queue panel lists your Afrolicious Promo Final Color Correction sequence from Adobe Premiere Pro. The Queue in AME allows you to render several movies at the same time. Not only that, but AME can use the Dynamic Link between it and other applications in the Adobe CS6 Production Premium Suite. This means that you can have sequences from Adobe Premiere Pro in the Queue as well as compositions from After Effects.

Next to the Queue is the Preset Browser where you can choose among dozens of render presets for various devices and outputs.

Before you render your master file, let's add a few more renders to the Queue using various presets.

Encoding video for web and mobile

There was a time not too long ago when the dominant devices for viewing movies were televisions and film projection systems in movie theaters. Today, movies can not only be produced by anybody with a video camera and a computer, but can be shown on a variety of different devices, including high-definition computer monitors, tablet devices, and smartphones.

To ensure that your movie will download as quickly as possible and look as good as it possibly can on any given device, it's best to create separate rendered movie files that are intended to play on specific types of devices. Because screens for mobile devices and computer monitors vary in size, and because higher-quality movie files are larger files to download, you want to give the end users options so they can make efficient use of their bandwidth and the capabilities of their movie viewing devices.

Encoding a movie file to be played on a variety of devices requires compressing the raw video in your edited Adobe Premiere Pro sequence to yield a movie file that can be streamed or downloaded as fast as reasonably possible from the Internet, yet still maintain maximum image quality.

In this exercise, you'll apply a variety of export presets in AME to your final edited sequence in Adobe Premiere Pro to create separate exports for different types of devices.

1 With the Afrolicious Promo Final Color Correction sequence in the Queue, select it, and then browse through the Preset Browser. Let's apply a render preset to the Queue for Android tablet devices.

2 Under Devices, twirl open Android, and then double-click on the preset Android Tablet - 720p 23.976. Doing so creates another render instance in the Queue for your Adobe Premiere Pro sequence. Click on the Output File name for this new render, navigate to the Exports folder, and name this **Afrolicious Promo Final - Tablet**. Click Save.

3 Let's add a render for smartphones. Also under Devices, twirl open Apple, and then double-click on the preset Apple TV, iPad, iPhone 3G and newer - 360p Widescreen 23.976. This should create yet another render instance. Click on the Output File name for this render, navigate to the Exports folder, and name this **Afrolicious Promo Final - Smartphone**. Click Save.

4 Now let's add another render that could easily be uploaded to YouTube. Select Afrolicious Promo Final Color Correction in the Queue. Under Web Video, twirl open YouTube, and then double-click on the preset YouTube HD 720p 23.976. Another instance will appear. Click on its Output File name, navigate to the Exports folder, and name it **Afrolicious Promo Final - YouTube**. Click Save.

5 Under Web Video again, twirl open Flash, double-click on the preset
   Web - 1280×720, 16×9, Project Framerate, 4500kbps, and Format F4V. A fifth
   instance appears in the Queue. Click on its Output File name, navigate to the
   Exports folder, and name it **Afrolicious Promo Final - Flash**. Click Save.

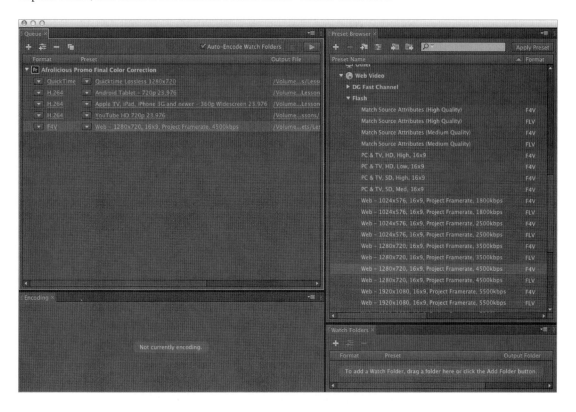

Adding an After Effects composition to the Queue in AME

As mentioned earlier, AME allows you to queue up not only Adobe Premiere Pro
sequences but also After Effects compositions.

In this exercise, you'll add an After Effects composition to your Queue in AME and
render it as a master file.

1 Click the Add Source button at the top left of the interface to bring up a
   navigation window. Navigate to the Lesson 06 folder, select Lesson_06_Finish.aep,
   and click Open.

2   In the Import After Effects Composition window that appears, you need to choose which composition in this project you want to add to the Queue. Click the disclosure triangle next to Comps to twirl it open, and then select Afrolicious_Outro. Click OK.

This After Effects composition will now be in the Queue under the five render instances you added previously.

3   Each item in the Queue has two down arrow menu buttons. Under Afrolicious_Outro, click the left menu button and choose QuickTime. Click the menu button to the right and choose the preset you made, Quicktime Lossless 1280×720.

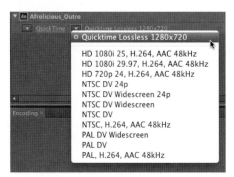

4   Click on the queued item's Output File name, and navigate to the Exports folder. Name this render **Afrolicious_Outro Master.mov**, and then click Save.

5   Click the Start Queue button. You should see multiple progress bars in the Queue panel as each of the movie files renders.

6   When the renders are complete, navigate to the Exports folder and verify that they are there.

As you've witnessed, Adobe Media Encoder CS6 allows you to easily set up exports of an Adobe Premiere Pro sequence and an After Effects composition using a library of export presets, so that you can make master copies for your archives as well as copies that will play on a variety of web and mobile devices.

Streaming vs. download

There is an important difference between streaming video and downloading video as it relates to creating video for the web:

- **Downloading video** involves copying a video file from one computer or server to another. The file then exists locally and can be copied elsewhere.
- **Streaming video** is video content that is a live playback of the video on a remote server that is then accessed via a web browser by the user. The movie file is not stored locally on the end user's computer and therefore cannot be copied. This is not the same as a progressive download, which does cache the video file on the user's computer and allows the user to start watching the video as the video is still downloading.

Rendering your compositions in After Effects

With its multiprocessor rendering engine, After Effects CS6 has the power to tackle even the most complicated compositing and motion graphics render tasks, saving you time and allowing you to meet your deadlines.

1 Open After Effects CS6. Choose File > Open Project, navigate to your Lesson 06 folder, select Lesson_06 Start.aep, and click Open. Now let's open the Render Queue.

2 Press Command+Option+0 (Ctrl+Alt+0) to bring up the Render Queue. Much like the Queue in AME, the Render Queue in After Effects allows you to line up multiple compositions to be rendered and/or multiple instances of the same composition to be rendered.

3 In the Project panel, open the Comps folder, and then select and drag the Afrolicious_Outro composition into the Render Queue.

4 Any composition that is added to the Render Queue is given default settings. Click the disclosure triangles next to Render Settings and Output Module to twirl them open and see these defaults.

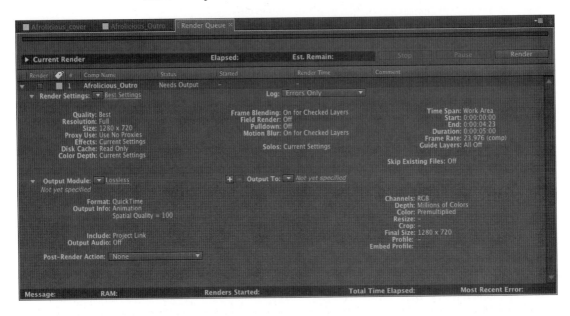

For the sake of simplicity, let's use a preset.

5 Click the menu button next to Output Module and choose H.264 from the menu.

6 Click on the "Not yet specified" text next to Output To, navigate to the Exports folder, and name this render **Afrolicious_Outro - h264.mp4**. Click Save.

After Effects CS6 has a render engine that gives you the option to use all of your CPU cores—not just one—and allocate a specified amount of your computer's RAM to each core. This enables After Effects to render multiple frames simultaneously, dramatically increasing the speed of your render.

7 Choose After Effects > Preferences > Memory & Multiprocessing (Edit > Preferences > Memory & Multiprocessing) to activate the multiprocessor render engine in After Effects CS6. Select the Render Multiple Frames Simultaneously check box. The RAM allocation per background CPU setting determines how much RAM will be allocated to each CPU core. Set this to 0.75 GB and click OK.

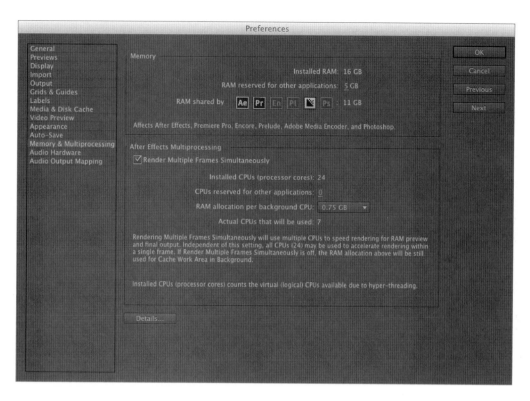

8   In the Render Queue, click Render. When Multiprocessor Rendering is turned
    on, it may take a few moments for the rendering to start. Once it starts, you
    should see a yellow progress bar move across the top of the Render Queue.
    When the yellow line gets all the way across, your render is finished.

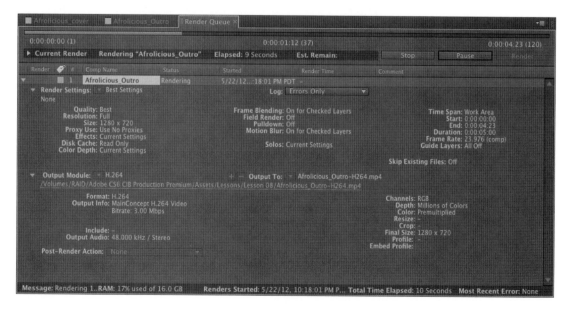

Sometimes you might need to render an After Effects composition but simultaneously continue to do other work in After Effects. In this case you could add an After Effects composition to the Queue in AME and have that render while After Effects is free to do other work.

Proxy rendering in Adobe After Effects

There may be times when you are working with an After Effects composition, either in After Effects or with an imported composition in Adobe Premiere Pro, in which you might want to have either a prerendered temporary low-resolution version or a final high-resolution version. The reason for these two scenarios is that having a completed render of your After Effects composition can greatly speed up the export of the final edit in Adobe Premiere Pro or a final composition in After Effects in which your prerendered composition is nested.

Adobe After Effects allows you to render out a composition and then automatically link the composition to the render on your hard drive. After Effects will then access the render and not do the raw calculations whenever the composition is accessed in the After Effects project or the Adobe Premiere Pro project in which the composition is imported.

A render of an After Effects composition that is linked in this manner is called a *Proxy*.

To set up a render of a Proxy in Adobe After Effects, go to the Output Module settings in the Render Queue, and choose Set Proxy in the Post-Render Action menu. After rendering the composition, After Effects automatically links the composition to the Proxy render on your hard drive. A link to a Proxy can be deactivated if further editing to the composition is required.

Archiving your project

When you finish a video project, it is good work practice to archive it properly. This ensures that, should you ever need to revisit the project in the future, you have everything you need in terms of project files and raw media to pick up where you left off.

When you're ready to archive your project, Adobe Premiere Pro CS6 and Adobe After Effects CS6 offer simple ways to bundle your project materials and project files. In Adobe Premiere Pro, use the Project Manager by choosing Project > Project Manager. In After Effects, use the Collect Files feature by choosing File > Collect Files.

Review questions

1 How would you perform white balancing to a video clip in Adobe Premiere Pro?

2 How do you send a clip from Adobe Premiere Pro to Adobe SpeedGrade?

3 How do you export a sequence from Adobe Premiere Pro?

4 How do you apply multiple preset render instances to a queued sequence or composition in Adobe Media Encoder?

5 How do you render a composition in Adobe After Effects?

6 How do you add an After Effects composition to the Queue in Adobe Media Encoder?

Review answers

1 One way would be to use the Three-Way Color Corrector effect. Use the Highlights eyedropper to sample an area of the video frame of an object that, in reality, is pure white and is intended to look pure white in the frame.

2 You would select the clip in your Project panel in Adobe Premiere Pro, and then choose File > Send to Adobe SpeedGrade.

3 Choose File > Export > Media, apply Export Settings, and then click Export.

4 Select the queued item, and then double-click on a preset in the Preset Browser.

5 Add the composition to the Render Queue, apply Render and Output settings, and then click Render.

6 Click the Add Source button, choose the After Effects project file, and then select the desired composition.

9 AUTHORING FOR DVD, BLU-RAY, AND THE WEB

Lesson overview

In previous lessons, you learned some of the basics of final color correcting your video and creating a final mix of your audio. When your project is complete, there are many different ways to deliver your media to the end user. In this lesson, you'll take your skills a step further and learn how to do the following:

- Send a sequence from Adobe Premiere Pro to Adobe Encore

- Customize a template menu design in Encore

- Program navigation and playback of a menu design in Encore

- Master a DVD or Blu-ray Disc in Encore

- Export your menu design as an interactive Flash movie

- Create simple customized interactivity in Flash Professional

 This lesson will take approximately 60 minutes to complete.

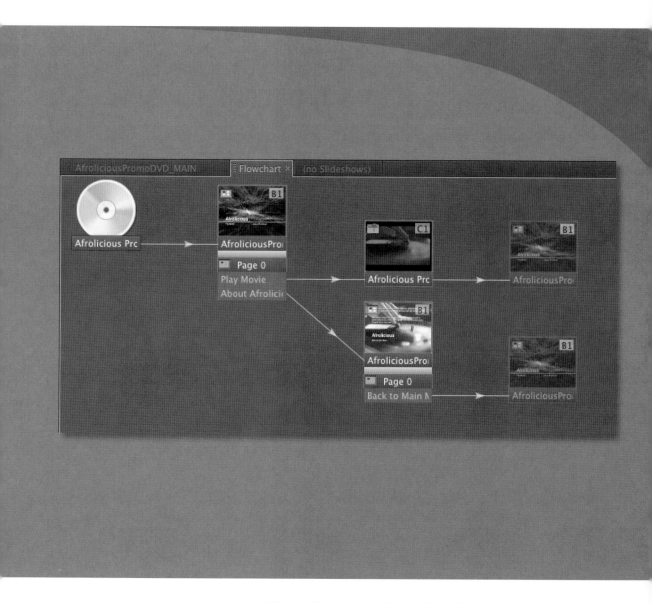

A DVD menu Flowchart panel in Adobe Encore CS6.

Preparing your final output sequence in Adobe Premiere Pro

If you are continuing from the previous lesson, feel free to continue with the Adobe Premiere Pro project you already have open. If you are starting at this lesson, navigate to the Lesson 09 folder on your hard drive and open the Adobe Premiere Pro project Lesson_09 Start.prproj. Save your Adobe Premiere Pro project file in the Lesson 09 folder as **Afrolicious Promo.prproj**.

Change your workspace to the standard Editing workspace.

1   Choose Window > Workspace > Editing.

You want your user interface to correspond to the instructions in this lesson, so you'll reset your Editing workspace to its default setting, just in case the workspace had been modified on your system.

2   Reset this workspace by choosing Window > Workspace > Reset Current Workspace, and then click Yes.

Because you are continuing with a previous version of this edit, you'll first save a new version of your sequence. This allows you to go back to the previous version if need be and is a recommended best practice in the video editing workflow.

3   In the Project panel, twirl open the Sequences bin.

▶ **Tip:** Press Command+C (Ctrl+C) to copy. Press Command+V (Ctrl+V) to paste.

4   Click on the Afrolicious Promo Final Color Correction sequence to select it. Choose Edit > Copy to copy it to your clipboard. Then choose Edit > Paste.

This will make a duplicate of this sequence outside of the Sequences folder.

5   To modify the name of the sequence, click on the name of the sequence to select it.

6   Change the name of the sequence to **Afrolicious Promo Final Output,** press Return (Enter), and drag it into the Sequences folder.

7 Double-click the Afrolicious Promo Final Output sequence to load it in your Timeline.

Note that the sequence appears in a new tabbed Timeline panel in front of your original sequence.

Having multiple Timeline panels open simultaneously can be useful in certain situations, but it can also be confusing. For the time being, you'll close the first Timeline to eliminate the possibility of accidentally modifying the wrong sequence.

8 In the Timeline panel, click the Afrolicious Promo Final Color Correction tab to select it.

9 Press Command+W (Ctrl+W) to close this sequence.

The new sequence is now the only one visible in the Timeline, which will ensure that you are looking at the most recent iteration.

10 Press Command+S (Ctrl+S) to save your Adobe Premiere Pro project.

About Adobe Encore

Adobe Encore CS6—a separate software application included with Adobe Premiere Pro CS6—allows you to create DVDs, Blu-ray Discs, and web DVDs, all from a single project.

Standard DVDs display movies in standard definition, or 720×480 pixels. This format is still in use, although it is being supplanted by the more modern Blu-ray Disc, which can display a movie in high definition (HD), or 1920×1080 pixels. A web DVD is a Flash .swf file that allows you to embed in a web page the same user experience as with the standard DVD or Blu-ray Disc.

Encore is now a fully native 64-bit application, enabling you to take advantage of all available RAM in your system, open and save projects faster, and get better, more responsive performance when handling large files and projects. DVD and Blu-ray Disc authoring enhancements include support for 8-bit color for highlight buttons; the ability to create much larger slide shows than before; and support for upper field-first video for better support of certain HD-format source files.

Using Dynamic Link to send your edit to Encore

Adobe Encore CS6 allows you to Dynamically Link an Adobe Premiere Pro sequence within an Encore project. This precludes having to do a video export of your Adobe Premiere Pro sequence before bringing it into Encore. In addition, after importing an Adobe Premiere Pro sequence to Encore, any changes that you make to the sequence in Adobe Premiere Pro automatically refresh in all instances of this sequence in Encore.

1 In your Adobe Premiere Pro project, select the Afrolicious Promo Final Output sequence in your Project panel. Choose File > Adobe Dynamic Link > Send to Encore. Encore will open if it wasn't already open.

   You should see a New Project window prompting you to enter a name for your Encore project and a location to save it.

● **Note:** An HD movie that is mastered to a standard DVD will not play in HD because standard DVDs only play at standard definition (i.e., NTSC 720×480 pixels or PAL 720×576 pixels). To output an HD movie so it will play from a disc in HD, you must set up your Encore project for Blu-ray.

2 Name your Encore project **AfroliciousPromo_DVD** and browse to your Lesson 09 folder. Select DVD for Authoring Mode.

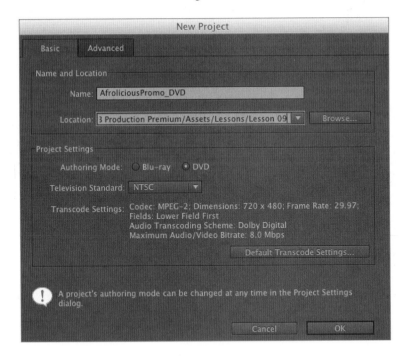

PAL system

DVDs distributed in North America and much of Central and South America conform to the NTSC standards, namely the standard definition frame size of 720×480 and a frame rate of 30 fps. However, DVDs produced for playback in a majority of other regions of the world, like much of Africa, most of Asia, and virtually the entirety of Europe, use the PAL (Phase Alternating Line) system. PAL is a video standard that is characterized by a 625-line image that plays back at 25 fps; a larger frame size yet lower frame rate than NTSC's standard definition. You have the ability to burn DVDs in Encore by using either the NTSC or PAL standard.

3 For Television Standard, choose NTSC or PAL, depending on the standard where you are located or the region in which your DVD would need to play. Click OK.

4 To ensure that your interface conforms to the instructions in this lesson, you'll choose a preset workspace. Because the first set of tasks you'll be doing involve creating the DVD menu layout, choose Window > Workspace > Menu Design. Then reset this workspace to its default setting by choosing Window > Workspace > Reset "Menu Design." In the window that appears, click Yes.

The Encore interface has a Project panel in which you should see a Timeline object as well as an Adobe Premiere Pro Sequence object.

The Timeline panel at the bottom shows your Adobe Premiere Pro sequence in the Timeline.

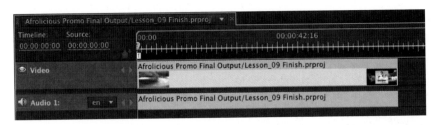

Encore was designed to make interactivity in a DVD menu system very easy to create and manage. The Flowchart panel shows a hierarchical view of your entire DVD authoring project. By selecting an object in the Flowchart panel or in the Project panel, you can see that object's properties in the Properties panel.

DVD region codes

You are able to use region codes to restrict certain areas of the world from accessing media. For instance, if a film is slated for a spring release in Japan and a fall release in the United States later that year, the Japanese distributors can restrict American playback devices from accessing the media on the disc. You are able to set up this type of digital-rights management through Encore. The following is a list of all region codes and a partial list of the corresponding nations:

0   Universally accessible

1   United States, Canada, Bermuda, U.S. territories

2   Europe, Japan, Middle East, Greenland

3   Taiwan, South Korea, Hong Kong, Southeast Asia

4   Mexico, South America, Central America, New Zealand, Australia

5   India, Russia, Afghanistan, Ukraine, most of Africa

6   China

7   Reserved by MPAA

8   Reserved for international venues such as airlines and cruise ships

ALL   All regions

The Properties panel allows you to apply various settings by choosing from drop-down menus or by using the pick-whip tools to link to objects in the Project panel. A *pick-whip* is an interface feature that allows you to intuitively link project items and properties together by literally drawing a line between them in the Adobe Encore interface.

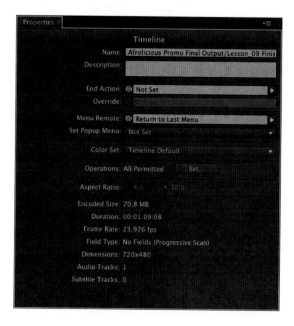

A Tools panel contains a Selection tool, a Move tool, and a Type tool.

Now that you have a basic familiarity with the interface, let's create some DVD menu pages.

Creating a simple auto-play DVD

There will be times when you'll want to create a simple DVD that has no interactive menus. It will simply play automatically when you put it in a DVD player.

Encore makes doing this very easy. Just import a video clip or Adobe Premiere Pro sequence into Encore, and put it in a Timeline. In the Flowchart panel, set the project's First Play to be your Timeline, and set the Timeline's End Action to loop back to the beginning of the Timeline (or No Action for a single play). Then do a build to disc.

Dynamic Link between Encore and Adobe Premiere Pro

To demonstrate the Dynamic Link between your imported sequence in Adobe Encore and the corresponding sequence in Adobe Premiere Pro, you'll perform a simple operation.

▶ **Tip:** Press Command+Tab (Alt+Tab) to switch between open applications.

1   In your Encore interface, click the Monitor tab to reveal it. If the Monitor tab isn't available, choose Window > Monitor to open it. Press the spacebar to play your Timeline. You should see your edited sequence in the Monitor.

    The edit starts with a fade up from black, yet it ends without a fade. What if you removed this opening fade-up in your Adobe Premiere Pro sequence? Would you have to reimport this sequence to Encore for this change to appear in your Encore Timeline? The answer is no.

2   Switch back to Adobe Premiere Pro. In your Afrolicious Promo Final Output Timeline, press Home to adjust your current time indicator (CTI) to the beginning of your sequence. Zoom in on your Timeline by pressing the equal (=) key until the first Cross Dissolve is visible on Video 2. Select this Cross Dissolve.

3   Press Delete to eliminate the Cross Dissolve. Save your Adobe Premiere Pro project by pressing Command+S (Ctrl+S).

4   Switch back to Adobe Encore. Select your Timeline and press the Home key. In the Monitor you should see that the opening fade-up no longer exists here either.

Any change that you save in your Dynamically Linked Adobe Premiere Pro sequence will automatically update in Encore. This feature is very useful for when you need to continue making changes to your edit even after you've started your DVD authoring in Encore.

Overview of DVD navigation

For the end user to navigate between DVD menu screens and to ensure that all of the DVD buttons function as intended, a fair amount of programming is required in Encore. Fortunately, programming the DVD navigation is very straightforward to do using Encore's intuitive tools.

In this lesson, you'll create a DVD menu system that has two pages, a Main page and an About page. The Main page will have two navigation buttons: one to play the movie and the other to go to the About page. The About page will display a block of text and have a button that sends the user back to the Main page.

Using Preset menus

Although you could create the static layout for the DVD menu pages in Photoshop Extended or Adobe After Effects, you'll use a menu preset that comes with Encore and then customize that preset.

Let's look at some of the presets to get an idea of how easy they are to use. You should see two panels at the lower right of the interface, Library and Styles.

In the Library panel, you can choose from different sets of DVD menu presets that include background images, placeholder text, and button rollover states. Browse through these in the Set drop-down menu.

1   For this lesson, choose the Entertainment set in the Library panel. Double-click the Electric Menu and locate Electric Menu in the Project panel.

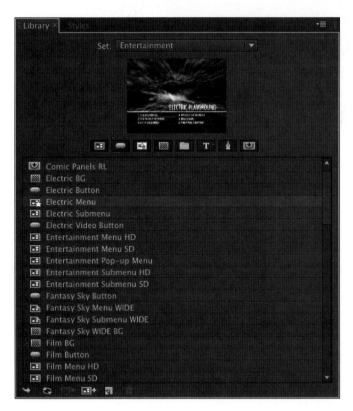

If you do not see these or any other DVD menu presets, you may need to download and install them first. Go to http://helpx.adobe.com/x-productkb/multi/library-functional-content-missing.html and follow the instructions.

2 Double-click on Electric Menu. Its properties will appear in the Properties panel and its layers will display in the Layers panel. Click the Properties panel's Basic tab and change the name of this menu to **AfroliciousPromoDVD_MAIN**.

3 Notice that the Layers panel shows all of the layers and folders. Twirl open the folder (+) 6. The Final Chapter. It contains a Highlight sublayer and a text sublayer. As you might have guessed, this DVD Menu preset was created in Photoshop. Each of the layer groups has a sublayer for the DVD navigation button rollover states.

Next, you'll customize this DVD Menu preset for your project.

Creating a custom DVD menu

A custom DVD menu, depending on the needs of a particular project, can be quite complex and include multiple menu screens, animated transitions between screens, photo slide shows, optional subtitles or closed captioning, chapter markers, alternate audio tracks, and even hidden "Easter eggs."

The example project will not require a complex DVD menu design but does require a bit of work on your part to customize it.

You'll need to edit and reformat the placeholder text on the AfroliciousPromoDVD_MAIN page. Then you'll replace the background image with one of your own.

1 In the Layers panel, you'll see six button sets, which look like folder icons with names. Hold down the Command (Ctrl) key and select the button sets 6. The Final Chapter, 5. Bellissimo, 3. Sci-fi Lullabies, and 2. The World of Music. Then

press Delete. All that should remain are the background image, the Electric Playground text layer, 1. The Beginning, and 4. Worlds of Wonder.

2   Choose the Text tool from the Tools panel. Click once on the Electric Playground layer in the Menu Viewer to make the text editable. Select all of this text by pressing Command+A (Ctrl+A) and change it to **Afrolicious**. To commit changes to this text object, click on a blank spot in the Layers panel.

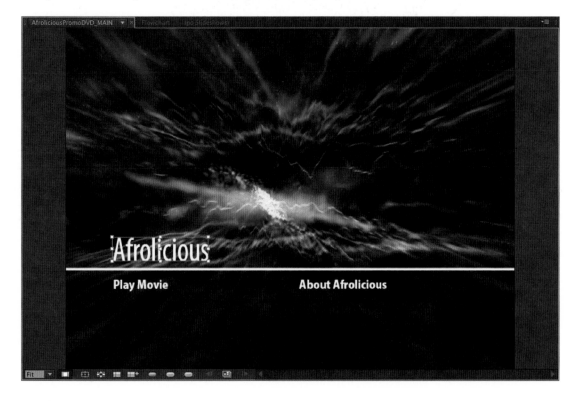

3   Now you'll change the text on the two button objects. In the Layers panel, double-click on the button set 4. Worlds of Wonder. A Rename Layer window appears. Type in the name **About Afrolicious** and click OK. Double-click on the button set 1. The Beginning and type in the new name **Play Movie**.

4   Twirl open the two button sets in the Layers panel. Note the two Highlight sublayers. Select the Highlight for About Afrolicious; you should see a green rectangle around the text as well as a thin, blue rectangle underneath the text. This thin, blue rectangle indicates the size of the menu button rollover state, which shows as a red underline. With the Selection tool, adjust the right edge of the blue rectangle until it is the same width as the About Afrolicious text.

5   Do the same for the Play Movie button. Select its Highlight sublayer, and then adjust the width of its thin, blue rectangle so that this button's rollover state is the same width as the text.

6   Select the Afrolicious text layer, hold down the Command (Ctrl) key, and click the About Afrolicious and Play Movie text sublayers. In the Character panel, set the font to Helvetica Neue bold. This will change the font to one you already used in your edit.

▶ **Tip:** As you move objects by dragging them in the Menu Viewer, hold down the Shift key to constrain movement to either the horizontal or the vertical axis.

7   Deselect all, and then select just the Afrolicious layer. Press the M key to activate the Move tool from the Tools panel, and then click and drag the Afrolicious text layer so that its left edge aligns with the left edge of Play Movie.

8   Press the V key to activate the Selection tool again. Hold down the Command (Ctrl) key and select the Play Movie and About Afrolicious layers in the Layers panel, so that all three text layers are selected. In the Styles panel, choose Basics from the Set menu, and then double-click on Drop Shadow Black (text) to give the text a black drop shadow.

Aside from changing the background, you've adjusted the preset to create a customized layout. Because the About menu page will have the same basic layout, let's duplicate the Main menu page.

9 In the Project panel, select the AfroliciousPromoDVD_MAIN menu object. Choose Edit > Duplicate, making a new menu object called Afrolicious-PromoDVD_MAIN copy. Double-click the copy, and then in the Properties panel, change the name to **AfroliciousPromoDVD_ABOUT**.

10 With the layers for AfroliciousPromoDVD_ABOUT showing in the Layers panel, double-click the Play Movie folder and rename it to **Back to Main Menu**. Select its Highlight sublayer, and use the Selection tool to adjust the width of the thin, blue rectangle so that it's the same width as the text. Deselect the button box for the About Afrolicious folder so that this text object is not interactive. Select the Highlight sublayer for About Afrolicious and press Delete.

11 Click the Show Safe Area button on the Menu Viewer. These safe guides show the title and action safe areas of a frame.

12 Select the About Afrolicious text layer, and then use the Move tool to drag the About Afrolicious text object to the top left of the title safe area.

13 In Mac OS Finder or Windows Explorer, navigate to the Additional Assets folder (Adobe CS6 Project Assets > Lessons > Lesson 09 > Additional Assets). Open the AboutAfrolicious file in a text editor. Select all of the text and choose Edit > Copy. Switch back to Encore.

14 Select the About Afrolicious text layer in the Layers panel. With the Type tool, click once in the Menu Viewer panel on the About Afrolicious text and press Command+A (Ctrl+A) to select all of the text. Then choose Edit > Paste. All of the text from the text document should now be on this layer, although it is not all visible. Adjust the bottom-right corner of the thin, blue rectangle around the text to increase the rectangle to the width of the title safe area and the height to the top half of the title safe area.

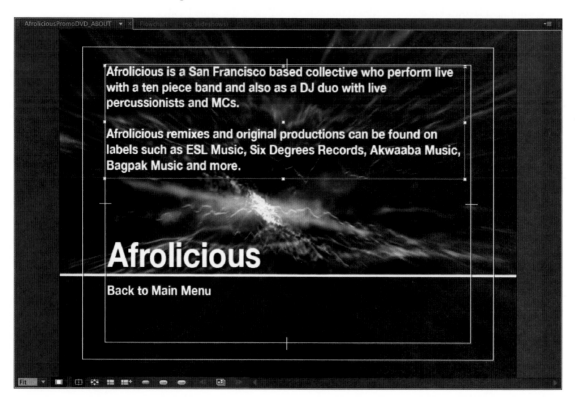

Next, you need to replace the background image of the About menu. To do this, you must first export a still from your edit.

15 Switch to Adobe Premiere Pro. In the Timeline for Afrolicious Promo Final Output, set your CTI on a frame that would serve as a good still image background for the About menu page. At the bottom of the Program viewer, click the Export Frame button. In the Export Frame window, name the exported frame **AboutMenuBG** and save it as a TIFF to your Lesson 09 folder. Click OK.

16 Go back to Encore. Choose File > Import As > Asset. Navigate to your Lesson 09 folder, select AboutMenuBG.tif, and then click Open. AboutMenuBG.tif will appear in your Project panel. Select it. With the AfroliciousPromoDVD_ABOUT menu open, drag and drop AboutMenuBG.tif into the Menu Viewer.

17 You'll see this image cover up everything else in the menu. Double-click on the AfroliciousPromoDVD_ABOUT menu in the Project panel to show its layers in the Layers panel. Select the AboutMenuBG.tif layer at the top, and then choose Object > Arrange > Send to Back.

18 Adjust the Zoom Level of the Menu Viewer to 50% to see the outer edges of the selected AboutMenuBG.tif layer. With the Move tool active, hold down Option+Shift (Alt+Shift) as you drag a corner of the image until its height matches the height of the menu frame. Adjust the position of the AboutMenuBG.tif layer so it is centered in frame. Set the Menu View magnification to Fit and deactivate the Show Safe Area button.

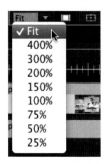

19 Press Command+S (Ctrl+S) to save your Encore project.

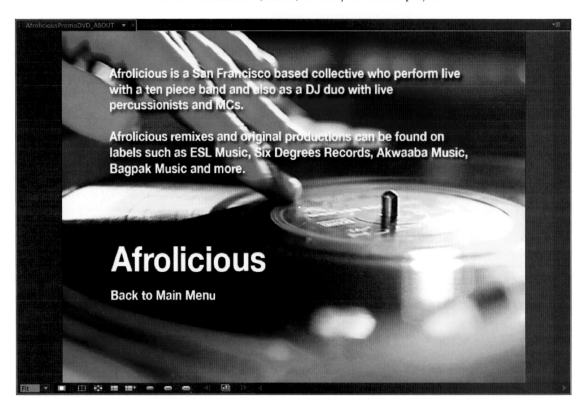

Programming navigation in DVD menus

Now that you've created the basic layout of your menu pages, it's time to program the buttons and playback options.

1   In the Layers panel for the AfroliciousPromoDVD_ABOUT menu page, select the Back to Main Menu button set and view its properties in the Properties panel. Among them is a Link property. Click the right arrow for the Link property, and choose AfroliciousPromoDVD_MAIN > Play Movie. This will ensure that clicking the Back to Main Menu button will send the user back to the Main menu and make the Play Movie button active.

2   In the Project panel, double-click on AfroliciousPromoDVD_MAIN. If there is anything still selected, press Shift+Command+A (Shift+Ctrl+A) to deselect all.

3 In the Layers panel, select the Play Movie button set. In the Properties panel, set the value for Link by using the pick-whip, which is the little swirl icon next to the word Link. Click once on the pick-whip and then, without letting go of your mouse button, draw a line all the way to the Afrolicious Promo Final Output Timeline in the Project panel.

● **Note:** A pick-whip is an intuitive user interface feature that allows you to link one project object with another by drawing a line between them.

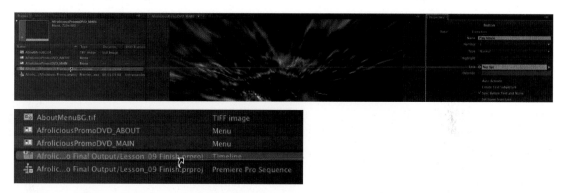

4 When you see this Timeline object highlighted by a green rounded rectangle, release the mouse pointer and verify that the value for Link is the Afrolicious Promo Final Output Timeline : Chapter 1. When the DVD menu is activated, clicking the Play Movie button will play the movie.

5 In the Layers panel, select the About Afrolicious button set. In the Properties panel, set the Link to AfroliciousPromoDVD_ABOUT > Back to Main Menu. When the DVD is activated, clicking this button will send the viewer to the About menu.

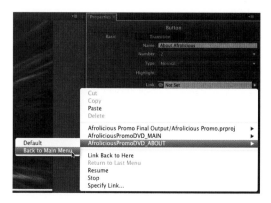

In the Flowchart panel you should see a DVD (or Project) icon labeled Untitled Project with a blue arrow linking it to a Timeline icon.

6   Select the untitled disc icon and go to its Properties panel. Change its Name to **Afrolicious Promo DVD**. Change First Play to **AfroliciousPromoDVD_MAIN : Play Movie** by clicking the right arrow icon for First Play and then accessing the menus. Notice how this changes the Flowchart so that when the DVD is first loaded, the Main menu plays first, not the Timeline.

7   In the Flowchart panel or in the Project panel, select the Afrolicious Promo Final Output Timeline, and then go to its Properties panel. Set the End Action to AfroliciousPromoDVD_MAIN > Play Movie. When the movie is done playing on the DVD, the Main menu will appear again.

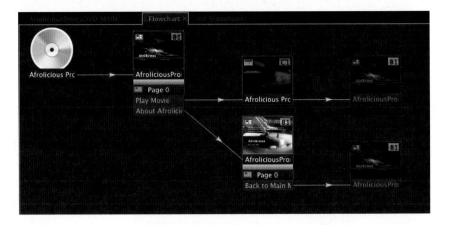

8   Press Command+S (Ctrl+S) to save your project.

Adding motion to DVD menus

DVD menus can be more engaging to the viewer if they include some motion, either with video clips or animations. Let's add a video clip to the background of the Main menu to give it some motion.

In the Menu Viewer panel, set the Zoom Level of AfroliciousPromoDVD_MAIN to 100%. Currently, there is a still image in the background. To replace this with a video clip, let's first import that video.

1   Choose File > Import As > Asset. Navigate to the Footage folder (Adobe CS6
    Project Assets > Footage), select Live_01.mp4, and click Open. This clip is
    approximately 20 seconds long, which is sufficient as a looping video background.
    More important, this clip is a well-composed shot that encapsulates the overall
    mood of the movie being presented on the DVD.

2   Select AfroliciousPromoDVD_MAIN in the Project panel. In the Properties
    panel, click the Motion tab. Using the Video property's pick-whip tool, select
    Live_01.mp4 in the Project panel, which should appear highlighted with green
    when selected. When you release your mouse pointer, you should see the first
    frame of Live_01.mp4 as the background of the Main menu page.

3   Press Command+S (Ctrl+S) to save your project.

Testing your project

If you create a navigation system on a DVD menu, it's important to make sure that all of the button links and other functionality work as intended before you output your project on an optical disc or as a Flash movie for the web.

In Encore, you can verify all of the links and other menu properties by checking and previewing your project.

1 Choose File > Check Project. A panel appears with properties that when chosen here, will be verified. Click Start to check your project. Any errors will show in the field at the bottom of the window. Close this panel.

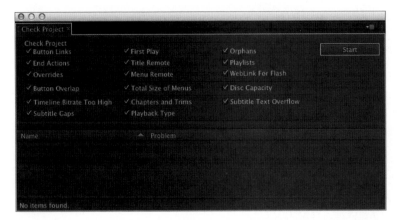

2 Now do a preview. Click the Preview button at the top of the interface to bring up a Project Preview window that has DVD menu controls at the bottom.

3 Because the Main menu contains motion, you need to click the "Render current motion menu or slideshow" button so you can see the video background in the preview.

This render may take a while, because the HD video content is being converted to standard definition. When it is done, you should see your DVD menu design as it would appear when viewed from a mastered DVD. Use the DVD menu controls to test your buttons and to otherwise make sure that the DVD pages look the way you want them to.

● **Note:** To see a finished state of how your Encore project should look, choose File > Open Project, navigate to the DVD Final folder (Adobe CS6 Project Assets > Lessons > Lesson 09 > DVD Final), and open AfroliciousPromo_DVD_Finish.ncor.

4 When you're finished, click Exit Here.

5 If everything looks good, you're ready to output. Press Command+S (Ctrl+S) to save your project.

Outputting your DVD or Blu-ray Disc

Encore enables you to output your project in a few different formats, including standard DVDs and the more modern Blu-ray Discs.

Although on-demand streaming HD video is now possible, Blu-ray Discs can play HD movies at a higher bitrate than on-demand streaming movies on the Internet; hence, Blu-ray Discs yield better image and sound quality.

Choose File > Build > Disc to open the Build panel. Here, you can burn your project to a blank DVD. You can also verify any settings related to encoding for different Region Codes or Copy Protection.

To burn a project to a blank DVD, click Build. Encore then prepares all of the files to format onto the blank DVD.

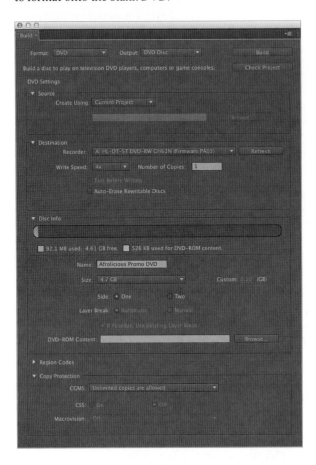

When authoring for DVD or Blu-ray, consider the amount of content that you need to put on the disc, and based on that, use the appropriate blank media.

Standard DVDs, which are used for standard definition video content, can have multiple layers on each side and can even be written on both sides of the disc, making the capacity as much as three times that of a single-sided, single-layer standard DVD. For instance, a single-sided, single-layer standard DVD holds approximately 4.7 GB, whereas a dual-sided, dual-layer standard DVD can hold approximately 17 GB.

Blu-ray Discs, which are used for HD video content, can also have multiple layers, and can hold between 25 GB and 50 GB, although new technologies are being developed to allow up to 128 GB capacity on Blu-ray Discs.

The amount (number of minutes) of video content that can fit on either of these types of discs depends on the bitrate at which the video was encoded before output. The capacity of a blank optical disc is measured in bytes, not minutes.

Should your project require more space than a blank disc allows, you can access your Encore Project Settings and adjust the Maximum Audio/Video Bitrate in the Default Transcode Settings. Generally, you would encode a standard DVD with a bitrate of between 3 Mbps and 8 Mbps. You would encode a Blu-ray Disc with a bitrate of between 5 Mbps and 15 Mbps.

If you intend to master to disc very little content relative to the capacity of your blank media, encode your DVD or Blu-ray content at the highest maximum bitrate possible to ensure the best possible image quality.

The balance between data compression and image quality

When you're at the output stage of creating a DVD for a lengthy movie, the capacity of the blank media and whether all of your content can fit on it is a primary factor to consider. Adobe Encore lets you adjust the data compression rate so your content can be reduced in file size to fit in the limited capacity of your blank optical media. However, the more that data is compressed, the more you sacrifice the image quality of your video content. You should strike a balance between a data compression rate that allows all of your content to fit on a blank disc while maintaining as good image quality as possible. These considerations need to be assessed on a project-by-project basis.

Flash content on the web today

The Adobe Flash Player software allows content encoded as .swf files to play in web browsers. The Flash Player software is still available for desktop operating systems, including Windows, Linux, and Mac OS. However, it has been steadily losing ground as a mode of sharing video content online as a result of H.264/MPEG-4 rapidly taking over the market of web video in recent years. In addition, Flash content is not supported on mobile browsers that run on Apple iOS-based devices. Although a version of the Flash Player is currently still available for the Linux-based Android mobile operating system, Adobe has discontinued development of its Flash Player for mobile devices in favor of HTML5.

Although the Flash Player is less favorable to an HTML5 solution due to its lack of compatibility on mobile devices, Adobe Flash Professional CS6 is still widely used and is at the cutting edge in the development of apps, games, and other desktop and mobile content.

Outputting your project as Flash for the web

Encore also enables you to output your project as an interactive Flash file for the web, so that all of the project content and menu functionality can be embedded in a web page and no optical media is required. Additionally, the Flash .swf file format can contain searchable metadata, allowing a web-embedded .swf to show up in search engines. Also, .swf files are still widely compatible with web browsers that run on desktop operating systems.

Let's output your Encore DVD menu as a website with embedded Flash content.

1   To do this, choose File > Build > Flash. Set your Destination Location as your Lesson 09 folder. Under Settings, choose FLV as your format. Set the Preset to FLV 1280×720 29.97fps Widescreen Medium Quality. Click Build.

A Build Progress window shows the progress bars.

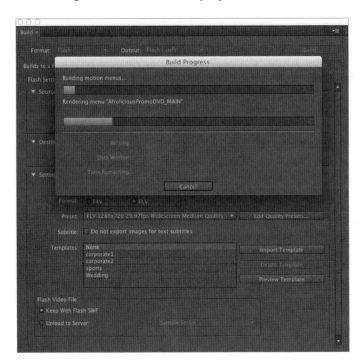

2 When all rendering is done, click OK. Then close the Build panel.

3 To find your Flash movie output on your hard drive, go to the Afrolicious Promo DVD folder in your Lesson 09 folder. You'll see an index.html file. Double-click that file to open it in a web browser. To see your Flash movie, you must have the Flash Player installed.

Introducing Flash Professional

Adobe Flash Professional CS6 is an authoring environment that is generally tailored for creating games, websites, animation, and multimedia content for desktop computers and mobile devices.

For a comprehensive tutorial on using Adobe Flash Professional CS6, check out *Adobe Flash Professional CS6 Classroom in a Book* (Adobe Press, 2012).

Creating interactivity with Flash Professional

Although this book can't cover all the tasks you can do with Flash Professional, you can perform a basic task. Let's say you want to embed your movie in a web page without the menu functionality. All you want is the movie with playback controls in a customized skin. To do that is very simple.

1 Open Flash Professional and choose File > New. In the Templates, choose Media Playback, and then choose Title Safe Area HDTV 720. Click OK. A new stage appears with title and action safe guides.

Next, you want to take a .mp4 export of your movie and bring it directly into your Stage.

2 Choose File > Import > Import to Stage. Navigate to the Additional Assets folder (Adobe CS6 Project Assets > Lessons > Lesson 09 > Additional Assets), select Afrolicious Promo Final.mp4, and then click Open. You'll see an Import Video window.

3 Under "Where is your video file?" choose "On your computer" and "Load external video with playback component." Then click Next, which will bring you to the Skinning settings. Choose a Skin preset, click Next, and then click Finish.

You should see an instance of your video in your Stage with playback controls at the bottom. In order to see the entire frame, you may need to change the view magnification, at the top right of the stage, to Show All.

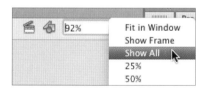

4   To publish this, choose File > Publish Settings. Select Flash (.swf). Click the folder icon to open the Select Publish Destination window and choose the Lesson 09 folder. Then in the Save As field in this same window, name your file **AfroliciousPromoFlash.swf**. Click Publish.

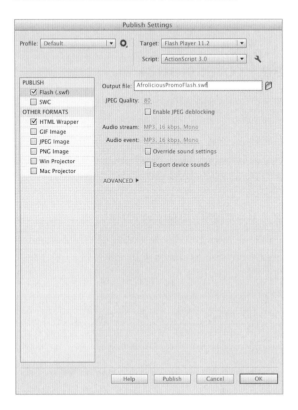

5   In your Lesson 09 folder, you should see AfroliciousPromoFlash.swf ready to be embedded in a web page. If you drag this file into a web browser window, you'll see your final movie with the playback controls you selected in Flash Professional.

Review questions

1 Why is it useful to send a sequence from Adobe Premiere Pro to Adobe Encore?

2 Where in the Encore user interface can you find the preset menu designs?

3 What is a pick-whip, and what is it used for?

4 How do you export your DVD menu design so that all of its functionality can be embedded in a web page?

5 How do you give your movie file customized playback controls?

Review answers

1 Thanks to the Dynamic Link feature, any changes applied to an Adobe Premiere Pro sequence that has been imported to Encore will automatically update in the Encore project without any intermediate rendering required.

2 The Encore Preset menu designs are in the Library panel.

3 A pick-whip is an interface feature in Adobe Encore that allows you to set values in the Properties panel by literally drawing a line with your mouse pointer between a property value and an item in the Project panel.

4 You can achieve this in Encore by choosing File > Build > Flash.

5 Create a project in Flash Professional using a Media Playback template.

INDEX

Production Notes

Adobe Creative Suite 6 Production Premium Classroom in a Book was created electronically using Adobe InDesign. Art was produced using Adobe Photoshop. The Myriad Pro and Warnock Pro OpenType families of typefaces were used throughout this book.

Team Credits

Writers: Bob Donlon, Adam Shaening-Pokrasso, Sam Young
Adobe Press Editor: Victor Gavenda
Senior Editor: Karyn Johnson
Production Editor: David Van Ness
Development Editor: Anne Marie Walker
Technical Editor: Simon Walker
Compositor: WolfsonDesign
Proofreader: Bethany Stough
Indexer: Jack Lewis
Media Producer: Eric Geoffroy
Cover Design: Eddie Yuen
Interior Design: Mimi Heft

Contributors

Authors

Bob Donlon   Bob is a 29-year veteran in the TV and multimedia industries, and has been using Adobe software since 1988. He is the founder and former general manager of Adobe TV. Bob currently serves as SVP, general manager, West Coast, at Wreckingball Media Group.

Adam Shaening-Pokrasso   Adam is a video producer and owner of a boutique animation, design, and production company in San Francisco called 12FPS. He produces media for numerous technology companies, has created graphics for award-winning documentaries, and exhibits media works around the world.

Sam Young   Sam is a video editor and motion graphics artist based in San Francisco. He has done work on music videos, corporate promotions, and documentaries. He enjoys coffee.

Contributors

Joe McGuire (music and talent)
John L Dretzka (graphic design)
Winston Merchan (production and editorial)

All video content was produced by 12FPS (12fps.com) in San Francisco, CA, courtesy of Afrolicious Music.

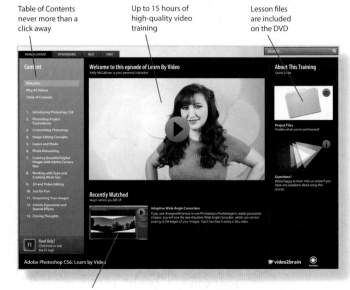

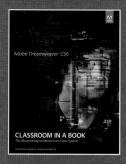

The fastest, easiest, most comprehensive way to learn
Adobe® Creative Suite® 6

Classroom in a Book®, the best-selling series of hands-on software training books, helps you learn the features of Adobe software quickly and easily.

The **Classroom in a Book** series offers what no other book or training program does—an official training series from Adobe Systems, developed with the support of Adobe product experts.

To see a complete list of our Adobe® Creative Suite® 6 titles go to
www.peachpit.com/adobecs6

Adobe Photoshop CS6 Classroom in a Book
ISBN: 9780321827333

Adobe Illustrator CS6 Classroom in a Book
ISBN: 9780321822482

Adobe InDesign CS6 Classroom in a Book
ISBN: 9780321822499

Adobe Flash Professional CS6 Classroom in a Book
ISBN: 9780321822512

Adobe Dreamweaver CS6 Classroom in a Book
 ISBN: 9780321822451

Adobe Muse Classroom in a Book
ISBN: 9780321821362

Adobe Fireworks CS6 Classroom in a Book
ISBN: 9780321822444

Adobe Premiere Pro CS6 Classroom in a Book
ISBN: 9780321822475

Adobe After Effects CS6 Classroom in a Book
ISBN: 9780321822437

Adobe Audition CS6 Classroom in a Book
ISBN: 9780321832832

Adobe Creative Suite 6 Design & Web Premium Classroom in a Book
ISBN: 9780321822604

Adobe Creative Suite 6 Production Premium Classroom in a Book
ISBN: 9780321832689

Adobe**Press**